CW00778989

Bourdieu's Field Theory and the Social Sciences

James Albright · Deborah Hartman
Jacqueline Widin
Editors

Bourdieu's Field Theory and the Social Sciences

palgrave
macmillan

Editors
James Albright
The University of Newcastle
Callaghan, NSW, Australia

Deborah Hartman
The University of Newcastle
Callaghan, NSW, Australia

Jacqueline Widin
University of Technology Sydney
Sydney, NSW, Australia

ISBN 978-981-10-5384-9   ISBN 978-981-10-5385-6   (eBook)
https://doi.org/10.1007/978-981-10-5385-6

Library of Congress Control Number: 2017947171

Cover image: © VisionsofAmerica/Joe Sohm
Cover design: Tom Howey

Printed on acid-free paper

This Palgrave Macmillan imprint is published by Springer Nature
The registered company is Springer Nature Singapore Pte Ltd.
The registered company address is: 152 Beach Road, #21-01/04 Gateway East, Singapore 189721, Singapore

The editors and authors respectfully dedicate this book to the memory and ongoing legacy of the oeuvre of Pierre Bourdieu.
"Bourdieu is now the name of a collective research enterprise that crosses the boundaries of disciplines and countries."
Loïc Wacquant, (University of California, Berkeley)
Le Monde | 23.01.2012

PREFACE

In conceiving this book, we were encouraged by Bourdieu's call for researchers in sociology, education, journalism and literature to 'think in a completely astonished and disconcerted way about things you thought you had always understood' (Bourdieu 1989, p. 207). We asked ourselves and our contributors to demonstrate what they were able to see differently through the lens of Bourdieu's field analysis.

Pierre Bourdieu is one of the foremost social philosophers and sociologists of the twentieth century. There are many books that include some discussion of his key heuristic concepts: field, habitus and capital. However, this book does what no other book does: it highlights the conceptual work at the heart of reflexive sociology. No other book has fully addressed the kind of thinking a researcher has to do to operationalise Bourdieusian concepts in field analysis. The book's focus on field theory and practice identifies and fills a gap in current publications; the authors provide examples of analysis of particular fields that are not usually given, for example, surfing, poetry and journalism. The book's chapters by prominent Bourdieusian scholars and recently graduated and current HDR students offer an extraordinary range of explorations and reflections of undertaking empirical studies utilising field analysis. Bridging commentary from the editorial team, synthesising key insights and challenges researchers face when putting field analysis into practice, links the chapters.

This book came about through discussions between Mike Grenfell, an internationally renowned Bourdieu scholar, and the editorial team. Mike was in Sydney for a conference and we discussed the various ways researchers were using Bourdieu's field analysis in the Australian context. The different projects which came to mind provided a solid basis for a collected edition; we were also able to attract interest from Bourdieu scholars outside of Australia. The book developed in stages, the first stage was to gather people together in a colloquium held in Sydney where the potential contributors to the book presented their Bourdieu-inspired research and thoughts around field analysis. The colloquium showcased a broad range of research applying field analysis, by presenters from Europe and the UK (via video links), Denmark, New Zealand along with Australian contributions. It also attracted an audience of researchers and research students interested in field analysis. The second day of the colloquium, a meeting to discuss the possibility of this book, was enthusiastically attended by most presenters. It seemed there were a need and an appetite for producing a book like this. The dedication of the contributors for the project has kept us going throughout the editorial process.

The chapters offer examples from a diverse range of discipline contexts: cultural studies, poetry, welfare systems, water management, education, journalism and surfing. The chapters and commentaries in this book provide demonstrations of theorising within practical examples of field analysis gathered in one accessible book. The chapters in their different approaches provide examples of how to clearly understand Bourdieu's field analysis and conduct rigorous and innovative research.

In our discussions about the book, we were aware that there are other edited books on Bourdieu's approach to research; we needed to consider questions such as what contribution to new knowledge will the book make? How could we, as editors, organise the diversity of areas and approaches to using field analysis? How can we make it into a cohesive story?

Considering these questions, it was clear that field analysis would be the central topic of the chapters; the editors and contributors all recognised that field analysis is an unappreciated area of Bourdieu's work and little attention is paid to it, as opposed to his concepts of 'habitus' or 'capital'. Specifically, the authors/contributors wished to address the way we operationalise field analysis and key ideas such as Bourdieu's ways of thinking about field analysis; the notion of homology; the strengths and limitations of field analysis; the way fields change and interrelate and ultimately the whole point of field analysis is that one starts asking questions about the field.

The book consists of sixteen chapters, with a substantial introduction and concluding chapter and commentary sections introducing the three parts. The chapters are divided into logical sections: the first contains studies which examine field as an object of study; in the second, the chapters address Bourdieu's key concepts of struggle, positioning and legitimacy/illegitimacy; and in the third, the authors work with extensions of Bourdieu's concepts. In each chapter, the author(s) address the way that field theory was used to examine the dynamics and relationships in the fields under study. The chapters specifically address what Bourdieu's field analysis allowed the researchers to see that they may not have otherwise identified. In some chapters, the authors describe how they worked with additional theories to extend their analysis of the field. The author's application of field analysis differed according to their field of study and the researcher's orientation; the book allows for varied emphases within Bourdieu's field theory and it makes connection between different practices. A question that we wanted to focus on was how do different researchers within their unique settings and resources make sense of their fields in different practical studies?

The book also wanted to attend to what one can and cannot do with using Bourdieu's field analysis? Chapters by Nash, Maton, Brook and Albright and Hartman describe how Bourdieu's field analysis is extended by including other analytical frameworks. In Maton's case, it was the addition of Legitimation Code Theory, Albright and Hartman used critical discourse analysis as another heuristic device. Brook explored the possibilities of connecting Bourdieusian field theorising with post-Foucauldian governmentality studies.

A feature of the book is the way that it draws the diversity of the fields and the methodological approaches together. The illuminating introduction by Jim Albright and Deborah Hartman and the likewise meticulous attention to the Bourdieu's theoretical categories in the concluding chapter by Mike Grenfell bookend the chapters focusing on particular fields.

The book will be useful to undergraduate and postgraduate scholars and researchers who are currently working with Bourdieusian methods or who would like to understand ways to do so. Bourdieu is widely known in cultural studies and education, particularly in Europe, the USA, Australia and New Zealand. His approaches are increasingly being taken up in health, social work, anthropology, family studies, journalism, communication studies and other disciplines where an analysis of the interplay between individuals and social structures is relevant. In addition to a general academic market, this book and chapters within it could be widely used in research methodology courses at postgraduate level.

We believe that this book has something useful for all Bourdieusian scholars. Whether the reader is interested in specific applications of field theory in their own field or particular methodological aspects of the application of field theory, the chapters in each section reveal the thinking and actions that researchers utilising field theory must embark upon. This is both the challenge and the joy of thinking like Bourdieu.

Callaghan, Australia   James Albright
Callaghan, Australia   Deborah Hartman
Sydney, Australia   Jacqueline Widin

Reference

Bourdieu, P. (1989). *Language and symbolic power.* (G. Raymond & M. Adamson, Trans.). Cambridge: Polity Press.

Acknowledgements

The editors would like to thank the University of Technology Sydney and the University of Newcastle for their financial and administrative support and encouragement for the intellectual development that occurred in the Colloquium *Beyond the fields we know*. We gratefully acknowledge all of the contributors to that colloquium in January 2013, which started the journey of this book. Sandris Zeivots documented the outcomes of the second day of the colloquium, and Geoff Evans skilfully facilitated the conversations that led to the shaping of this book. Terry Fitzgerald provided final proofreading support and helped us enormously in organising the manuscript for submission to Palgrave.

The impetus for the colloquium was the possibility that celebrated Bourdieusian scholar Mike Grenfell would deliver a keynote and contribute to the discussions at the colloquium. Unfortunately, Mike was ill and could not travel. His paper was read by Scott Brook on the day. We are very grateful that Mike continued his involvement in the project and contributed the important afterword chapter of the book.

Thinking like Bourdieu, in all aspects of life, is challenging. The editors would like to acknowledge and thank all of our mentors, collaborators, family and friends who continue to inspire and challenge us to step beyond the fields we know into unmapped intellectual and social terrains.

James Albright
Deborah Hartman
Jacqueline Widin

CONTENTS

1 Introduction: On Doing Field Analysis   1
   James Albright and Deborah Hartman

Part I Field as Both a Conceptual and Empirical
        Object of Analysis

2 Drought and Water Policy in the Western USA: Genesis
   and Structure of a Multi-level Field   21
   Joan Cortinas, Brian F. O'Neill and Franck Poupeau

3 Masculine Learner Identities in the Field of
   Student-Directed Musical Learning   39
   Garth Stahl and Pete Dale

4 Poetry and the Conditions of Practice: A Field Study   53
   Jen Webb

5 Academic Literacy Support: Challenging the Logic of
   Practice   67
   Jacqueline Widin

6   Transformations of the Danish Field of Welfare Work:
     Shifting Forms of Dominated Capital   81
     Jan Thorhauge Frederiksen

7   Breaking from the Field: Participant Observation and
     Bourdieu's *Participant Objectivation*   99
     Emma E. Rowe

Part II   Positionality, Struggle and Legitimation

8   Framing a "Community of Consumption": Field
     Theory, Multi-perspectival Discourse Analysis and the
     Commercialization of Teaching   117
     Jonathan Crichton

9   Reshaping the Field from the Outside in: Aboriginal
     People and Student Journalists Working Together   133
     Bonita Mason, Chris Thomson, Dawn Bennett and Michelle
     Johnston

10   Cultural Innovation on the Fringe—the Fields of
     'Limited' and 'Extensive' Production   149
     Mark Gibson and Tony Moore

11   Bourdieusian Reflexivity in Insider Research in Higher
     Education: Considering Participants as a Critical
     Audience   165
     Katrina Waite

12   Positioning Participation in the Field of Surfing: Sex,
     Equity, and Illusion   181
     lisahunter

Part III   Explorations utilising Bourdieu and Other
           Methodological Approaches

13   Conceptualising Strategies Open to Players Within
     the Field of Australian Boys' Education   203
     Deborah Hartman and James Albright

14   Field Theory, Space and Time   217
     Chris Nash

15   Governing Cultural Fields   235
     Scott Brook

16   Thinking like Bourdieu: Completing the Mental
     Revolution with Legitimation Code Theory   249
     Karl Maton

17   Afterword: Reflecting In/On Field Theory in Practice   269
     Michael Grenfell

Index   293

EDITORS AND CONTRIBUTORS

About the Editors

James Albright Since leaving teaching in 1998, Prof. James Albright (University of Newcastle, Australia) has undertaken research and scholarship in Canada, the USA and Singapore. His co-edited book, *Pierre Bourdieu and Literacy Education* (2008), which is used in advanced courses internationally, addresses literacy education as a sociological field. His other book with D.L. Carlson is *Composing a Care of the Self: a critical history of writing assessment in Secondary English Education*. Boston, MA: Sense Publishers (2012). Prof. Albright was the inaugural director of the Educational Research Institute Newcastle (ERIN). He is the editor-in-chief of the new open-access journal, *Education Science* (MDPI, Basel, Beijing & Washington).

Deborah Hartman is lecturer in Family Studies and Associate Director of the Family Action Centre, at the University of Newcastle, Australia. In her roles as an educator, researcher and practitioner in the fields of Family Studies and Education, she has always been instrumental in developing innovative education and curriculum development programs. She combines a professional background in primary and indigenous education, academic interests in language and sociology, families and diversity in trans-disciplinary research and teaching in family studies. She is currently applying the tools of field analysis to research into the growth of the study of families internationally.

Jacqueline Widin has extensive experience in the teaching and research field of English as an additional/international language and in the broad field of language, literacy and social justice. She has a particular interest in the relationship between language teaching and learning, human rights and sociopolitical dynamics with the language education field. She is currently a Senior Lecturer at the University of Technology Sydney and coordinates the Applied Linguistics and TESOL programs, she also regularly along with teaching and researching outside of Australia. She is the author of *Illegitimate Practices: Global English Language Education (2010)*, her other publications include *Symbolic Violence and Abuse in Language Education 2015 (book chapter), Maintaining the status quo: symbolic violence in higher education 2014* (co-authored with J. Watson).

Contributors

Dawn Bennett is John Curtin Distinguished Professor and Director of the Creative Workforce Initiative with Curtin University. Her recent research focuses on identity development, employability, graduate transition and creative labour markets, with a particular focus on the impact of identity development on higher education learning. An active violist, Dawn serves on numerous editorial boards and convenes the Australian Learning and Teaching Fellows' network. She is on the board of directors for the International Society for Music Education and the Music Council of Australia, serves as a commissioner with the ISME Commission for Education of the Professional Musician, and chairs the Curtin Academy.

Scott Brook is Associate Professor at the University of Canberra, Australia, where his research is focused on cultural field studies, creative labour and cultural policy. He is currently a Chief Investigator on 'Working the Field', a major Australian Research Council-funded study of how creative graduates sustain cultural vocations. He is also active in the Australian cultural policy and arts sectors, having given evidence at a Senate Inquiry into Commonwealth arts funding, undertaken cultural planning scoping studies for local governments and received project funding and commissions from a range of bodies, including Copyright Agency Limited, SBS and the Australia Council.

Jonathan Crichton is Senior Lecturer in Applied Linguistics and Member of the Research Centre for Languages and Cultures, University of South Australia. His research focuses on language as a form of expertise in professions and organisations. His publications include *The Discourse of Commercialization* (2010) and, co-edited with C.N. Candlin, *Discourses of Deficit* (2011), *Discourses of Trust* (2013) and *Communicating Risk* (2016) and, co-authored with C.N. Candlin and S.H. More, *Exploring Discourse in Context and in Action* (2017), all with Palgrave.

Pete Dale, Ph.D. studied at Sunderland Polytechnic 1989–1992. On graduating, he played in several indie/punk underground bands (Pussycat Trash, Red Monkey, Milky Wimpshake) and set up the cult DIY label/distributor Slampt which ran very successfully between 1992 and 2000. Taking up school teaching in 2001, Pete completed an MA in Music (2005) and then a Ph.D. at Newcastle (2010) whilst simultaneously working as a teacher. He gave up his teaching job to work as an early career fellow at Oxford Brookes in 2012, subsequently becoming Senior Lecturer in Popular Music at Manchester Metropolitan University in 2013. His monographs include *Anyone Can Do It: Tradition, Empowerment and the Punk Underground* (Ashgate, 2012), *Popular Music and the Politics of Novelty* (Bloomsbury Academic, 2016) and *Engaging Students with Music Education: DJ Decks, Urban Music and Child-centred Learning* (Routledge, 2017).

Jan Thorhauge Frederiksen is Associate Professor at the Section of Education, Department of Media, Cognition and Communication, University of Copenhagen. He works primarily in sociology of education and professions, and his previous research is focused on welfare professions, professional training and inequality in education. Currently, his work examines the ways in which changes in recruitment to professional training affect professional work practice and professional boundaries

Mark Gibson is Head of Communications and Media Studies at Monash University. His research interests include cultural industries and cultural policy, everyday life and theories of power in communications and cultural studies. Recent projects he has been involved in include a study of fringe, independent and avant-garde cultural production in Australia and *Creative Suburbia*, examining the prospects for creative industries development in outer suburbia. He is author of *Culture and Power—A History of Cultural Studies* (Oxford, Berg: 2007) and was, until recently, long-term editor of *Continuum—Journal of Cultural Studies*.

Michael Grenfell has held Chair positions in Ireland, Scotland and England, including 1904 Chair of Education in Trinity College Dublin, Research Director at the University of Southampton and Adjunct Professor at the University of Canberra, Australia. He has an extensive background of research on Bourdieu, with whom he worked on various projects including three periods as visiting scholar at the *École des Hautes Études*, Paris. His publications include *Bourdieu: Agent Provocateur* (2004), *Arts Rules: Bourdieu and the Visual Arts* (2007, with C. Hardy), *Bourdieu, Language and Linguistics* (2007), *Bourdieu: Key Concepts* (Routledge, 2012), *Pierre Bourdieu* (Bloomsbury, 2014) and *Bourdieu and Data Analysis* (Lang, 2014).

Michelle Johnston lectures in film, television and screen arts at Curtin University. She specialises in multi-cam television production and has nearly 20 years of experience working in media and the television industry. Michelle has produced five series of an Aboriginal community television program called Noongar Dandjoo and is currently involved in a service-learning program for Curtin media students working with Aboriginal community groups. Her research interests include Indigenous community media, action research and cross-cultural collaboration.

lisahunter researches pedagogy, physical culture, health, social space and symbolic violence and sex/gender/sexualities. She is an independent scholar in Australasian contexts without fixed institutional bonds. Recent publications include *Pierre Bourdieu and Physical Cultures* (2015); 'If you see what i mean? Visual narratives' in *Narrative research in practice: Stories from the field* (2015); 'What a queer space is HPE, or is it yet?' in *Sport, Education and Society* (2017) and 'Desexing surfing? (Queer) pedagogies of possibility' in *Radical Politics, Global Culture: A Critical Surf Studies Reader* (2017). lisahunter has a developing interest in indigenous/first nations/Aboriginal ontologies, meditation and movement.

Bonita Mason The authors are Curtin University academics from Western Australia. Dr. Bonita Mason, a lecturer and Walkley award-winning journalist, has worked with national and regional Aboriginal organisations in Australia. Her award-winning Ph.D. advocated critically reflexive journalism research and practice. Chris Thomson is a lecturer, researcher and journalist specialising in sense-of-place theory and real-time collaborative Aboriginal affairs reporting. As a Higher Education Academy Principal Fellow and Australian Learning and Teaching Fellow,

Prof. Dawn Bennett's research focuses on developing graduate employability. Dr. Michelle Johnston is a film and television program maker who specialises in participatory action research and Aboriginal community engagement.

Prof. Karl Maton is Director of the LCT Centre for Knowledge-Building at the University of Sydney in Australia. He is the creator of Legitimation Code Theory (LCT), which is being widely used to shape research and practice in education, sociology and linguistics. His most recent books include *Knowledge and Knowers: Towards a realist sociology of education* (2014, Routledge), which sets out key ideas of the theory, *Knowledge-building: Educational studies in Legitimation Code Theory* (2016, Routledge), a primer for using the approach. See: http://www.legitimationcodetheory.com

Tony Moore is an Associate Professor in Media Studies at Monash University, where he was also Director of the National Centre for Australian Studies (2010–2013). Tony is author of *Dancing with Empty Pockets: Australia's Bohemians, The Barry McKenzie Movies* and *Death or Liberty: Rebels and Radicals Transported to Australia 1788–1868*, recently adapted as a major documentary. A former ABC TV documentary-maker and commissioning editor at Pluto Press and Cambridge University Press, Tony heads up a major Australian Research Council project examining the connection between emerging creative arts and popular culture, entitled *Fringe to Famous*.

Joan Cortinas Muñoz is a postdoctoral researcher at the UMI/IGlobes (CNRS/University of Arizona) research centre in Tucson. He holds a Ph.D. from the *Ecole des Hautes Etudes en Sciences Sociales* of Paris. His research focuses on public policy changes in two different fields: social policy and water supply policy. His investigation on social policy changes since 1980 has been focused on Spain and France. His research on water supply policy in semi-arid regions is centred on the study of the West of the USA.

Chris Nash is Professor of Journalism at Monash University, and previously the Director of the Australian Centre for Independent Journalism at the University of Technology, Sydney. He has had an award-winning career as a journalist and filmmaker, and in 2016 authored *What is Journalism? The Art and Politics of a Rupture*. He is particularly interested in methodological issues arising for journalism as a discipline in the humanities and social sciences and as a contemporary art form in its own right. He is interested in journalism about the political economy of cities, and environmental and social sustainability.

Franck Poupeau is Senior Researcher at the CNRS. After a postdoctoral study of school choice practices and urban segregation in Paris and its suburbs, he studies the struggles for access to natural resources—water in particular—and utility providers, in the context of expanding areas of poverty in Andean and North American cities. He is the coordinator of several projects on environmental conflicts and water management.

Brian F. O'Neill is a doctoral student in sociology at the University of Illinois at Urbana-Champaign, USA where he is a teaching assistant and researcher. He is affiliated with the French unit, UMI-iGLOBES based in Arizona, and the Centre for Research and Documentation on the Americas at Sorbonne-Nouvelle, Paris-3, where Franck Poupeau is his research director. His work to date has, and continues to focus on, water professionals and policies in the Western USA. Additionally, he has recently begun investigating individuals with rare chronic illness and their access to health care in the context of US health policies.

Emma E. Rowe is an early Career Researcher and Lecturer in the School of Education, Deakin University. Emma's Ph.D. was the recipient of the 'Outstanding Dissertation Award' from the American Association of Research in Education, Qualitative Research SIG (2015). Her monograph is published by Routledge and is entitled, *Middle-class school choice in urban spaces: the economics of public schooling and globalized education reform* (2017). Emma's work is also published in *Journal of Education Policy, Critical Studies in Education* and *International Studies in Sociology of Education*. Emma contributed to the UNESCO Global Education Monitoring Report (Australia) and the International Handbook on Urban Education.

Garth Stahl, Ph.D. is a Senior Lecturer in Literacy and Sociology at the School of Education at the University of South Australia. His research interests lie on the nexus of neoliberalism and sociocultural studies of education, identity, equity/inequality and social change. Currently, his research projects and publications encompass theoretical and empirical studies of learner identities, gender and youth, sociology of schooling in a neoliberal age, gendered subjectivities, equity and difference, and educational reform. Of particular interest is the exploration of counternarratives to neoliberalism around 'value' and 'respectability' for working-class youth.

Chris Thomson is a lecturer at Curtin University where he teaches online journalism, photojournalism and specialist Indigenous reporting. In 2010, Chris set up Australia's first independent, metropolitan news website which he still edits and operates. Before that he was a foundation journalist and national columnist with Fairfax's WAtoday.com.au news website. His research interests include sense of place journalism, and how grassroots news providers are influencing Australia's news agenda.

Katrina Waite is a Lecturer in the Institute of Interactive Media and Learning at the University of Technology Sydney, Australia. Her research is focused on the sociology of higher education, including the use of utopian methods in the practice of developing higher education curriculum and the practices of students and staff in university decision-making.

Jen Webb is Distinguished Professor of Creative Practice at the University of Canberra, Australia; she is also Director of the Centre for Creative and Cultural Research and a poet. Her recent works include the scholarly volumes *Researching creative writing* (Frontinus, 2015) and *Art and human rights: Contemporary Asian contexts* (with Caroline Turner; Manchester UP, 2016) and the creative volumes *Stolen stories, borrowed lines* (Mark Time Press, 2015) and *Sentences from the archive* (Recent Work Press, 2016). Research for this chapter was supported by the Australian Research Council for the project 'Understanding creative excellence: A case study in poetry' (DP130100402).

LIST OF FIGURES

Fig. 4.1	The sub-field of contemporary poetry	59
Fig. 6.1	Cloud of modalities 1990	90
Fig. 6.2	Cloud of individuals, 1990	91
Fig. 6.3	Cloud of modalities, 2010	92
Fig. 6.4	Cloud of individuals 2010	93
Fig. 8.1	Multi-perspectival approach (Candlin and Crichton 2011b; Crichton 2004, 2010)	123
Fig. 13.1	The field of boys' education	209
Fig. 14.1	Harvey (2006, p. 135): A general matrix of spatialities	225
Fig. 16.1	Specialisation plane (Maton 2014, p. 30)	256
Fig. 16.2	Knowledge-code dispositions	261
Fig. 16.3	Knower-code position	263
Fig. 16.4	Relativist-code experiences	264

LIST OF TABLES

Table 6.1   Cohorts by profession   87
Table 13.1   The work of texts   213

CHAPTER 1

Introduction: On Doing Field Analysis

James Albright and Deborah Hartman

Adopting Bourdieu's reflexive approach to any object of study carries with it certain risks. His reputation as one of the pre-eminent sociologists of the latter half of the twentieth century invites disputation, which has risen, at least in part, from how his theorising matured over this time, the range of research he undertook, and how his work had been translated and appreciated in Anglophone circles. In this book, contemporary researchers will find productive, "generous" and, equally, "generative" interpretations and applications of Bourdieu's reflexive sociology that engage and build upon it. Interpretations and critical appraisals of Bourdieu's work continue to provide constructive openings for research across many fields of inquiry.

Attending to how researchers employ Bourdieusian field analysis is instructive (Albright 2006). As outlined in our Forward, this book's contributors provide descriptions of their work in operationalising Bourdieusian concepts within field analysis. This introduction provides readers with an understanding of field with specific reference to the mature Bourdieu's conceptual and analytical moves in *The social structures of the*

J. Albright (✉) · D. Hartman
University of Newcastle, Callaghan, Australia

J. Albright et al. (eds.), *Bourdieu's Field Theory and the Social Sciences*,
https://doi.org/10.1007/978-981-10-5385-6_1

economy (2005), *On the state: Lectures at the College de France, 1989–1992* (2014), and elsewhere. In the first, he argues and demonstrates through a meticulous examination of the buying and selling of houses how field analysis uncovers the unexamined assumptions of traditional economist explanations of the market. Bourdieu reveals how the State constructs the market through housing policy that favours dominant actors over others the market, which can decide, for example, whether to promote private housing or collective provision. He describes how the State consecrates symbolic constructions, which constitute, in a strong sense, for buyers and sellers the relative value of houses, neighbourhoods and towns.

Field emerged in Bourdieusian reflexive sociology as conceptual arma-ture that attempts to overcome inhibiting binarisms of objectivity and subjectivity, resistance and agency, structuralism and phenomenology. Bourdieu's project was to ground a reflexive analysis and critique con-stituted within his concept of social fields to construct a science with an attitude (Ladwig 1996). His reflexive sociology places a methodological obligation on its practitioners to address their own positionality within the field and social space in general. Theorising "science" as historically and socially constituted practice, field analysis admits no a priori episte-mologically privileged positions to claims about knowledge and the con-struction of knowledge.

Of particular relevance in undertaking field analysis is Bourdieu's cri-tique of the scholastic disposition. He argued that the freedom and privi-lege to indulge in scholarly language games and contempt for ordinary language, largely invisible to scholars, to the extent that the gulf between the logic of practice and the logic of scholarly fields is justified and per-petuated in intellectual fields that purport to neutrally and scientifically analyse practice (Bourdieu 2000). Bourdieu long posited that the efforts of the enquiring subject to negate himself as an empirical subject, to dis-appear behind the anonymous record of his operations and his results, are doomed in advance to failure (Bourdieu 1988, p. 25).

For Bourdieu, actors in any field employ two types of knowledge of the field: the first is a logic of practice, or a practical feel for the game—an ability to understand and negotiate one's cultural field. The second is a reflexive relation to that field and one's own practices within it. For Bourdieu, the logic of practice, although allowing people to be quite successful in a field, can also be quite limiting, as it is formed largely by the constraints of the field itself. While a player may have a good feel for what is happening in his or her field, and know the written and unwritten conventions governing it, and what is appropriate in certain circumstances, what is possible is largely determined by these constraints. Yet, the field is constantly being transformed by the agents' actions. Bourdieu reflexive stance requires researchers to examine their social and cultural origins and categories, positions in the field, and a move away from an "intellectual bias" or tendency to see practices as ideas to be contemplated rather than as conceptual complications to be resolved. For Bourdieu, reflexivity is "the systematic exploration of the unthought categories of thought which delimit the thinkable and pre-determine the thought" (Webb et al. 2002, p.75). One of the clearest examples of Bourdieu commencing an investigation in this manner can be found in his first lecture on the State (Bourdieu 2014, pp. 3–22). He begins by examining the the values, assumptions, questions and approaches to understanding what may be understood as the state, as an "unthinkable object".

Further, Bourdieu (1990) argued that Nietzsche's notion of genealogy assists in overcoming researchers' tendencies to unquestioningly reproduce the common sense of the field. In this regard, in his "Lecture 28", illustrated by how the French Revolution may be understood in the development of the modern state, Bourdieu posits that the division between sociology and history is not justified and that all sociology should be historical (Bourdieu 2014, pp. 322–353). Bourdieu's (1993) sociology is reflexive when radical doubt is combined with genealogical analysis.

Through self-reflexivity and genealogy, researchers construct the properties of fields, understand how they emerged, and name how they affect agents' relational positions, actions and interests. Yet, in order to practice this kind of methodology, researchers walk a fine line between the logic of discovery and the logic of validation. Often discovery is seen as a matter of chance, based on intuition, while validation is considered scientific, distinct from interest and intuition. Yet for Bourdieu, the discovery moment is every bit as scientific as the validation processes. Discovery comes out of social philosophy—it is the basis of speculation which leads to the hypothesis and therefore the research project or program. Furthermore, empiricism is not necessarily scientific, unless the theorising that grounds it is sound. Researchers can easily forget the importance of different contexts and rely on untested assumptions. Bourdieu's relational approach to social research takes pains to show how invention and validation, collectives and individuals, and systems and individual agents are related to and dependent upon each other, rather than privileging one over the other (Webb et al. 2002).

Field analysis broadly consists of three methodological moves. First, the field being studied needs to be related to the broader field of power. Second, the structure of relations between positions taken up by individuals and groups as they contest for legitimating needs to be identified. The forms of economic and cultural capital that are up for grabs and the distribution of capitals within the field need to be described; that is, dominant and subordinate positions within the field are sketched. The difficulty here is that these relations can shift from site to site within the field. Third, the class habitus that individuals bring to the positions they take up in the field and the social trajectories they take up in it need to be identified (Swartz 1997, pp. 141–142).

First Move: Relations to the Broader Field of Power

Bourdieu's reflexive sociology does not totalise its objects of analysis. Identifying the positions, values and discourses in a field does not mean that everything is known about that field. Indeed, Bourdieu's original concept of field is as a conceptual heuristic, existing only relationally, as a set of possibilities that could be made by people or institutions engaged in a particular activity (Grenfell and James 2004; Nash 1999). He defined a field as a meta-theoretical open concept that circumscribes the structure of a space within which agents operate. As a metaphor for social space, Bourdieu's concept of field grew out of his work on French intellectual and artistic worlds as a way of drawing attention to specific interests governing those cultural worlds (Bourdieu 1984; Swartz 1997; Webb et al. 2002). In two of his early studies, he applied the concept to the French education and higher education systems (Bourdieu 1988, 1996; Bourdieu and Passeron 1990). Concisely, a field is

> [A] network or configuration, of objective relations between positions. These positions are objectively defined, in their existence and in the determinations, they impose upon their occupants, agents or institutions, by their present and potential situation (situs) in the structure of the distribution of species of power (or capital) whose possession commands access to specific profits that are at stake in the field, as well as by their objective relation to other positions (domination, subordination, homology, etc.). (Bourdieu and Wacquant 1992, p. 97)

In earlier work, Bourdieu and Nice (1980, p. 147) described practices as being over-determined. Struggles within fields produce cultural distinctions that are at the same time social distinctions, (re)producing social patterns and conflict from one field to another. Bourdieu contended these effects are more structural than intentional. Inequitable systems of difference for individuals and groups are inscribed in the practical logic of habitus that underlies the connection across fields "…[s]ince fields vary historically in their degree of autonomy from the economy, the polity, and class structure, no universal classification system connecting the various fields can be established" (Swartz 1997, pp. 134–135).

Bourdieu's genealogical approach contends that there is an historical tendency for fields to increase their autonomy from the field of power, which is played against the dominance of economic fields and economic capitals over cultural fields and capitals (Bourdieu and Wacquant 1992). The historical play of relative autonomy of a field can be described and analysed against its capacity to retranslate and interpret the demands of overlapping and intersecting fields on its own terms, especially within the field of power. "External influences are always translated into the internal logic of fields, mediated through the structure and dynamic of the field" (Bourdieu and Wacquant 1992, p. 105). Further, "autonomy is reflected in the field's ability to legitimate existing social relations within itself through a defence of its doxa, reason, and value for the field's existence" (Swartz 1997, pp. 126–127). Highly autonomous fields acquire forms of symbolic power to regulate the exchange of capitals within them. Less autonomous fields are subject to greater outside influence upon the contested value of capitals within them.

Field analysis situates individuals and groups, organisations and institutions along axes of difference within fields in terms of dominance and subordination, exclusion and usurpation, reproduction and change. Inter-field homologies and differences can then be found for actors along lines of class, gender, race, etc. The "homology of position among individuals and groups in different fields means that those that find themselves in dominated positions in the struggle for legitimation in one field tend also to find themselves in subordinated positions in other fields" (Swartz 1997, p. 130). Intra-field homologies can be found that reveal that a position taken up in a field affects an individual's or group's trajectory through it, a homology between the space of field occupied and the space of works done in it (p. 132).

In *The social structures of the economy* (2005), published in French in 2000, Bourdieu employed a range of qualitative and quantitative methods fit for purpose to uncover the policy and regulatory changes that have structured the French financial and building industries. Using correspondence analysis of available national statistics, what is revealed is the relation between class and the housing market and how what is being sold is not homes but credit. Bourdieu's interest in credit and housing can be traced back to early in his career (Bourdieu et al. 1963). In the 1990s, he returned to consider how the economic field might be productively understood and researched. He argues for "a realist definition of economic reason as an encounter between dispositions which are socially constituted (in relation to a field) and the structures, themselves socially constituted, of that field" (Bourdieu 2005, p. 193), within which he undertakes an analysis of "the economic habitus" and the many forms of capital that at work in its structuration.

In his *On the state: Lectures at the Collège de France, 1989–1992* (2014), he theorises the State as a homologous meta-field, closely associated with what he terms, the field of power, that exercises relative symbolic (and in the last resort, physical violence) domination over social space. Early within the lectures, Bourdieu employs examples of French housing market policy formation to clarify how the State may be understood, (Bourdieu 2014, pp. 13–17, 31). And, in considering his study of French housing policy, Bourdieu lays bare his methodology in the simplest of terms. He argues that State is not found in policy but in the contest of policy making, in what he calls "state action", which is a complicated space of competing agents. By way of example, he sketches the work of "commissions", who work closely with associations, authorities, banks and industry, in a "complex balance of forces", each their own valued expertise and esteem, in a struggle to determine a decision that has "material and symbolic" consequences. Bourdieu argues that "State" is discursive "shorthand" for "a set of extremely complex structures and processes". In attempting to understand how French housing policy is made, he argues that conceptualising of the State, better termed, the Field of Power, entails "thousands" of agents in "articulated and opposing sub-fields, etc., in complex relationships" (Bourdieu 2014, pp. 110–111).

Bourdieu's genealogy of the State elaborates a history of the development of the construction of juridical, bureaucratic and political sub-fields within what is in part the field of power. Bourdieu's argues that the origins of the modern state are a history of "progressive constitution of a differentiated space, an assemblage of fields—juridical field, administrative [bureaucratic] field, intellectual field, political field in the strict sense" (Bourdieu 2014, p. 310). Each are "differentiated" spaces of "mutual competition" that were constructed through struggles, over the law, the general common good, etc., and populated with historic and epistemic actors that employ various strategies in important struggles or "games". Intra sub-field struggles within the field of power are complicated by inter competitions over relative autonomy and influence in governing society. Bourdieu cites the "revolt of the juridical field against the bureaucratic sub-field that was part of the process of the [modern state's] constitution" (p. 311). His thesis is further elaborated in the second chapter of his *The social structure of the economy (2005)*, where he outlines the genesis and structure of the bureaucratic sub-field of the field of power as it related to French housing policy in the 1970–1980s. Of particular interest is his comments regarding the small sub-field of the high civil service, which enjoy relatively high levels of autonomy and is particularly engaged in debates about the very nature of the State. Yet, even here, "competitive struggles ... occur [that] owe their logic in part to external pressures, injunctions or influences" (p. 93).

SECOND MOVE: RELATIONS, CAPITALS, DISTRIBUTIONS, POSITION TAKING AND STRATEGIES

Bourdieu's understanding of the State, the field of power, as a meta-field is focused on its active use of power as "an organizing principle of differentiation and struggle throughout all fields" (Bourdieu and Wacquant 1992, pp. 229–230). Individuals and groups, organisations and institutions that hold dominant positions and capital in social space occupy the field of power. Bourdieu notes that the state is divided between those who hold cultural and economic capital. Contests in fields draw unequally from these sources of capital to make distinctions and derive position. Bourdieu notes the greater the difference held by positions in fields between cultural and economic capital, the more likely they are to be opposed in struggles within the field of power (Swartz 1997, pp. 137). Bourdieu's framework posits a homologous polarity in economic and cultural capital to that of the field of power and other relatively autonomous fields within social space. The identification of the distribution of capitals in a field and the resonance of these capitals in intersecting fields is important when studying contesting relations.

Bourdieu described the field of power as a meta-field. The field of power is "an organizing principle of differentiation and struggle throughout all fields" (Bourdieu and Wacquant 1992, pp. 229–230). Individuals and groups, organisations and institutions that hold dominant positions and capital in social space occupy it. Contests in fields draw unequally from these sources of cultural and economic capital to make distinctions and derive position. Bourdieu notes the greater the difference held by positions in fields between cultural and economic capital, the more likely they are to be opposed in their struggle within that field (Swartz 1997, pp. 137).

The structures operating in the field largely determine the possibilities for what is thinkable and unthinkable or expressible or inexpressible (Grenfell and James 2004). The ways fields are structured shape what we know and how we come to know it—the limits of knowledge produced and what can be recognised or goes misrecognised. He argues that it is the second dimension along which fields are structured is the opposition between old and new. Bourdieu argues that influxes of new players or agents in a field can be forces for transformation or conservation, depending on the situation in the field and the forces within and external to the field. While fields are likely to have their own species of valued cultural capital, Bourdieu argues that all fields are structured largely in the same ways.

The internal mechanisms operating within relatively autonomous fields shape what is possible within any given field. In any field, there are struggles for legitimisation—the right to exercise the "symbolic violence" of the domination of one set of ideas over others. This legitimisation produces an orthodoxy, or doxa in a field. While there are always struggles within fields, strongly autonomous intellectual fields, such as physics, for example, have internal mechanisms and structures that define the boundaries of these struggles and determine the nature of the field by defining: (1) the agreements about what is at stake; (2) who the players are and what positions they occupy; (3) a consensus regarding the rules by which the field works; and (4) a shared interpretive frame that allows those in the field to make sense of what other actors are doing in the field in a particular situation.

The similarities of structure, along the opposition between field-specific cultural capital and economic capital, and between old and new, are what Bourdieu calls homologies between fields. Bourdieu suggests that although fields may be relatively autonomous, there are homologies within and across fields. This means that all fields develop positions of dominance and subordination, and mechanisms of reproduction and change, and actors within the fields have strategies of exclusion and usurpation. However, the notion of homologies suggests that, through the distribution of various types of capital, those who find themselves in a dominated position in the struggle in one field also tend to find themselves in subordinate positions in other fields. So, Bourdieu argues struggles in the cultural field tend to produce cultural distinctions, such as gender or class, that are also social distinctions.

Bourdieu (2005) writes that there are even more significant homologies between the field of power (the State), economic fields and intellectual fields. These homologies offer a strong explanatory lens for understanding the cultural struggles within and across these fields. He suggests that the amount that can be explained about fields by the logic of the field varies according to the autonomy of the field (Bourdieu 2005).

Dominant actors within fields lay claim to the imposition of the legitimate vision and division of the social world. Those who deal professionally in making things explicit have two things in common. First, they strive to set out explicitly practical principles of vision and division. Second, they struggle, each within their own field, to impose these principles and have them recognised as legitimate categories of construction of the social world. Yet, in every field, the implicit presuppositions of players in each field that make up the illusio of the field are not completely known or explicit to the players. The dispositions of the players, shaped in some ways by the illusio of the field, ensure that all players see the game as important and worth playing.

What may be explained about fields by the logic of the field varies according to the autonomy of the field. He further argues that contrary to what appears to be the case, the political field is increasingly autonomous and governed by its own logic. In contrast, the journalistic field and the social science field are relatively lacking in autonomy and subject to the external power, particularly from the state. He also suggests the journalistic field is increasingly important to other fields as it has a strong tendency towards its heteronomous or commercial pole, and this tendency is influencing other fields in the same direction (Bourdieu 2005). When considering the field of power, Bourdieu has theorised that fields in modern states contest over "statist capital" circulating within the field of power (Bourdieu 1989; Bourdieu and Wacquant 1992, pp. 111–115). As a form of "meta-capital", statist capital exercises power over the exchange rates of economic and cultural capital. Recursively, holders of economic or cultural capital constitute the state through struggle over the symbolic and legislative capital of the state.

One of the charges put to Bourdieusian field analysis has been that "the productive nature of Bourdieu's model needs more elaboration. Further, the production and shape of homologies across fields require clarification. If one were to grant that structural homology exists between individuals or groups that exist across different fields, we would need to know the social process through which this 'objective' alliance or opposition obtains" (Swartz 1997, p. 135). Bourdieu goes to some pains in his genealogy of the State and his analysis of French housing policy to provide an understanding of the processes that "permit strategic linkages between groups (and not others)" (p. 135). Within his analysis, he describes methodological insights derived from using correspondence analysis to go move from "description" to "explanation" and

> bring to light the structure of positions or – and this amounts to the same thing – the structure of distribution of specific interests and powers that determines and *explains* [emphasis in original text] the strategies of agents and, consequently, the history of main interventions which led to the elaboration and implementation of the law on building subsidies. (Bourdieu 2005, p. 102)

Bourdieu's analysis of the work of "commissions" allows him to draw lines between the housing, banking, intellectual and civil service fields (pp. 114–118).

In *The social structures of the economy*, Bourdieu (2005) provides his mature rationale for the benefits of conducting field analysis, in this case, how to understand "economic reason". He argues, "We must ... attempt to construct a realist definition of economic reason as an encounter between dispositions, which are socially constituted (in relation to a field) and the structures, themselves socially constituted, of that field" (p. 193). He begins by outlining "the economic field" and follows with an analysis of the "economic habitus" and the volume of capitals that help structure it. Within the economic field, the four capitals (cultural social, economic and symbolic) found in most fields are at play. Economic players' "goodwill" and "brand name" form some of their symbolic worth. In addition, they hold commercial (distribution and marketing) and technological (science and IT) capitals. The key protagonists within the economic field are firms, with which the State plays an important role.

Bourdieu contends that economic reason tends to elide the intersection of the State within the field.

Economic reason, Bourdieu (2005) contends, fails to appreciate that "It is not prices that determine everything, but everything that determines prices" (p. 197). Field to relative extent through the competitive struggle between those firms that occupy dominant positions with the economic field and those that do not. Smaller firms develop niche strategies to survive and rarely challenge the larger. Moderately sized firms follow the logic of market orthodoxy determined by the dominant players. While economic reason focuses on agents' choice and agency, Bourdieu's analysis reveals that "brutal objectivity and universality" (p. 200) forges the stable logic of the economic field.

Change in the economic field usually comes from outside. One source of change is when actors threaten the field's relative autonomy by calling upon the State to intervene. Bourdieu argues that the economic field is a social construct where "the different agents engaged in the field contribute to varying degrees through the modifications they manage to impose upon it, by drawing, particularly, on the state power they are able to control and guide" (Bourdieu 2005, p. 204). He illustrates this through an analysis of French housing policy since the 1970s, which wound down social housing and freed up the availability of housing loans as part of a shift to neoliberalism within the field of power (Bourdieu 2008). State interventions realign the relative value of the capitals of firms and change their strategies for gaining or maintaining market share.

Interestingly, Bourdieu describes several sub-fields within the economic field. Firms constitute structures with their own relative autonomy to the larger economic field in which owners and managers vie to determine the firm's direction. After detailed description of the French housing market, Bourdieu's (2007, 2008) reworking of earlier conceptions of "the domestic economy" brings analytical sharpness to illustrate what happens when it meets the economic field. In the exchange, the often-anxious buyers must negotiate the relative weight of debt against their aspiration for a desirable home. The transaction is complex and uncertain. Buyers are "assisted" by sales agents who, while they must make a sale, recognising the economic constraints that shape buyers' purchases, having them recognise the logic of necessity to often settle for less in what Bourdieu describes as "a work of mourning" (Bourdieu 2005, p. 171). Bourdieu describes as "petit-bourgeois suffering" the great sacrifices that many buyers make to either enter the housing market or gain the house of their dreams.

Third Move: Identifying Class Habitus and Social Trajectories

For Bourdieu, the point of research is to make sense of why things happen and the bases for the presence of social distinctions. As well as the concept of the educational, social science, political and journalistic fields as relatively autonomous social fields, two other concepts, habitus and cultural capital, are needed to fully explain why and how social distinctions operate. It is the relationship between an individual's habitus dispositions and the structure of the social field which together shape his or her practices (Bourdieu 1993; Bourdieu and Passeron 1990).

Habitus, according to Bourdieu, is the system whereby our experiences as individuals growing up, shape our ways of thinking, acting and feeling to the extent that they become dispositions or tendencies that we can enact in a wide variety of social situations. As actors faced with an array of choices in a field—such as education—our habitus means that we have inclinations to behave in some ways rather than others. Schooling acts to create a general disposition towards a cultured habitus, thereby enabling new creative responses capable of transcending the social conditions in which it was produced.

While Bourdieu largely used habitus to describe and explain class relations, it has and can be used in an analysis of differences across gender, race, location or any other category, such as the intellectual habitus of the education researcher. The concept of habitus is multi-layered, with both individual and collective aspects that include a complex interplay between the past and the present. While a person's individual history has formed their habitus, so too has the collective history of their family, class and gender. The habitus within social groups (such academics in a particular field) differs to the extent to which individuals' social trajectories diverge from one another. Similarly, current social situations are not just acted upon, they are internalised to become another layer of the habitus.

Habitus can be expressed bodily through durable ways of standing, speaking, walking and thereby thinking and feeling. It can also be expressed through agency, allowing a person to draw on a repertoire of possible actions in any situation, that can either be transformative or constraining, depending on the situation.

While habitus allows for individual agency, it also predisposes us towards excluding certain practices unfamiliar in our cultural situations (Bourdieu 1993; Bourdieu and Passeron 1990; Reay 2004). It shapes our dispositions towards or away from certain practices. For Bourdieu, this means that practices or actions cannot be understood simply in such objective terms as the rules, values and discourses of a field. Nor can they be understood purely subjectively in terms of individual uncontextualised choices or decisions. People do think and act in strategic ways and try to use the rules of the game to their own advantage. Yet at the same time, he argues, they act unconsciously, unaware that their goals, motives and aspirations are not spontaneous or natural, but shaped by their habitus. Bourdieu argues that the habitus of a player combines with the structure of any field to render some thoughts and actions unthinkable. What is thinkable and unthinkable within various discourses is performed in actors' habiti.

Bourdieu's conceptualisation of field is inextricably linked with and came later than his other key theoretical and methodological tools and concepts of habitus and capital. He argues that any change or new entry into a field shifts the boundaries among all other positions in the field. For fields to operate there must be agents with the appropriate habitus to be capable and willing to invest in the field. New arrivals to fields must be willing to pay the price of entry, involving recognition of the importance of the game and the practical knowledge of how to play it. Bourdieu and Wacquant (1992) argue that the competitive logic of fields helps create the conditions for the misrecognition of power relations in ways that contribute to the maintenance of the existing social order. According to Bourdieu and Wacquant, established agents in a field tend to pursue conservation strategies and challengers are likely to opt for subversive strategies. Challengers oblige the old guard to mount a defence of its privileges. All actors in a field share a tacit acceptance that the struggle is worth pursuing and the deep structure of the field imposes and legitimises specific forms of struggle. For example, in academia, personal insults and physical violence are considered unprofessional but challenging the degree of objectivity in an opposing viewpoint is considered fair play (Bourdieu 1991; Swartz 1997).

In Bourdieusian studies (Bourdieu and Wacquant 1992), there is an increasing emphasis on moments of misalignment and tension between habitus and fields which may give rise to social change. The same habitus can lead to very different practices and stances depending on the state of the field.

In *Homo academicus*, Bourdieu (1988) distinguishes between empirical individuals and epistemic individuals. He distinguishes between the ways terms, such as names of people, are used in ordinary language and how they are used in sociological analysis. In ordinary language, when a particular individual is named, the name is merely a label, identifying or indicating a person recognisable as a real person, different to others. The label or name identifies the person but does not describe or analyse the differences.

On the other hand, epistemic individuals are constructed through sociological analysis by reference to the terms in the analysis. Bourdieu argued that sociologists construct epistemic individuals by reference to the particular characteristics important in any analysis, such as their position as an established incumbent or challenger. These characteristics are of course different from those used in ordinary description of an individual or in other scientific analyses of individuals, such as psychoanalysis. A Bourdieusian field analysis indicates that certain players in the field take on or represent epistemic positions in both the discourses of the field and in the social field where they operate. While all players in a field seek to influence the field by the texts they produce, the texts of epistemic players are highly significant in that they show how the field as a whole is constructed by the various moves players make through texts. The meta-field of power and the economic field are constructed within struggles to monopolise the naming function of official discourse and so to legitimate common values and representations. Actors

> must at the same time produce a discourse, and produce a belief in the universality of their discourse by palpable production in the sense of the evocation of spirits, phantoms – the state is phantom – of the thing that will guarantee what they are doing: 'the nation', the workers', the people', 'the state secret', national security', 'social demand,' etc. (Bourdieu 2014, p. 63)

In sum, Bourdieu's moves, reflexive and nonlinear, produce these productive understandings of the nature of the State and the field of the economy as "happenings". The objects researchers study are genetic, provisional and dynamic.

REFERENCES

Albright, J. (2006). Literacy education after Bourdieu. *The American Journal of Semiotics, 22*(1–4), 107–128.

Bourdieu, P. (1984). *Distinction a social critique of the judgement of taste* (R. Nice, Trans.). London: Routledge & Kegan Paul.

Bourdieu, P. (1988). *Homo academicus* (P. Collier, Trans.). Cambridge: Polity Press.

Bourdieu, P. (1989). Social space and symbolic power. *Sociological Theory*, 7(1), 14–25.

Bourdieu, P. (1991). *Language and symbolic power* (G. Raymond & M. Adamson, Trans.). Cambridge: Polity Press.

Bourdieu, P. (1993). *Sociology in question* (R. Nice, Trans.). London: Sage.

Bourdieu, P. (1996). *Noblesse d'état. The state nobility: Elite schools in the field of power* (L. Clough, Trans.). Cambridge, UK: Polity Press.

Bourdieu, P. (2000). *Pascalian meditations.* Cambridge: Polity Press.

Bourdieu, P. (2005). *The social structures of the economy.* Cambridge: Polity.

Bourdieu, P. (2007). *Sketch for a self-analysis* (R. Nice, Trans.). Chicago: University of Chicago Press.

Bourdieu, P. (2008). *The bachelors' ball: The crisis of peasant society in Béarn.* Cambridge: Polity.

Bourdieu, P. (2014). *On the state: Lectures at the Collège de France, 1989–1992.* P. Champagne, R. Lenoir, F. Poupeau, & M. C. Rivière (Eds.). Cambridge: Polity.

Bourdieu, P., Boltanski, L., & Chamboredon, J. C. (1963). *The Bank and its clients: Elements of a sociology of credit.* Center for European Sociology of the Ecole Pratique des Hautes Etudes.

Bourdieu, P., & Nice, R. (1980). The production of belief: Contribution to an economy of symbolic goods. *Media, Culture & Society*, 2(3), 261–293.

Bourdieu, P., & Passeron, J. (1990). *Reproduction in education, society, and culture* (R. Rice, Trans.). London: Sage in association with Theory, Culture & Society, Dept. of Administrative and Social Studies, Teesside Polytechnic.

Bourdieu, P., & Wacquant, L. (1992). *An invitation to reflexive sociology.* Chicago: University of Chicago Press.

Grenfell, M., & James, D. (2004). Change in the field—changing the field: Bourdieu and the methodological practice of educational research. *British Journal of Sociology of Education*, 25(4), 507–523.

Ladwig, J. (1996). *Academic distinctions.* New York: Routledge.

Nash, R. (1999). Realism in the sociology of education: 'Explaining' social differences in attainment. *British Journal of Sociology of Education*, 20(1), 107–125.

Reay, D. (2004). 'It's all becoming a habitus': Beyond the habitual use of habitus in educational research. *British Journal of Sociology of Education*, 25(4), 431–444.

Swartz, D. (1997). *Culture and Power: The sociology of Pierre Bourdieu.* Chicago: The University of Chicago Press.

Webb, J., Schirato, T., & Danaher, G. (2002). *Understanding Bourdieu.* London: Sage.

PART I

Field as Both a Conceptual and Empirical Object of Analysis

Part 1 presents, within the constraints of what space has allowed, accounts from six studies from across remarkably disparate domains of human activity. Appreciating how researchers have employed Bourdieu's methodology within the particularities of their own fields of inquiry may assist in understanding the kind of operational thinking needed when conducting field analysis. Part 1's studies have been chosen as examples of research conceptualising and problematising a field, as 'a system of relations among selected, abstracted, and simplified properties, which is deliberately constructed for the purpose of description, exposition, and prediction...' (Bourdieu 1977, p. 75).

The selected chapters of this Part have focused on the work that must be done prior to field work. For example, in Chap. 1, Joan Cortinas, Brian Neill and Franck Poupeau analyse the methodological conditions for applying the notion of the field to water policy. This chapter is one of the few to undertake field analysis in environmental studies, socio-technical systems or public policies (some exceptions include Bourdieu's analysis of housing policies or Vincent Dubois' researches on cultural policies). Often, research in this field is conducted through the lens of applied research. In their study, Cortinas, Neill and Poupeau have used field theory to understand the logics of decision-making and the coalitions involved in water policy, which allowed for a comprehensive analysis of the large multiplicity of institutions and agents, from federal to municipal levels, including states and counties involved in the management of water.

The next two chapters in this Part shift focus to the employment of field in education in the arts. In Chap. 2, an example of locating case study within field analysis, Garth Stahl and Pete Dale address issues of gender and equity within a specific site of music education. Jen Webb, in Chap. 3, provides her thinking when constructing poetry as a field of cultural production. Stahl and Dale draw upon empirical evidence from a small-scale study of white working-class boys' conceptions of music-making in the north-east of England where they showed themselves to be capable of high levels of engagement, enthusiasm and success despite generally being considered 'low achieving' and 'highly disaffected' in formal schooling. Webb argues that operationalising field theory enabled her to develop an evidence-based consideration of changes in poetry as a field, which highlighted the role of relations within it, with a particular focus on the 'game' of position-taking, and contemporary ways of translating symbolic capital to economic capital.

Chapters 4 and 6 investigate the field of higher education. Jacquie Widin, in Chap. 4, theorises the Australian higher education field, which she argues is dominated and dominating within the broader national and international fields of power, and is itself a contested, uneven space. In this chapter, multiple case studies are referenced to exemplify the stratifications, differentiations and complexities of the power relations within and surrounding the field. Emma Rowe, in Chap. 6, presents a reflexive self-analysis of her own positionality within participant observation as a method in the academy. This chapter illuminates through field analysis the barriers, provocations, ethical contentions and epistemological contests that arise when engaging in participant observation.

In the remaining chapter in this Part, Chap. 5, Jan Thorhauge Frederiksen constructs the Danish field of welfare work to understand the changes in its structure through geometric data analyses between 1980 and 2013. Examining the institutions and agents of the Danish welfare state, who are organised by several welfare professions—teachers, social workers, physiotherapists, social educators, nurses, librarians, police officers and others—Frederiksen illustrates, through field analysis, that Danish welfare policies and administrative reforms are changing its iconic welfare state often in unintended ways through shifting professional recruitment, and hierarchies. His analysis reveals that dominant struggles within the field of power affect the structure of the welfare state.

As examples of research conceptualising and problematising particular fields, each provides readers with in situ access to aspects of the three methodological moves outlined in the Introduction. Diverse in how they collected their data, providing examples of a range of quantitative and qualitative methods, these chapters' authors focus on their meta-methodological concerns in relating the focus of their study to the broader field of power, determining the structure of relations in determining the forms of economic and cultural capital at stake, and the habitus of actors, their positionality and strategies.

Four important considerations emerge when reading across these chapters. No one chapter addresses all of these concerns. Nor are the concerns found to be addressed equally in them. The first is that field theory is not a method so much as it is an orientation in which a variety of methods can be employed. Methodological choices are determined by the object of the analysis and less so by the meta-methodological theoretical concerns that guide the research. The second is that to varying degrees, these six studies are mindful of relating their analysis to the field of power, even when conducting small-scale case studies. Next, in relative degrees, each provides a genealogy, which attempts to historise their field analysis. And, finally, these researchers' employment of Bourdieu's concepts of capital and habitus is not 'cherry-picked'. Capital and habitus form part of their analysis that is framed within a fully conceptualised understanding of their place within field theory.

Methodological diversity is represented across all the studies presented in this collection. Readers may find Chap. 6's discussion of 'participant objectivation', which Rowe contends is underdeveloped and underexplored in social sciences, especially the political and ethical responsibilities of doing ethnographic research within Bourdieusian field analysis, provocative. Chapter 4 presents an example of case study research where sites within an Australian technology university, are constrained by powerful national and international institutions, the field of higher education and the broader field of power, which is constituted by interplay of 'governmental departments, institutions such as Government ministries, Australian aid agencies, Australian foreign relations organisations, international aid and finance organisations, Australian universities and universities outside of Australia' (Widin, this volume).

With respect to early analytical moves in relation to the field of power, Chap. 1 is exemplary in how field analysis permits Cortinas, Neill and Poupeau to construct a view of US water policy as a complex, hierarchical world involving various semi-autonomous levels. Their analysis provides a picture of the field of power as partially constituted in the actions of dominant coalitions of water policy interests.

Additionally, Cortinas, Neill and Poupeau illustrate the genetic nature of field analysis in providing a framework for understanding US water policies through time, as well as across levels of action. Chapter 3 also reveals the social scientist as historian. Webb's construction of the sub-field of poetry engages readers in a recount of how the institutions, agents, publishing practices and audience engagement, the forms of capital and consecration, the conditions for entry to the field, etc., have evolved in the past half-century.

Finally, and importantly, as editors, we have attempted to bring together a collection of researches that counter the tendency to cherry-pick from the Bourdieusian tool chest. The theoretical borrowings of Bourdieu's notions of capital and habitus are common across many fields of research. We have tried to demonstrate that any appropriation of one entails them all in order to fully engage their full analytical worth. In this first Part, in Chap. 2, Stahl and Dale theorise how the fields they create influence their habitus in order to understand discursively what 'achievement' and 'success' mean. They demonstrate how boys' habitus moves across fields (the formal schooling, the student-led learning culture) the boys negotiate doxic conceptions of how learning is constituted. Again, in Chap. 5, Frederiksen illustrates how relations of dominance manifest between specific welfare professions and between forms of capital, revealing a changing set of relations between capital possession and welfare work, i.e. a changing class-structure of welfare work. These chapters represent in their own ways rich, deep and reflexive engagement with the fields that are the object of their studies.

REFERENCE

Pierre, B. (1977). *Outline of a Theory of Practice* (R. Nice, Trans.). Cambridge: Cambridge University Press.

CHAPTER 2

Drought and Water Policy in the Western USA: Genesis and Structure of a Multi-level Field

Joan Cortinas, Brian F. O'Neill and Franck Poupeau

INTRODUCTION

The objective of this text is to analyse the methodological conditions for applying the notion of field to a specific kind of policy: water policy. This research, based on a collective work that has been conducted since September 2014 on water conflicts and on the management of the "mega-drought" affecting the Western USA, constitutes a challenge for several reasons. Indeed, the notion of field has never been applied to the area of environmental studies, as it has essentially been applied to intellectual, cultural and political fields. Water is not a symbolic good like literature, art

J. Cortinas · F. Poupeau
UMI iGLOBES, CNRS/University of Arizona, Tucson, AZ, USA

B.F. O'Neill (✉)
Department of Sociology, University of Illinois at Urbana-Champaign, Champaign, IL, USA

© The Author(s) 2018   21
J. Albright et al. (eds.), *Bourdieu's Field Theory and the Social Sciences*,
https://doi.org/10.1007/978-981-10-5385-6_2

or ideas, and even if it is often presented as essential for life, with symbolic properties (Bachelard 1999), modern water services mainly deliver a material good, on an economic market with private or public modes of management. As the field of water policy in the Western United States chiefly concerns physical flows of water, it is not only regulated by intellectual norms (Bourdieu 1991) or by "juridical infrastructure" (Bourdieu and Christin 1990, p. 65), but it is framed by material infrastructures, mainly socio-technical systems such as rural irrigation systems, urban networks and megaprojects (dams, canals, etc.). Moreover, water regulation differs from residential housing (Bourdieu 2005), where the market is regulated by the state, local authorities and laws implemented to facilitate access to homeownership. The water market is regulated by the complex status of companies in charge of delivering the service and by economic forces impacting the relation between offer and demand (Lorrain and Poupeau 2016). Consequently, water policy is not based along lines of more traditional analysis of the public versus the private sector.

The field of water policy is also characterised by "multi-level regulation", involving not only international, federal and state norms, but also local levels (municipality, county, etc.) of administration. For example, the current debate over the looming water crisis faced by the Western USA reveals a complex architecture of laws and institutions, which is partly due to the decentralised nature of the American government. However, the notion of field has never been used for a multi-level analysis. To understand the logics of drought management, one must understand not only the processes of decision-making, but also how institutions at different levels of action work together and/or compete in order to produce new water policies and to impose a legitimate model of water management. The necessity to consider the interconnections between the different institutions involved in the responses to drought thus constitutes the main challenges of the field analysis of water policy in the Western USA. That is also one of the main differences with the works presented in *The Social Structures of Economy* (2005), with Pierre Bourdieu's sociology of housing policies, and *The Bureaucrat and the Poor* (2010), with Vincent Dubois' study of welfare policies. Both pioneer attempts to apply the notion of field to public policy as they consider the administrative and political levels of action in a separate and successive way, paying attention to the top-down appropriations of general norms by local powers in the logic of "*passe-droit*", or to the making of bottom-up public policy "from the counter" of territorial administrations. But both works do not articulate the different levels of action in a common frame of analysis—a multi-level field of public policy.

Although the actions of the different agents or institutions involved in water policy are not explicitly coordinated (except in the case of official agreements), which in turn creates conflicts and tensions, the responses to the repeated announcement of water shortages are related to the way water policies have been historically implemented since the beginning of the twentieth century, and this history still structures the relations between contemporary institutions and levels of action (Cortinas et al. 2016). Instead of being considered as a common good, water has been a resource used by economic, professional and bureaucratic elites to strengthen their power by promoting a model of hydraulic society which corresponds to their vision of "modern" capitalism (Worster 1986). And if water management refers to economic development (mining extraction, agro-industry, urban sprawl, seasonal migrations, extension of a lifestyle characterised by huge consumption, in other words, as a way of implementing the "American Dream"), the problem is to determine whether there is an autonomy of water policy towards these external determinations and to what extent it can be considered as a field.

The notion of field is used as an operative notion, a model of understanding, more than a fixed and closed theory. It is generally accepted that the study of a field must follow three steps (Bourdieu and Wacquant 1992; Grenfell 2014): (1) determining the relation of the considered field to the field of power; (2) mapping out the different agents competing; and (3) analysing their habitus and the system of dispositions involved in the field. But before being able to apply this methodology, built to study more homogeneous samples of populations (artists, intellectuals, editors, etc.), it is necessary to determine to what extent water policy constitutes a field. This demonstration implies that we determine not only the existence of a "common issue" for which the field agents would compete (i.e. a minimal agreement on the object of their disagreements), but also the existence of field effects that define, at the same time, the boundaries of the field, which are frequently the object of symbolic struggles. The first step of this work will thus consist in asking if there is a specific capital that is associated with the field of water policy and if it reveals a "common issue" shared by the agents involved in this field; this analysis is based on a research related to the institutional responses to the drought faced by the Western USA (principally Arizona and California), not only in the 2010s, but since the emergence of water policy as a specific domain of action structured by public authorities and private forces. The second step will detail the methodological hurdles encountered in the delimitation of the boundaries of the field and the different epistemological decisions made to determine the existence of "field effects", with the definition of active institutions and pertinent variables. The third step will outline some principles of analysis applied during the fieldwork realised to collect the data necessary to build the relational analysis of the field. This paper does not propose a complete field analysis but, rather, a description of the background of the study of the field, of its issues and limits, from the nature of the "capital(s)" concerned to the painstaking operations involved in the definition of institutions and factors determining water policy. In opening the "black box" of the research process, it operates a "pre-construction of the relevant variables" that prepares the way for the "construction of the scientific object".

CONFLICTS AND COMMON ISSUE

The definition of a common issue constituting the field of water policy leads first to a determination regarding what the social agents are really competing about, and thus to pay attention to their practices. Managing water is not only building technical systems (tunnels, canals, dams, urban networks, etc.) and regulating flows: it is also managing skills defined as technical and professional (engineering), managing economic markets (development of the service, prices, contracts, etc.), managing water rights and their repartition; and finally, managing water is managing power: power over the city, over the power of producing goods, collecting taxes, etc. When people and groups struggle to impose a model of water management in their city or in their region, they also compete to determine the appropriate skills that are necessary to implement this model, whatever this model might be. Many analysts make the hypothesis that water managers utilise what is referred to as "best practices" in order to realise the "common good", but a sociological frame of analysis leads to the idea that, before all, water managers try to implement strategies in order to define the water policy that corresponds to their practices and their capacities. As a consequence, the imposition of a legitimate model of water management helps them to maintain their power and the power of their organisation on the field of water management.

Conflicts related to the distribution of the Colorado River waters in the Western USA constitute a key entry point to understand how water policies are shaped in relation to the field of power. First of all, this is an arid land facing global transformations: since the nineteenth century, the economic development of this region has been based on the exploitation of its natural resources through mining, agriculture and now urban development. Second, public policies in the urban east, developed notably through programs implemented by federal agencies, have highly contributed to setting water infrastructures that gradually transformed the fearful semi-arid west into the breadbasket of the east and, later, into a thriving and autonomous centre of economic development. More specifically, huge and massive infrastructures such as dams, aqueducts and hydroelectric power plants have been promoted since the beginning of the twentieth century in order to support the irrigation of agricultural land and the growth of urban cities. These technical systems have been implemented by programs coming from federal agencies since the 1920s. Third, centralised decision-making authorities came up against powerful collective resistance, ranging from community-based protests to the environmental movement and legal and administrative actions, situated in a field of power involving local economic elites and federal administrations (Walton 1993; Espeland 1998). Indeed, the management of water has been the product of the struggles of various social organisations, local decision-makers and federal elites. Policies allowing for the shared use of the Colorado River are affecting cross-border issues between the American states and at the USA and Mexico border regions (respectively, Arizona and Sonora). Finally, the Western USA appears to be a land of conflicts for the control of natural resources, at least since the nineteenth century (Poupeau et al. 2016). Nowadays, debates over water management are generated by the "mega-drought" affecting the region since the beginning of the 2000s (Fleck 2016). This mega-drought is not only a natural disaster but also the results of the historical transformations affecting the West for more than a century.

WATER POLICY AND THE FIELD OF POWER

In order to analyse the relation of water policy to the field of power in the USA, the main levels of action were occurring in different coalitions built over time. This constitutes a pertinent starting point for a multi-level field analysis. On each level, the notion of field of power allows for a determination of a space where agents work to preserve, but also transform the balance of capital that exists in the field. The crisis occasioned by the drought and the struggles to define the legitimate model of water policy in the Western USA involve a specific form of capital: an institutional capital giving the power to manage water and to impose a specific model of managing water. However, as the field of water policy is not a homogeneous micro-cosmos with social agents interacting at the same level of action, but a complex and hierarchical world involving various levels (from federal to municipal), in which different processes of autonomisation appear in relation to the field of power, as a function of the effective level of action of the dominant coalitions of water policy.

All along the twentieth century, as the environmental norms of water policy were broadly applied, the coalition between federal authorities, their engineers and local elites had to give place and importance to local agents in charge of water regulation on their territorial levels. Federal authority had to intervene when absolutely necessary, that is, when moments arose when states or local administrations seemed to be unable to reach agreements. Federal powers appeared as a kind of arbiter at a very far distance from the field—a situation referring to the decentralisation of the American government, coupled with the great proliferation of water agencies—of the so called the hydraulic bureaucracy (Gottlieb and FitzSimmons 1991). At least until the 1960s, the strong willingness to develop the West led to the building of expensive megaprojects like the Hoover Dam. That "mastery of nature" (Teisch 2011) could only have been achieved by allowing local managers to have some autonomy and to defer to local expertise—a key characteristic of the field for many managers even today. It was also during this period that federal agencies were beginning to institute special programs for its "best and brightest". The idea was to move engineers into positions of "management" often at large regional offices or in Washington DC, with the appropriate MBA or other advanced management degree to go with it. As they could accumulate expertise in water and engineering, they could become "professionals", some of whom would go on to become international consultants late in their careers, and some are still active in this way. No longer explicitly dealing in engineering matters, they could make and enact policy, often at local and regional scales, at least in the USA.

Therefore, an independence of local and regional authorities from the state and federal levels (and the link that binds them all, the original agreement of 1922) appears to factor into the equation very little when examining the actual practices of water agencies. They seem to be very autonomous and forming their own unique sub-fields where different battles for local resources are fought, while at the same time espousing that "we are all in this together". Furthermore, there is a very close linkage to this structure, the ways that the agents are acting and their autonomy that can be found in the legal structure of the Colorado River Basin. Indeed, all the states and all the agents are linked to the Colorado River and the federal agencies, and the agreements and court cases that have been reached at the highest levels of the juridical and bureaucratic fields have maintained these linkages. However, each state has within it a unique legal structure for water. No two states are identical, and there is so much nuance in each state code that people have been very successful at being water lawyers in very small geographic areas protecting, sometimes, very large amounts of water and highly sought after water rights from the early nineteenth century. It is this, at times blurry, combination of capitals—legal, political and technical—which appear time and again that make an analysis of this field so complex and so different from other studies that have utilised Bourdieu's tools. However, the field theory remains useful to understand how the historical moments identified about the general arrangement of the US water policy, constitute a multi-level system, one that frames the trajectory of the different classes of water professionals. Certain types of water managers or water professionals seem to have been developing along with the development of the field of power, as it moved over time into a *laissez faire* capacity, which has allowed each state to develop its own water management policies and culture, on local levels of action, while also creating a field with considerable inertia.

Mapping the Field: A Provisional Definition of the Institutions Involved in Sharing Water from the Colorado River

If the task of defining the limits of the field of water policy developed to deal with drought does not consist exclusively in drawing up a list of the agents concerned in the process, this "mapping" of relevant institutions (Bourdieu and Wacquant 1992) presupposes methodological choices concerning the selection of agents engaged in struggles to define water policy. The struggles for the management of water from the Colorado River involve many institutions, which operate in what can best be described as a fragmented managerial approach. Some agencies deal with water quality and water concessions (State Water Control Board of California); others concern themselves with environmental questions (protection of flora and fauna); and yet others focus on water delivery infrastructure (State Water Project). In California alone, there are over two thousand institutions with responsibilities in the water sector. Every institution has its own level of competence and, consequently, a certain degree of autonomy.

Furthermore, the institutional architecture of water management varies from state to state. The sector is characterised by an extremely decentralised model including state institutions which essentially focus on incentivising and defining broad-ranging guidelines for water management, rather than exercising a capacity of constraint and coercion over actors in the water sector. In California, the most important tool applied by the Department of Water Resources is planning, a political instrument that consists in defining guidelines for water management and objectives to be attained by the ensemble of institutions supplying water to various users. While there are no coercive powers associated with these guidelines, incentives—essentially subsidies—are offered to convince the various agencies to follow the norms decreed. On the other hand, in Arizona, due to the complexity of legislation in the sphere of water management, state institutions play a much more active role than they do in California in terms of developing water management models for individual agencies.

Confronted by such a situation, it was necessary to make a series of methodological choices to construct the object of the study. The first task was to identify institutions with a direct link to the Colorado River Basin at various existing levels of government. In each of the states of the basin, a list of official institutions basically responsible for negotiations concerning the distribution of water from the river was established. In Arizona, the Arizona Department of Water Resources is primarily responsible for this task, while in California, the mission is carried out by the Colorado River Board of California, a body which, independent from the political system, is made up of institutions that have contracts with the Bureau of Reclamation, the federal agency responsible for the Colorado River (Pisani 2002). In Nevada, the Southern Nevada Water Authority carries out water distribution negotiations, which is essentially a metropolitan water agency. But these are just a few examples.

This first sample also encompasses departments responsible for regulating water in each individual state. These departments exert influence by means of two different mechanisms. On the one hand, they have the capacity to implement existing laws, which essentially, following the introduction of the Groundwater Management Act (1980) in Arizona, concern groundwater sources. On the other, they have the power to grant land use permits in specific territories and to establish guidelines for water management plans. Another task was to identify organisations that are supplied with water from the Colorado River in function of the type of consumer they serve, namely municipal agencies, operating either on their own or with other agencies under the aegis of "water districts," and irrigation agencies delivering water to the agricultural sector.

Beyond water agencies in individual states, cities and irrigation districts, conflicts over potential risks of restrictions for the use of water from the Colorado River reveal the importance of the role played by environmentalist organisations which, since the late 1990s, have exerted an influence over water policy in the American West via the elaboration of certain agreements, laws and regulations concerning drought; via participating in meetings and symposia focusing on responses to drought; and via legal challenges to water projects (such as the desalination plant near San Diego). Associations of urban and rural water agencies lobbying the political authorities about issues of drought management were also considered. An example of such bodies is provided by the Association of California Water Agencies (ACWA), which represents hundreds of water agencies. The informative interviews realised during the research revealed that the president of the association has played a leading role in the elaboration of the Governor of California's 2013 Water Plan. These initial lists of the managers and users of water from the Colorado River, which include hundreds of institutions, demonstrate the need to construct a sample that facilitates the task of collecting qualitative and quantitative data.

Following on from this initial list, a series of informative interviews was conducted to verify the pertinence of the methodological choices made. The aim was to move on from the phase of the preliminary delimitation of the field based on the institutions involved in managing water from the Colorado River, to a delimitation considering information deriving directly from water policy decision-makers. In this adjustment phase of the definition of the limits of the field studied, emphasis was initially placed not only on the water agencies with the highest degree of demographic and political influence, which are also, in a de facto manner, active within the institutions officially responsible for managing the distribution of water from the basin, but also on the irrigation districts receiving the greatest quantity of water from the Colorado River and/or prioritised in terms of the use of Colorado River water. These interviews enabled the examination of the influence wielded by the office of the Secretary of the Interior, the "River Master", and, consequently, of the federal sphere, in the elaboration of measures taken to counter the effects of the drought. In effect, the Secretary of the Interior is the only official with the right to introduce water-use restrictions in the American West. Alongside the Bureau of Reclamation, a federal agency, it is the political authority responsible for administering the nation's natural resources.

Urban water agencies, which are, to varying degrees, dependent on water from the Colorado River, were also studied in more detail in function of their access to other sources of water and of their relative priority in terms of appropriation of rights and demographic dynamics—expansion or stabilisation. Indeed, it seemed to be indispensable to consider the relative influence of these water agencies regarding positions taken vis-à-vis the responses to the issues of the Colorado River in particular and the drought in general. Of all the towns and cities that it was possible to include in the study, only those with the largest populations (Phoenix, Las Vegas, Tucson, Los Angeles, San Diego) were retained, as well as a small number of expanding centres which, due to their dependence of water from the Colorado River, are particularly active in terms of the elaboration of water policy (Gottlieb 2007; Ross 2011). In effect, small, rapidly growing cities attempt to get around current environmental regulations to procure the new sources of water required for their development, while cities with relatively stable populations tend to favour conservationist measures to secure their supplies (Benites-Gambirazio et al. 2016). The end result of these various methodological choices was a new list of 95 institutions located in the four states in the Colorado River Basin that are suffering most egregiously from the effects of the drought (Nevada, Colorado, Arizona and California). Complemented by research on documents and interviews, this list makes it possible to establish all the variables that could be considered as potentially relevant to an understanding of responses to the drought.

THE PRE-CONSTRUCTION OF RELEVANT VARIABLES

By delimiting the field based on a list of institutions exercising a field effect, it was possible to develop a database in which the rows represent the water agents included in the analysis and the columns represent the variables that, in the field work, were revealed to be indispensable in terms of understanding water policies. However, the elaboration of the list of relevant variables was by no means a straightforward task in comparison with the study of easily identifiable populations of individuals such as intellectuals, writers, artists and economists, for which variables such as social origin, academic qualifications and so on appear to be all important (Bourdieu 1977; Sapiro 1996; Lebaron 1997). Compared to the field of publishing analysed by Bourdieu, it was also difficult to find unique economic indicators, since the institutions active in the field of water policy include not only regulation agencies, but also service providers and irrigation districts buying, selling or regulating highly variable volumes of water. Furthermore, in the field of water policy, the relationship between institutions and their directors does not necessarily display the same degree of homology in terms of social characteristics as it does in studies of the employer class ("patronat") (Bourdieu and de Saint Martin 1978), or publishers (c.f. Bourdieu 1996, 2008). In all the states included in the sample, there are water sector professionals who hold director-level positions and who organise their careers by moving from one institution to another without owning the organisation they direct. While these positions are not occupied by chance, in the sense that they demand accredited, recognised skills, they nevertheless do not display the same degree of homology apparent in other studies of fields.

To define an ensemble of effective variables, the identification of existing conflicts in each of the regions studied over water shortages and the Colorado River was used as a tool to reveal the stances taken by the main protagonists of policies designed to deal with the drought. This applies not only to organisations in individual states, but also to the instruments of public action they choose and the ways in which they use them. This initial phase enabled us to highlight issues differentiating the various states, for example water access, water usage and water rights. In Nevada, these issues are largely urban (Las Vegas accounting for the clear majority of the population and of revenue generation), while in California, they are, for the most part, rural (despite urban growth, agriculture still accounts for almost 80% of water use). In other states, like Colorado and Arizona, the rural–urban split is more sharply contrasted, but while Colorado benefits from an upstream access to water from the river, the downstream location of Arizona does not provide it with priority rights.

An examination of the documents of various institutions revealed the existence of a degree of consensus about approaches to counter the effects of the crisis. The real problem was, beyond the obligatory conservation mandates deriving, for example, from the governor, to ascertain what policies are really implemented by each of the institutions. To resolve this problem, it was necessary to analyse, on a case-by-case basis, the priority objectives of public action. This made it possible to discern, among the objectives described, the priority actions of each institution, as well as the instruments required to implement them. The analysis of the differences in the stances taken by the institutions was thus based on collected data from a wide range of sources, including newspaper articles—essentially interviews—in which various officials of the institutions included in our sample spoke about the drought and various responses to it and the water plans of each of the institutions, which present guidelines for the water policies of each institution. The results of these analyses served as the basis for the elaboration of further interviews with each of the institutional managers in our sample.

Based on these analyses and of the interviews conducted with many of the managers of the institutions concerned, an ensemble of priorities has been defined, as well as a list of the most frequently applied water policy instruments. These priorities and instruments fall into several categories: attempts to meet future urban and agricultural water needs (mainly managed by the water agencies), but also relatively diverse responses to environmentalist objectives, which can themselves be categorised into two groups, with an ecological radicalism that seeks to call into question the use of water as an economic growth factor and a form of "business environmentalism" (Taylor 2016), the intention of which is to supply solutions to the water crisis from a sectorial perspective (quality of water, endangered species, etc.). Different instruments are applied to these priorities. Alongside traditional supply and demand management tools applied by water managers concerned with "good practices", there are the instruments of an approach to water governance characterised by, among other things, closer coordination between institutions, thanks to which rules better adapted to drought risks can be applied. In this same register, organisations not involved in bureaucratic administration promote extra-institutional consultation between protagonists in the water sector with a view to developing collective solutions to the crisis. Finally, environmentalist groups, many of them local, mainly use protest and the law against water management policies subordinated to economic development.

This simultaneously systematic and differentiated understanding of the field's issues made it possible, above all, to identify the social origins of the power of the protagonists of drought management. These can be divided into two categories. The first category encompasses the large cities retained in the study that have a growing demographic and economic influence, which means that they are a major electoral target likely to interfere with decision-making processes in terms of water management in times of drought and that they have a major impact on the official organisations that negotiate the distribution of water from the Colorado River. The second category includes the irrigation districts, the biggest of which are in California. When water shortages arise, irrigation districts have priority over the cities due to water rights legislation in the American West. These conflicts and the issues associated with them provide an insight into the centrality of water rights in the stances taken by the institutions of the West, highlighting, as they do, the role played by dependence on water from the Colorado River. This part of our research also enabled to identify the most influential environmentalist organisations in each state. Interviews with managers and directors permitted to identify different professional careers. Some of our water actors had local careers, others federal or state and others academic and NGO careers. Consequently, the database included some information on the academic backgrounds and professional trajectories of the water managers.

The Role of Institutional Capital in the Field of Water Policy: Outline of an Initial Interpretative Model

By defining the limits of the field and locating potentially efficient variables, it became possible to elaborate an initial, non-quantitative model of the field's structure designed to orient an analysis of multiple correspondences based on data collected on the institutions and the relevant variables. Consequently, the fieldwork (based on interviews and observations of meetings) functioned not so much as a kind of "empirical validation" of hypotheses but, rather, as a sort of complement to the elaboration of research hypotheses and the consolidation of relevant variables. In view of the sheer quantity of prosopographic work needed to build a complete database of the institutions retained for the study, the elaboration of the relevant variables had to be consolidated prior to conducting a statistical analysis, by conceptualising the principles structuring the field. The idea was therefore to define these efficient variables in terms of "capitals", the varying amount of which provides agents with a greater or lesser degree of influence in the definition of water policy. Besides economic capital, offering the capacity to manage water flows, the concept of institutional capital also provides a key to understanding the structure of the field of water policy in the American West. Bourdieu's study of the field of publishing was used as a comparative model to imagine a space primarily structured, first, by the total volume of economic and institutional capital available and, second, by the way in which they were distributed.

The notion of institutional capital covers four components, each of which was highlighted in the field study. The first concerns the effective capacity to develop and apply norms and regulations to the water sector. This regulatory role is the purview of political officials from the federal and state government. It also concerns federal agencies, notably the Bureau of Reclamation, and the water agencies of individual states. The second component of institutional capital refers to the position of an institution within other managerial institutions further up the hierarchical chain in terms of institutional capital. For example, the fact that a small water agency is a member of an executive board of a regional agency gives it more influence within the field than it would have if it remained isolated. The third component is linked to the capacity to manage large volumes of water. As an efficient variable within the field, the volume of water functions in two ways. First, it provides a degree of influence linked to the capacity of consumption: the greater the volume of water purchased by an institution, the greater the influence of that institution on the financial results of the selling agency, and, consequently, the more impact it has as a buyer. This explains why large cities such as Los Angeles and Phoenix have a major influence not only on the decisions of the water agencies that sell them water, but also, due to their electoral impact, on governors. The electoral impact of these centres of population is particularly substantial in states such as Arizona and Nevada where over 80% of the population lives in the big cities or their suburbs. Second, the volume of water managed, considered as an efficient variable within the field, is also linked to water rights. Thus, water from the Colorado River is legally allocated to a series of agencies that have contracts with the federal government. The fourth component is linked to the legal structure regulating the use of water from the Colorado River in the American West. Access to water in the region is governed by a doctrine dating from the fifteenth century, referred to as "prior appropriation": the first person to arrive on a piece of land and use the available water in a "reasonable" and "beneficial" way has priority over someone who arrives there later in terms of the use of that water.

The institutions capable of accumulating the greatest amount of capital, both institutional and economic, can therefore be defined as occupying a dominant position within the field of water policy. In this perspective, the primary axis of the analysis would differentiate institutions in function of the volume of capital they possess, with, on the top, federal and state bodies, and the major urban water agencies and irrigation districts of California. On the basis of this axis representing the amount of capital possessed by various institutions are to be found local environmentalist organisations fighting for or against specific projects—a desalination plant, saving a protected zone, etc.—and small cities and irrigation agencies that distribute a discrete volume of water from the Colorado River and that benefit from a relatively limited number of co-presences within institutions with a greater degree of institutional capital. This opposition between a regulatory function and a commercial function, or between an institutional capital and an economic capital, helps to explain, at least partially, the polarisation of the field of water policy between ecological and economic priorities, and sheds light on why water conservation policies promoted to different degrees (of application and, doubtless, sincerity) by all institutions, enjoy varying degrees of autonomy vis-à-vis the imperatives of economic development.

Conclusion—Genesis and Structures of a Multi-Level Field

This text has presented the preliminary steps of a field analysis related to water policy in Western USA. In order to understand the structure of the field, the analysis started by understanding its genesis, starting with the building of water infrastructures since the nineteenth century to the management of the drought affecting the southwest in the twenty-first century (Pincetl 2011). This history of the formation of a system of specialised institutions dedicated to water revealed the multi-level dimension of a policy where federal powers interfere with state administrations and a diversity of local interests. The relational notion of field is thus a way to highlight structural principles, which take into account the multiple layers of institutions and its managers, and instruments that contribute to the framework of water policy through time and across levels of action. The study of water policy leads to a study of systems of multi-level actions where the relations between the agents are operating in social spaces that might appear more complex and undetermined than the cultural or the economic field. The problem is now to determine what is providing coherence to such a system of relations where social practices operate at different levels of action (international, federal, regional, municipal, etc.), and where systems of position takings related to the drought refer to the system of positions in the field of water policy.

References

Bachelard, G. (1999). *Water and dreams: An essay on the imagination of matter.* Dallas: Institute for Humanities & Culture.

Benites-Gambirazio, E., Coeurdray, M., & Poupeau, F. (2016). Une promotion immobilière sous contraintes environnementales. *Revue française de sociologie, 57*(4), 735–765.

Bourdieu, P. (1977). La production de la croyance [contribution à une économie des biens symboliques]. *Actes de la recherche en sciences sociales, 13*(1), 3–43.

Bourdieu, P. (1991). Le champ littéraire. *Actes de la recherche en sciences sociales, 89*(1), 3–46.

Bourdieu, P. (1996). *The rules of art: Genesis and structure of the literary field.* Stanford University Press.

Bourdieu P. (2005). *The social structures of the economy.* Cambridge: Polity Press.

Bourdieu, P. (2008). A conservative revolution in publishing. *Translation Studies, 1*(2), 123–153.

Bourdieu, P., & Christin, R. (1990). La construction du marché [Le champ administratif et la production de la 'politique du logement']. *Actes de la recherche en sciences sociales, 81*(1), 65–85.

Bourdieu, P., & de Saint Martin, M. (1978). Le patronat. *Actes de la recherche en sciences sociales, 20*(1), 3–82.

Bourdieu, P., & Wacquant, L. (1992). *An invitation to reflexive sociology.* Chicago: University of Chicago Press.

Cortinas, J., Coeurdray, M., Poupeau, F., & O'Neill, B. (2016). Water for a new America: The policy coalitions of the Central Arizona Project (Part 1). In F. Poupeau, H. Gupta, A. Serrat-Capdevila, M. A. Sans-Fuentes, S. Harris, & L. Hayde (Eds.), *Water bankruptcy in the land of plenty* (pp. 65–78). Leiden: CRC Press.

Espeland, W. (1998). *The struggle for water: Politics, rationality and identity in the American Southwest.* Chicago: The University of Chicago Press.

Fleck, J. (2016). *Water is for fighting over, and other myths about water in the west.* Washington: Island Press.

Gottlieb, R. (2007). *Reinventing Los Angeles: Nature and community in the global city.* Cambridge, MA: MIT Press.

Gottlieb, R., & FitzSimmons, M. (1991). *Thirst for growth: Water agencies as hidden government in California*. Tucson: University of Arizona Press.

Grenfell, M. (2014). *Pierre Bourdieu: Key concepts* (2nd ed.). London: Routledge.

Lebaron, F. (1997). La dénégation du pouvoir [Le champ des économistes français au milieu des années 1990]. *Actes de la recherche en sciences sociales, 119*(1), 3–26.

Lorrain, D., & Poupeau, F. (2016). How socio-technical systems and their operators work. In D. Lorrain & F. Poupeau (Eds.), *Water regimes: Beyond the public and private sector debate* (pp. 187–200). London: Routledge.

Pincetl, S. (2011). Urban water conflicts in the Western US. In B. Barraqué (Ed.), *Urban water conflicts* (pp. 237–246). Paris: UNESCO-IHP.

Pisani, D. J. (2002). *Water and American Government: The Reclamation Bureau, National Water Policy, and the west, 1902–1935*. Berkeley: University of California Press.

Poupeau, F., Coeurdray, M., Cortinas, J., & O'Neill, B. (2016). The making of water policy in the American Southwest: Environmental sociology and its tools. In F. Poupeau, H. Gupta, A. Serrat-Capdevila, M. A. Sans-Fuentes, S. Harris, & L. Hayde (Eds.), *Water bankruptcy in the land of plenty* (pp. 101–118). Leiden: CRC Press.

Ross, A. (2011). *Bird on fire—Lessons from the world's least sustainable city*. New York: Oxford University Press.

Sapiro, G. (1996). La raison littéraire [Le champ littéraire français sous l'Occupation (1940–1944)]. *Actes de la recherche en sciences sociales, 111*(1), 3–35.

Taylor, D. E. (2016). *The rise of the American conservation movement: Power, privilege, and environmental protection*. Durham: Duke University Press.

Walton, J. (1993). *Western times and water wars: State, culture and rebellion in California*. Berkeley: University of California Press.

Worster, D. (1986). *Rivers of empire: Water, aridity and the growth of the American West*. New York: Oxford University Press.

CHAPTER 3

Masculine Learner Identities in the Field of Student-Directed Musical Learning

Garth Stahl and Pete Dale

INTRODUCTION

In this chapter, we employ Bourdieu's approach to field theory to investigate a specific case study of the musical practices of an all-male, peer-led, extra-curricular music program. Our interest is in how disadvantaged boys engage with their learning in a field they create actively outside of their formal schooling (cf. Stahl and Dale 2012, 2013). After being first influenced by Lewin's *Gestalt* theory, Bourdieu applied, developed and refined his version of field theory over the course of his oeuvre (cf. Hilgers and Mangez 2015 for a genealogical analysis). As a conceptual tool in Bourdieu's toolbox, his version of field theory allows for an exploration of space, whether social or physical, as relational. More specifically, field represents a particular social space that involves a hierarchical network or configuration of relations between subject positions. As we operationalise Bourdieu's approach to field theory, we consider the

G. Stahl
University of South Australia, Adelaide, Australia

P. Dale (✉)
Manchester Metropolitan University, Manchester, UK

© The Author(s) 2018
J. Albright et al. (eds.), *Bourdieu's Field Theory and the Social Sciences,*
https://doi.org/10.1007/978-981-10-5385-6_3

applicability and the potential for exciting theoretical provocations while considering the intricacies and complexities of this theory.

In our analysis, it is essential to our understanding of Bourdieu's field theory that it is theorised in tandem with the generative capacity of the habitus where individuals are agentic in their learning (Stahl and Dale 2015). The young men in this small case study were capable of high levels of engagement, enthusiasm and success in their music-making, despite generally being considered "low achieving" and "highly disaffected" in their formal schooling. Considering the relationship between field and habitus, our interest is in how the *field of learning* created by these young men influences their habitus, the "mental and corporeal schemata of perception, appreciation, and action" (Bourdieu and Wacquant 1992, p. 16), and vice versa. We are also interested in the extent to which the field of music-making adopts socially validated learning processes that serve in direct contrast to the field of formal schooling. Field theory requires an investigation of how power manifests and how value is generated in relation to the logic of the field. For Bourdieu (1985),

> the social world can be represented as a space (with several dimensions) constructed on the basis of principles of differentiation or distribution constituted by the set of properties active within the social universe in question, i.e., capable of conferring strength, power within that universe, on their holder. Agents and groups of agents are thus defined by their relative positions within that space. (p. 724)

The theory of field—in relation to habitus and capitals—has much to lend the investigation of the "social and symbolic value of music" (Burnard 2012, p. 100). Through this chapter, we analyse how working-class boys' learner identities function in learning cultures and how such fields give rise to new "patterns of thought" and new identities. As the boys' habitus moves across two fields (mainly the formal schooling and the student-led learning culture), we see them negotiating differing conceptions of learning while simultaneously drawing on historically validated working-class dispositions which greatly influence their learning practices.

This chapter first outlines the (dis)engagement of working-class boys with formal schooling as a historic phenomenon. These young men, who were labelled as "problematic" and "non-starters" in their formal schooling, were passionate and critically engaged with their music practices. We then discuss the main tenants of Bourdieu's theoretical toolkit with specific attention to field and habitus. In theorising the relationship between habitus and the field of learning, we consider the overlaps between learner and social identities. In the discussion, we show the merits and weaknesses of Bourdieu's field theory, focusing on three key areas: the field as competitive; enculturation and the capacity of the habitus to rebuff the field; and dispositions in reference to the logics of the field.

WORKING-CLASS BOYS AND SCHOOLING

In society, today boys increasingly find themselves attempting to negotiate successful learner identities in educational environments shaped by neoliberal reforms with a very narrow definition of success (MacLeod 2009; Stahl 2015). Such educational spaces trap working-class boys in a binary between either action (which fixes boys as "arrogant" and "loutish") or, alternatively, passivity (which fixes them as "apathetic non-workers") (Francis 2006; Stahl 2015). The study of working-class boys' problematic experiences with formal education has a long-standing history in the social sciences (Willis 1977; Humphries 1981). In contemporary neoliberal times, within the field of formal schooling, we frequently see learning cultures shaped by high-stakes testing where achievement becomes a site of "value" and "devaluement" (Stahl 2012, 2013, 2015). Working-class boys have not found it easy to "slip seamlessly in and out of different social fields" or negotiate often paradoxical fields (Ingram 2011, p. 301), and exposure to contrasting logics can result in a fractured identity. In Reay's (2002) case study, *Shaun's Story*, she utilises Bourdieu's concept of "the duality of the self" to illustrate the fractured relationship of "white working-class masculinities with educational success" and the "heavy psychic costs" involved in embodying "tough boy on the street versus good boy in the classroom" (p. 222).

In line with other scholars, we contend the neoliberal agenda of formal schooling, where "learning equals earning" is pervasive (Brown 2013, p. 685), has a tremendous influence on the boys' habitus, their masculine identities, and their learner identities (Phoenix 2004; Burke 2007; Davies and Saltmarsh 2007; Stahl 2015). As neoliberalism structures teaching and learning in competitive and confounding ways, we focus on what boys actually want to achieve and how their engagement with (or, as often as not, disengagement from) achievement-oriented activities shapes their habitus (Connolly 2006a; Atencio et al. 2009). By not exploring where boys thrive as learners, we know little about the identity work surrounding boys' learning. In her study of working-class boys' engagement with their education in Belfast, Ingram (2009) argues "learning and schooling are enmeshed. If you oppose one, you oppose the other" (p. 429). While this phenomenon may be alarmingly prevalent, we now consider field theory can be used to study how boys engage with their learning practices in an informal learning culture.

Working with Field Theory

A central element of Bourdieu's work is his attempt to undermine the dualisms of objectivism and subjectivism, structure and agent, where the tools of habitus and field intend to offer an "alternative conceptualization of the individual as socially embedded" and shaped by one's location within social fields (Kenway and McLeod 2004, p. 528). For Bourdieu, fields designate "bundles of relations" where there is often struggle over different types of capital, whether economic, social, cultural or symbolic (Bourdieu and Wacquant 1992, p. 16). The game occurs in fields that are always competitive, where the accumulation of capitals and status is always at stake. It is assumed that agents tend to perceive the field in terms of stakes, logics and beliefs tied to that field. Field theory requires an understanding that fields are *relational* and not composed of one entity but instead a *system of relations*. As sites of endless change, fields are "where agents and institutions constantly struggle according to the regularities and the rules constitutive of this space of play" and where there exists a set of logics particular to that field (Bourdieu and Wacquant 1992, p. 102). While participants possess capitals that can or cannot be operationalised in the field, capitals are not always operationalised with equal ease. There is a skill required to play the game successfully and secure one's own value. Each field, composed of specific rules, is to varying degrees, autonomous, though also simultaneously influenced by other overlapping and competing fields. Therefore, the players, in this case young males, often occupy more than one social field simultaneously and are exposed to competing and contrasting logics of practice.

Grenfell (2008) writes that even though a field is profoundly hierarchised and characterised by struggle, "dominant social agents and institutions having considerable power to determine what happens within it, there is still agency and change" (p. 73). To maintain the equilibrium, the field mediates what social agents do in specific contexts, but within the dialectic of field/habitus, there is often tension. Habitus is where one's perceptions and conceptions are conditioned by the structures of the environment in which they are engendered, yet the habitus does not operate identically for all people and is deeply dependent on capitals and field. Therefore, habitus and field operate in two interrelated and overlapping ways:

> On one side, it is a relation of conditioning: the field structures the habitus, which is the product of the embodiment of the immanent necessity of a field (or of a set of intersecting fields, the extent of their intersection or discrepancy being at the root of the divided or even torn habitus). On the other side, it is a relation of knowledge or cognitive construction. Habitus contributes to constituting the field as a meaningful world, a world endowed with sense and value, in which it is worth investing one's energy. (Bourdieu and Wacquant 1992, p. 127)

Bourdieu therefore posits a circular relationship between structures and practices, in which "objective structures tend to produce structured subjective dispositions that produce structured actions which, in turn, tend to reproduce objective structure" (MacLeod 2009, p. 15). As a cultural reproduction theorist, a main tenant of the Bourdieusian approach is that structural (dis)advantages are internalised through socialisation and, as a result, they produce certain forms of behaviour.

The Field of Learning

We conceptualise the peer-led extra-curricular music program attended by the young men in this case study as a "learning culture". We define learning culture loosely as the *cultural practices through which students learn* and where agents take up certain cultural roles and enact certain practices around learning processes (James et al. 2007; Perkins 2013). Practices are what people do and how they talk about what they do, so that learning cultures become formed and reformed, structured through "the actions, dispositions and interpretations of the participants" (James et al. 2007, p. 4). Innate to our understanding of how field and habitus work together, we theorise learning as a process of meaning-making which is socially constituted (Stahl and Dale 2015). Despite being constrained by fields, individuals are agentic in their learning. According to Bourdieu, "social structures and cognitive structures are recursively and structurally linked, and the correspondence between them provides one of the most solid props of social domination" (Bourdieu and Wacquant 1992, p. 14). Therefore, the individual and their learning are not merely constructed through their experiences within the field but also through their relationship with their subjectivities; in this case, the subjectivities are either a "good learner" or a "poor learner".

THE CASE STUDY: A LEARNING CULTURE OF YOUNG DJs AND MC-ERS

Conducted in a north-eastern city in England, the case study involved young men (11–16 years of age) who engaged in practices of DJ-ing and MC-ing (cf. Stahl and Dale 2012, 2013, 2015). In their formal education, our participants' learning experiences were shaped by the institutional discourse of high-stakes education, where the rhetoric of "learning equals earning" was pervasive (Brown 2013, p. 685). Academic achievement tied to employment contributed to how these young men saw their formal learning. Given the post-industrial context and limited employment opportunities, the way learning was positioned by the school environment was, of course, highly problematic. The inner-city secondary school had an attainment level below national averages where students often came from significantly disadvantaged backgrounds in relative terms. At the time our research was undertaken, data from the Fischer Family Trust (commonly used to measure socio-economic advantage/ disadvantage across the UK school system) placed the school on the 97th percentile. In order to access the identity negotiations of these young males in the field of extra-curricular peer-led music production, we focused upon how boys conceptualised their learning. In contrast to their standards-driven field of formal schooling, the learning culture of music production was a field where the boys felt successful and valued. Our participants found ways to take ownership of their learning and thus constitute themselves as subjects of value (Stahl and Dale 2012, 2013). These boys, who were the lowest achievers in the core subjects of the UK's National Curriculum (English, Maths and Science), were nevertheless able to demonstrate a love of learning and their work on the DJ decks and as MCs on the "mics" made them the envy of their peers.

As historically informed, the habitus carries with it specific histories; the "residue of specific cultural, social, and personal histories" (Atencio et al. 2009, p. 5). For white working-class boys, the practice of learning has been tied to traditional working-class values, dispositions focused on "sameness" and "ordinariness" and a commitment to collective well-being that has been documented in other studies focusing on working-class identities (Skeggs 2002; Reay 2003; Connolly 2006a, b; Ingram 2009; Stahl 2013). In operationalising habitus, it is essential to acknowledge how it is influenced greatly by the past as it negotiates different fields and capitals. Furthermore, different dispositions within the habitus are pulled to the forefront according to the logic of the field. This pull of dispositions is often in relation to an agent's "ability to perform in appropriate ways in a given environment (field) by alignment with the recognized 'tastes' and 'preferences' associated with that social space" (Hart 2013, p. 51). As working-class males draw on certain historically informed dispositions, such as social cohesion and social solidarity (through a history of union action and community involvement), they confirm in their learning practices their gendered, classed and ethnic subjectivities inside and outside of schooling (Mac an Ghaill 1994; Stenning 2005; Stahl 2015). Our research showed how, in the learning culture, working-class dispositions contributed to a conception of learning around collaboration in contrast to the logic of competition in the field of formal schooling (Stahl and Dale 2015).

PUTTING FIELD THEORY TO WORK

Within a field, what positions agents is the possession of capital and how the capital is recognised. It is through recognition that capital is given power relevant to the purposes of a particular field. Positions in the field contribute to the production of an agent's habitus, or particular ways of thinking, being and doing (Reay 2004; Stahl 2015). The relations between positions in the field are particularly significant in analysing the field where it is socially recognised knowledge that is paramount with a "corps of specialists" functioning as "the exclusive holder" (Hilgers and Mangez 2015, p. 7) which, in turn, directs how the game is played. However, while the field structures the habitus, there is space for improvisation as the habitus is "creative, inventive, but within the limits of its structures" (Bourdieu and Wacquant 1992, p. 19). As a result of the internalisation of external structures, habitus reacts to the solicitations of the field by "actions [that] are not purposeful but, rather, continuously adaptive" (Robbins 2000, p. 29). The habitus is permeable and responsive, internalising the logics of the field, but it also has the capacity to rebuff. In relation to the fields it encounters, the habitus is agentic and it seeks to accrue value and symbolic power (Skeggs 2004; Stahl 2015).

In her work on music conservatoires, Perkins (2013) documents how dominant institutional practices orient students towards particular ways of learning. Through these practices, she contends "the knowledge generated of learning cultures is situated, located as it is in one space and one time" (p. 13). While the institution of formal schooling in our case study may structure the habitus around learning in certain ways, this is certainly not all-encompassing. While these young men languish in their formal schooling, they are able to construct a learning culture which is centred around collectivism, where status and esteem can be conferred upon hard work, sustained effort and "a 'practice makes perfect' determination" (Stahl and Dale 2013). While Butler (1999) completely rejects the Bourdieusian project on grounds of rigid determinism, arguing the field/habitus relationship as one where habitus encounters the field and submits due to the compelling authority of the field, our study shows how the habitus is in constant negotiation with every field it encounters. For the habitus to simply submit to the field would mean that each field has the same authority and that the habitus is simultaneously submitted to multiple interlocking fields. Therefore, in operationalising Bourdieu's conceptual toolkit in reference to our case study, we see numerous provocative questions: how do these experiences with different fields of learning influence the habitus of these young men? With overlapping and conflicting fields, which field has more salience in structuring the habitus? As we consider our research, we problematise three key areas: the field as competitive; enculturation and the capacity of the habitus to rebuff the field; and dispositions in reference to the logics of the field.

The Field as Competitive

Burnard (2012, p. 72) has argued that DJ-ing is a site of collective and individual creativities where success is determined by the creation of a "'buzz', 'atmosphere', 'mood', and 'vibe' in the spatial interaction between them and the crowd". In our study, competition definitely manifested although creating a powerful musical moment appeared to be much more about the process than the product. Through making a musical moment, certain boys became more legitimate than others, yet these moments came and went with them so did the recognition. According to Bourdieusian logic, the strategies of the player always operate in relation to the volume and structure of his or her capital. Each field has distinctions that are symbolically valued and co-opted by certain agents, often at the expense of others. In Bourdieu's approach to field theory, distinction becomes a key focus for symbolic struggles in which agents attempt to establish superiority. Therefore, in Bourdieusian terms, the creation of quality music within the field becomes a form of distinction; however, it is a fleeting moment and, as a capital, it does not secure long-term status or positioning.

Bourdieu and Wacquant (1992) argue that symbolic capital is valued and accumulated according to the logics and practices which comprise each field, where individuals (and groups) struggle over "embodied meanings and practices which constitute the social field/s, and where positions of power are delineated according to prevailing ways in which the embodied self is recognized and legitimized" (Atencio et al. 2009, p. 4). While fields are certainly competitive, field theory pushes us to question the overemphasis on agents accruing capital and symbolic power. The habitus seeks to accrue value in fields where it judges the accrual of value as a viable possibility. As agents negotiate the field, their strategies depend on: "(1) 'their position in the field' (the volume and composition of capital); (2) 'the perception that they have of the field' (habitus); and (3) 'the state of the instruments of reproduction' (field)" (Yang 2013, p. 7). In reference to this case study—which is situated in the field of formal schooling—the hegemonic logic is the accumulation of capital (qualifications), but that logic does not structure the habitus of every individual as successful learners or accumulators of this valuable field-specific capital the boys largely do not engage with institutional discourses. The habitus easily available to them within these field structures are largely "oppositional, disengaged or unsuccessful". This is characterised by many teachers and gender theorists as a problem created by the boys and their masculine identities rather than as a failure of this system to engage them as learners. Instead, their habitus, as generative, looks for fields (the musical learning culture) where they can gain validation and draw on historically constituted dispositions associated with working-class masculinity (cooperation, caring) that are not valued in the highly pressured formal schooling environment.

Enculturation and the Capacity of the Habitus to Rebuff

When thinking critically with field theory, we must consider the degree to which the habitus is influenced by the field. As a result of the internalisation of logics of the fields, habitus reacts to the solicitations of the field as it is "continuously adaptive" (Robbins 2000, p. 29). We know the habitus is always co-constructed with the field(s) but certain fields, it would appear, have more influence than others. The habitus is permeable and responsive; it both internalises and rebuffs new experiences. For Bourdieu, habitus constitutes the field as meaningful where it can enact and accrue value and where "it is worth investing one's energy" (Bourdieu and Wacquant 1992, p. 127). While the boys exist in a formal schooling structure where they are consistently devalued, they are still able to rebuff discourses which label them "low level learners" once they shift field. Being the product of history and experience, habitus: "may be changed by history, that is by new experiences, education or training … Dispositions are long-lasting: they tend to perpetuate, to reproduce themselves, but they are not eternal" (Bourdieu 2002, p. 29). The habitus carries with it the generative seeds (closely aligned with their working-class dispositions) which allow it to resist and to actively structure spaces where the value is possible. Therefore, in this research, agents are active in the fields where the logic—in this case, the learning around collaborative music-making—fits with their habitus where there exists continual synchronicity. Against the pressures of formal schooling with the emphasis on the attainment of qualifications, the boys' habitus experiences disjuncture. As the habitus negotiates a field where it feels like a "fish out of water" (Bourdieu and Wacquant 1992, p. 127)—where the disjuncture is seen as an impossibility—the habitus looks for fields, such as the learning culture of music-making, where it can draw on dispositions and capitals to accrue value.

Dispositions in Reference to the Logics of the Field

Employing a Bourdieusian toolkit, we theorise how creating music in a learning culture influences dispositions in the habitus in line with the logic of the field. In his argument concerning habitus as distributed cognition, Connolly (2006a) states the tool is valuable in that it helps us move away from the idea that a boy's masculine identity is static and fixed; that it is something simple acquired and then located in their head and that is remains the same and unchanged regardless of the different contexts he will move between. (p. 144)

There is

no core masculine identity that an individual boy (or group of boys) has and which they then take with them and express across a range of contexts and situations. Any expression of masculinity can only be understood, and is actually only ever made possible, by the context within which it takes place. (Connolly 2006a, p. 150)

Throughout our research, we were aware of the hyper-masculine safety net which furthers anti-educational stances and often creates particular barriers to learning. However, bad-boy, anti-school masculinities, though potent, are not the only identity discourse drawn upon by boys (Archer and Yamashita 2003; Martino and Pallotta-Chiarolli 2003; Nayak 2006). For the "hard" boys in our study, who were frequently labelled in a negative manner by their teachers, the field of the learning culture was a way to legitimately contend with the hegemonic masculine identity, to express themselves without appearing weak. Because the "hard boys" are making music and perceived by their peers as musicians, they were able to shift between alternative identity positions as learners (Stahl and Dale 2013). Some fluidity of learner identity thus became possible, with elements of homology arising between learners' habitus inside and outside of the school context.

In learning cultures, practices of learning become formed and reformed, structured through "the actions, dispositions and interpretations of the participants" (James et al. 2007, p. 4). While social fields are structured according to symbolic forms, which are often valued according to the dominant practices, we see this is less apparent when habitus and field are more closely aligned (cf. Yang 2013, p. 10–11). As Bourdieu makes clear, when habitus and field do not accord there are disjunctures, but in a peer-led learning environment, the habitus and field are closely aligned, whereas in the boys' formal schooling, the disjunctures are more divisive and, as a result, they tap into specific repertoires of "hard" masculinity as their social positioning is more vulnerable. The habitus, as generative, allows for the boys to disassociate from the accumulation of capital (qualifications) innate to the hegemonic logic of the field of formal schooling. More precisely, the habitus, in order to accrue value, steers the boys away from the dominant logics of the formal schooling, propelling it to a field where the habitus understands the logic and has the capital to compete. However, the opportunity to DJ and MC within the school context to some extent disrupted this dominant logic, opening up at least some possibility for more positive learner identities amongst the "bad boys".

Bourdieu's theory of field—when applied to fields with radically different logics—requires theorisation with the generative capacity of the habitus. As the habitus seeks to gain validation, it looks for fields (and arguably constructs fields) associated with dispositions that are historically constituted and culturally validated which, in this case, is working-class masculinity (cooperation, caring). Therefore, what we see here is a learning culture that appears as a counter-field (an inverted field with apparently opposite logics) compared to the boys' formal schooling. Nevertheless, through the welcoming of DJ-ing and MC-ing as acceptable activities for the classroom, a possibility arose whereby the out-of-school learning environment could, to at least some extent, coalesce with the field of formal schooling.

References

Archer, L., & Yamashita, H. (2003). Theorising inner-city masculinities: Race, class, gender and education. *Gender and Education, 15*(2), 115–132.

Atencio, M., Beal, B., & Wilson, C. (2009). The distinction of risk: Urban skateboarding, street habitus and the construction of hierarchical gender relations. *Qualitative Research in Sport and Exercise, 1*(1), 3–20.

Bourdieu, P. (1985). The social space and the genesis of groups. *Theory and Society, 14,* 723–744.

Bourdieu, P. (2002). Habitus. In J. Hillier & E. Rooksby (Eds.), *Habitus: A sense of place* (pp. 27–34). Aldershot: Ashgate.

Bourdieu, P., & Wacquant, W. (1992). *An invitation to reflexive sociology.* Cambridge: Polity Press.

Brown, P. (2013). Education, opportunity and the prospects for social mobility. *British Journal of Sociology of Education, 34*(5–6), 678–700.

Burke, P. (2007). Men accessing education: Masculinities, identifications and widening participation. *British Journal of Sociology of Education, 28*(4), 411–424.

Burnard, P. (2012). DJ cultures. In P. Burnard (Ed.), *Musical creativities in practice* (pp. 100–122). Croydon: Oxford University Press.

Butler, J. (1999). Revisiting bodies and pleasures. *Theory Culture Society, 16*(2), 11–20.

Connolly, P. (2006a). The masculine habitus as 'distributed cognition': A case study of 5- to 6-year-old boys in an English inner-city, multi-ethnic primary school. *Children & Society, 20*(2), 140–152.

Connolly, P. (2006b). The effects of social class and ethnicity on gender differences in GCSE attainment: A secondary analysis of the Youth Cohort Study of England and Wales 1997–2001. *British Educational Research Journal, 32*(1), 3–21.

Davies, B., & Saltmarsh, S. (2007). Gender economies: Literacy and the gendered production of neo-liberal subjectivities. *Gender and Education, 19*(1), 1–20.

Francis, B. (2006). Heroes or zeroes? The discursive positioning of 'underachieving boys' in English neo-liberal education policy. *Journal of Education Policy, 21*(2), 187–200.

Grenfell, M. (2008). *Pierre Bourdieu: Key concepts.* Durham: Acumen.

Hart, C. S. (2013). *Aspirations, education and social justice: Applying Sen and Bourdieu.* London: Bloomsbury.

Hilgers, M., & Mangez, E. (2015). Introduction to Pierre Bourdieu's theory of social fields. In M. Hilgers & E. Mangez (Eds.), *Pierre Bourdieu's theory of social fields* (pp. 1–36). Abingdon, Oxfordshire: Routledge.

Humphries, S. (1981). *Hooligans or rebels? An oral history of working-class childhood and youth 1889–1939.* Oxford: Basil Blackwell.

Ingram, N. (2009). Working-class boys, educational success and the misrecognition of working-class culture. *British Journal of Sociology of Education, 30*(4), 421–434.

Ingram, N. (2011). Within school and beyond the gate: The complexities of being educationally successful and working class. *Sociology, 45*(2), 287–302.

James, D., Biesta, G., Davies, J., Gleeson, D., Hodkinson, P., Maull, W., et al. (Eds.). (2007). *Improving learning cultures in further education (Improving Learning Series).* Abingdon: Routledge.

Kenway, J., & McLeod, J. (2004). Bourdieu's reflexive sociology and 'spaces of points of view': Whose reflexivity, which perspective? *British Journal of Sociology of Education, 25*(4), 525–544.

Mac an Ghaill, M. (1994). *The making of men: Masculinities, sexualities and schooling.* Buckingham: Open University Press.

MacLeod, J. (2009). *Ain't no makin' it.* Boulder, CO: Westview Press.

Martino, W., & Pallotta-Chiarolli, M. (2003). *So what's a boy?* Maidenhead: Open University Press.

Nayak, A. (2006). Displaced masculinities: Chavs, youth and class in the post-industrial city. *Sociology, 40*(5), 813–831.

Perkins, R. (2013). Learning cultures and the conservatoire: An ethnographically-informed case study. *Music Education Research, 15*(2), 196–213.

Phoenix, A. (2004). Neoliberalism and masculinity: Racialization and the contradictions of schooling for 11-to-14-year-olds. *Youth Society, 36*(2), 227–246.

Reay, D. (2002). Shaun's story: Troubling discourses on white working-class masculinities. *Gender and Education, 14*(3), 221–234.

Reay, D. (2003). A risky business? Mature working-class women students and access to higher education. *Gender and Education, 15*(3), 301–317.

Reay, D. (2004). It's all becoming habitus: Beyond the habitual use of habitus in educational research. *British Journal of Sociology of Education, 25*(4), 431–444.

Robbins, D. (2000). *Bourdieu and culture.* London: SAGE.

Skeggs, B. (2002). *Formations of class & gender: Becoming respectable.* Nottingham: SAGE.

Skeggs, B. (2004). *Class, self, culture.* London: Routledge.

Stahl, G. (2012). Aspiration and a good life among white working-class boys in London. *Journal of Qualitative and Ethnographic Research, 7*(8–9), 8–19.

Stahl, G. (2013). Habitus disjunctures, reflexivity and white working-class boys' conceptions of status in learner and social identities. *Sociological Research Online, 18*(3).

Stahl, G. (2015). *Aspiration, identity and neoliberalism: Educating white working-class boys.* London: Routledge.

Stahl, G., & Dale, P. (2012). Creating positive spaces of learning: DJers and MCers identity work with new literacies. *The Educational Forum, 76*(4), 510–523.

Stahl, G., & Dale, P. (2013). Success on the decks: Working-class boys, education and turning the tables on perceptions of failure. *Gender and Education, 25*(2), 1–16.

Stahl, G., & Dale, P. (2015). DJ and MC Habitus and 'Skillz' in Peer-led Learning Cultures. In P. Burnard, Y. Hofvander Trulsson, & J. Soderman (Eds.), *Bourdieu and the sociology of music education* (pp. 127–143). Hants: Ashgate.

Stenning, A. (2005). Where is the post-socialist working class? Working-class lives in the spaces of (post-)socialism. *Sociology, 39*(5), 983–999.

Willis, P. (1977). *Learning to labour: How working class kids get working class jobs.* New York: Columbia University Press.

Yang, Y. (2013). Bourdieu, practice and change: Beyond the criticism of determinism. *Educational Philosophy and Theory, 45*, 1–19.

CHAPTER 4

Poetry and the Conditions of Practice: A Field Study

Jen Webb

INTRODUCTION

Contemporary poetry is a mode of social activity, and an expressive medium that, like art more generally, is simultaneously set apart from the everyday world and threaded right through it. Comparatively, few people routinely choose poetry as their reading matter, but will turn to it when they need to apply balm to a broken heart, or want to (attempt to) express the ineffable. Analysis of the practice, along with the conditions of its production and its reception, could thus shed light on aspects of contemporary society.

However, the sociological literature includes remarkably little work on poetry or its producers. There is little consideration of how poets approach the making of their work, or its dissemination; how they interact as competitors and collaborators; or how explicitly they understand and negotiate the frameworks within which they are operating. Answering the question "Why no sociology of poetry?" P.J. Ward suggests that it is because poetry is not "social": the recondite nature of

J. Webb (✉)
University of Canberra, Canberra, Australia

© The Author(s) 2018
J. Albright et al. (eds.), *Bourdieu's Field Theory and the Social Sciences*,
https://doi.org/10.1007/978-981-10-5385-6_4

53

its expression "truncates the very thing that in all other cases language strives to achieve" (Ward 1981, p. 202), while Kurt Wolff responds that a study of poetry would primarily address explorations of meaning, not of social organisation (Wolff 1986, p. 348).

In response to this gap in the literature, I recently completed a field study of poets and poetry. The aim was to draw on and extend Pierre Bourdieu's work on the field of cultural production, focusing on this section of the field. This chapter outlines the approach we took and the framework within which we approached this project. I begin by setting out the sociological approaches to the broader field of cultural production, and then discuss the focus and the findings of this project.

BAD BEDFELLOWS?

In 1980, Pierre Bourdieu announced that "Sociology and art do not make good bedfellows" (1993a, p. 139), and this has been echoed by many subsequent researchers. César Graña describes the relationship as characterised by "ceremonial academic warfare" (1989, p. 17), and Vera observes that this is a battle fought on both intellectual and institutional grounds (1990, p. 5). Bourdieu's position is that artists are to blame for the conflict, because they are attached to the "universe of belief" (1993a, p. 139) that enjoys a special ("magical") status, and that sociologists are also to blame because they take a reductive approach to analysis of the field. This results in confirmation of the already known, rehearses the clichés of the art field, and fails to interrogate sociologists' own preconceptions. Those who do attempt to analyse the universe of art tend to present art is fully homologous with the wider social field: as Stanley Katz writes, "Insofar as social scientists have been interested in art, they have been concerned with art in its social context" (2006, p. x). The result is that their findings overlook the particularities of art's traditions, logics, values and practices, the contexts in and through which agents enter and remain within the field, and the conditions of production of art.

Art is, after all, a social practice, but it is not fully homologous with social conventions; hence, neither social nor economic features satisfactorily explain its internal operations. When, for example, Becker writes that art is simply "the work some people do" (1982), or when Janet Wolff cites Mayakovsky to the effect that "art is always 'manufacture'" (1981, p. 13), the risk is that readers will assume this means art is fundamentally an economic activity like other economic activities. Overall, sociology has largely failed to acknowledge what Bourdieu makes clear: the need to interrogate how individuals enter the field; the internal shape and dynamics of the field; how art objects are constituted, framed, and disseminated; and how artists and artworks operate in their social contexts.

Eduardo de la Fuente argues that what he describes as "the new sociology of art" (2007) erodes the barriers between sociological and humanist frameworks and pays serious attention to the social character of artworks. Examples are found in studies of specific art forms (see, e.g. Grenfell and Hardy 2007), and such collections as Inglis and Hughson (2005) and Becker et al. (2006). Hanquinet and Savage's 2016 Handbook includes contemporary modes, as well as accounting for globalisation and the rise of social media and art's intersection with popular culture. But while there is, thus, a developing focus on the art world, virtually no attention is paid to poetry. Explaining this absence, Phil Cohen (2005, n.p.) observes that "poetry constitutes a small, semi-autonomous province within the federal republic of letters". In this, he gestures towards Bourdieu's concept of cultural field, pointing to the need for a close study of the field.

Mapping the Field

Any attempt to conduct a field study needs to begin with the "construction of the object" of study, with identification of the principles of relationality, rigour, and other social dimensions associated with that field (Bourdieu and Wacquant, 1992, p. 224). This involves mapping work: delimiting the area of investigation, and identifying the positions available within that field; how institutions and agents take up their position in that field; what forms of capital are required to occupy and retain such a position; and how the struggles to preserve or change the field manifest (Bourdieu 1983, p. 312). Such an operation permits the building of understandings of the organisational principles at stake, and the relational, processual, institutional, and individual practices and processes involved. It offers a "heuristic efficacy" (1983, p. 311), providing pathways towards understanding how elements in a domain of practice are constituted, how they interact and operate, and how they are operated on.

Working from these principles, the poetry project began by constructing the "object" of contemporary poetry, identifying the conditions of access to the field, the habitus of the individuals who enter and remain within the field, the modes of capital, how agents engage in struggles for position, and the doxa—the values, the beliefs—that directs such struggles.

Of particular importance, since three of the investigators of this field study are themselves poets and hence "insiders" who share the illusio of the field, it was necessary to take a reflexive approach to our research. This led us to apply techniques that would allow us to break with the common sense and commonplaces shared by members of a field of practice: to apply a "radical doubt" to all we know of the field and to achieve this primarily by relying not on what we know of the field, but by investigating its "social history": how has this field emerged in history; how does it constitute itself; and what are the principles of belief and values held by its members? We relied on observation, conversation, and analysis: fieldwork in the form of visits to, and participation in, sites of poetry practice; interviews with 75 poets, at different stages of their careers and in nine different nations; and extensive reading of the extant literature. This is manifestly an imperative where an insider is investigating their own field, but it applies equally to any field study because:

> The preconstructed is everywhere. The sociologist is literally beleaguered by it, as everyone else is. The sociologist is thus saddled with the task of knowing an object—the social world—of which he is the product, in a way such that the problems that he raises about it and the concepts he uses have every chance of being the product of this object itself. (Bourdieu and Wacquant 1992, p. 235)

Bourdieu's charts of the field of class relations (1993b, p. 38 et seq) locate the field of power at the dominant pole of the field of class relations, and the field of cultural production at the (economically) dominated but (symbolically) dominant space of the field of power. This grounds his depiction of the art world as "the dominated of the dominant": possessing authority with respect to the rest of the social world, but a weak player in the field of power because artists "possess all the properties of the dominant class minus one: money" (Bourdieu 1993b, p. 165).

When he charts the structure of the field of cultural production, Bourdieu describes a bifurcated field. One pole is dominant (but poor), committed to autonomous production; the other pole is dominated (but rich), committed to heteronomous production. The field is also organised in terms of its varying forms of consecration: from the rearguard (those artists and artworks that have remained important and known), through the "bourgeois" (older consecrated avant-garde) and the "charismatic" (the consecrated avant-garde) to the contemporary avant-garde.[1] Those positions with little or no consecration are the location for new and emerging artists, new modes that have not yet been properly acknowledged by the field's gatekeepers, or those working for a market (because in this case, the works are committed to other fields than art).

The relationship between the field of cultural production and the field of power is quite clearly articulated. Art is woven into the fabric of the political field because it is hailed as a representative of the nation to itself and others. Virtually, all contemporary nations have a version of a ministry or department of the arts, and the policies and funding mechanisms to actualise its role. They maintain national galleries, libraries, and art schools, and regulate education in the arts. With reference specifically to poetry, many nations and regions (though not Australia) fund a poet laureate whose responsibility includes marking key events and ideas in their nation or region. Other support may be provided poetry, such as the provision of a specialist poetry library. Globally, the UNESCO Creative Cities Network is an enticement for cities that already possess a significant creative infrastructure to bid for UNESCO City of Literature status, which raises the profile of literature and therefore of poetry in named cities. Overall, though, poetry has a low profile with respect to the field of power. The making of literary works is rarely taught in art schools; where creative writing is taught at university level, poetry typically is an add-on, if it is included at all; poetry is not reliably included on the lists of national literary prizes; and it is very difficult to find contemporary poetry in any brick-and-mortar bookstore.

Poetry is not, in short, precisely like the other art forms. While there is significant overlap among them—particularly in the habitus of poets, which (as for other artists) generates creative thinking and practice, commitment to the logic of capital-A Art, and a shared belief in the ideal of fully autonomous work—the field can be better understood as a series of sub-fields laminated together. An obvious distinction is between the autonomous and heteronomous poles of the field, a distinction so comprehensive that Lahire argues that the cultural field is not in fact a field, but a pair of subfields: "the consecrated avant-garde" and the "subfield of large-scale production" (2010, p. 453), with different conditions for entry and rewards for participation. The field divides too according to modes of practice. Music, for example, uses a different medium, has different conditions for entry, constructs different objects, and has different traditions and histories from literature. And the sub-field of literature itself is divided: though all the forms it contains are expressive modes, and all use the same medium, language, they use it in very different ways to achieve very different outcomes. Novels, nonfiction, and scripts are typically committed to communicating ideas and story, while poetry typically commits itself not to communication, but to imagery: "A poem should not mean./But be", wrote Archibald MacLeish (1985, p. 106), and this depiction resonates for many poets.

There is a logic to this insistence on the non-instrumentality of poetry: it is almost impossible for poets to operate at the heteronomous pole of the field, because there is no popular audience and no large-scale market-oriented production for contemporary English-language poetry. Therefore poets who are operating in terms of a practical sense of the field will be likely to value, and compete for, what is available to them: mystery; art for art's sake. Success in this operation is likely to provide practitioners with pretty much the only modes of capital available to them: social (participating in the right networks); cultural (knowledge, competencies, and taste); and symbolic (prestige and reputation: that which provides the conditions to acquire and use other kinds of capital).

Figure 4.1 adapts the key points of Bourdieu's diagram of the field of cultural production (1993b, p. 49) to accommodate the contemporary shape of the sub-field of poetry. As is evident, the same modes of consecration apply, and the same bifurcation is in place.

This diagram should be read as a partial and contingent depiction of the field, as is any diagram of social activity. It is always subject to change, both as tastes and practices change, and as practitioners compete for consecration, shifting positions. As poets develop their capacity and capital, as technology affords new modes of practice and channels of dissemination, and as social values change, the positions themselves changed. In nineteenth- and early twentieth-century Australia, for example, poetry that accorded distinction, and was consecrated, is the poetry that now is found primarily in the mass audience/low consecration zone: bush poetry, rhyming, or sentimental verse. Modernist avant-garde poets were then found in the low audience/low consecration zone, struggling to achieve acceptance in the field. Today, poets in that zone are likely to be rappers and spoken-word artists, or digital poets who focus on technology rather than language; this approach leaves all but the most effective (and the most networked) excluded from consecration.

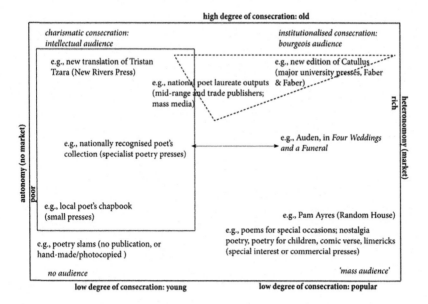

Fig. 4.1   The sub-field of contemporary poetry

While it is inevitable that, across time, poets and poems will shift between categories of consecration (from no audience through to high consecration, or vice versa), what does not seem to change is the gulf between autonomy and heteronomy. It is possible to straddle those domains, as is the case with Auden's "Funeral Blues", but this was only because it was included in a very successful movie. More typically, agents belong only to one or the other pole. The U.K.'s Pam Ayres, for example, has made an income from her work over a long career. Her publisher, Random House, is an appropriate outlet for her work: it is regularly ranked one of the world's largest publishers,[2] but though it publishes a few luminaries such as Billy Collins, Mary Oliver, and Maya Angelou, it does not publish arcane, emerging, or avant-garde poets. Collins, Oliver, and Angelou possess sufficient symbolic capital, by virtue of their longevity and quality, to be included alongside Ayres in Random House's poetry stable, but this co-presence does not afford her distinction, because her work is directed outside the field, as a mode of entertainment, and not as capital P Poetry. Despite her public success, her practice does not accord with the values of the field. This is an example of the effect of the battle in the nineteenth-century French poetry community to achieve autonomy (Bourdieu 1984, p. 3), which resulted in a commitment to "art for art's sake", and to the valuing of poetry that aims at the new, that refuses convention, that does not seek the applause of those without poetic credentials. We distinguish ourselves, Bourdieu wrote, by the distinctions we make: "Taste classifies, and it classifies the classifier" (1984, p. 6). Those who make and read autonomous, experimental, and consecrated poetry achieve distinction in the field by displaying "the pure gaze" which "implies a break with the ordinary attitude towards the world" (1984, p. 31). Those who make and read popular or nostalgic poetry and doggerel distinguish themselves negatively with respect to the field, demonstrating an absence of informed judgment or taste, and a refusal to see the world outside of the lens provided by the doxa (1984, p. 240). They may operate effectively within the economic sphere, but cannot achieve field-specific capital.

POETRY AND CAPITAL

Where the poets compete for position in the field, then, they are competing for a range of capital forms. No poets in the field study said that they earned money by selling poems or by winning prizes: not surprisingly—it is very rare to make any real income from poetry.[3] What they identified as the reward for their work was first the personal satisfaction that comes from the making process, and next, and most importantly, the prestige attendant on being recognised as a poet, and the distinction that such recognition accords. They operate, therefore, to maximise their accumulation of symbolic capital (1991, p. 238). The possession of high levels of symbolic capital is evidenced by the number and the prestige of prizes and awards they have won; the number of books published with prestigious imprints; and the extent to which their work has been translated into other languages, and been included in important international anthologies.

Cultural capital, which Bourdieu refers to, variously, as incorporated capital (1991, p. 230), a "feel for the game", or informational capital (1987, p. 4), involves the competencies that allow agents to perceive and appreciate certain products or practices and to be familiar with the codes and markers of the field (Bourdieu 1984, p. 2). Its possession equips poets to move strategically, and achieve success according to the logic of the field. What this means in concrete terms was more vaguely articulated by the poets we interviewed, because it is, after all, a more intangible form of capital; it is, however, very dependent on social capital: though most poets are tertiary educated, there is very little formal training in poetry, which means they need to train themselves. This usually happens either through their watching and modelling themselves on others, or they being mentored by more established practitioners.

What is clear is that economic capital has a very limited place in the field. Virtually, no poets make a living directly from their writing, and, as Bourdieu observes, poetry's "emancipation … from the rule of money and interest" (2010, p. 222) means it is both free to, and required to, focus on acquiring capital in other forms. Of course, this is true of most artists in any medium; but though there are examples of artists in other modes supporting themselves from their art, this is not the case for poets. Individual poems earn only a pittance in most publications, and very often are published without any economic exchange. Book collections are more likely to be produced by small presses than by established publishers that pay advances and invest in promoting sales. Very few major publishers contract poetry collections. Other than the handful of university presses on the annual Publishers Weekly rankings of the leading publishers, few if any publish poetry; those few typically release only curriculum-oriented anthologies, or new editions of classical works.

One reason the capital associated with the field of poetry is so resistant to economic capital—or, more precisely, why it is so difficult to leverage the field-specific capital—is because the community of contemporary poets operates as a closed shop. As Bourdieu notes about the nineteenth-century battle for autonomy waged by poets, while they won that war and thus achieved a sense of artistic "purity", they lost social relevance; in the main, poets have "only their competitors as clients" (1996, p. 82). Very few people outside the field would recognise the names of any recent or contemporary poets except for the most notorious and famous: Seamus Heaney; Sylvia Plath; Maya Angelou; and Les Murray. Without name recognition, and without an audience willing to purchase the products, there is little opportunity to earn a living from poetry.

The Poetic Habitus

Poets do, of course, have to support themselves financially, but their habitus does not direct them to successful professional careers, in most instances. Fortunately, for contemporary poets, the higher educational context, with burgeoning creative writing courses, provides a genuinely fruitful site for them to translate their symbolic capital into the economic. Of the 75 poets in the study, 40 are employed in the university sector. Often, this occurs not (only) because of their distinction as poets, but because of their networks: tenured academics in their social circles invite them to teach a course, which often translates into an ongoing role. For poets, social capital is a very important aspect of their careers. It often begins at the earliest stages: growing up in a home with collections of books, and/or parents who read or recited poetry; joining the right poetry group; and being mentored by poets who know how to play the game. This results in being invited to read their work at the "right" venues; being reviewed by important critics; and having collections of poetry published by professional, widely distributed publishers. The most successful poets in the study are those who are intensively and extensively connected to, and embedded within, a community of practice. The least successful—least known, least published—of the poets, by contrast, report high degrees of isolation with respect to the poetry community.

The possession of relational networks is, therefore, one of the conditions for entry to the sub-field of poetry; the other key condition is the possession of the artistic habitus. Bourdieu and Haacke (1995) discuss this in some detail, identifying such elements as heterodoxical tendencies; a degree of social or political disinterestedness; the possession of technical skills and knowledge of art; and, overall, a feel for the game—the deeply installed dispositions that make the individual entirely at home in the field and able to navigate it successfully.

Australian rapper poet Omar Musa is an example of this habitus and its importance in generating the sorts of moves that lead to successful navigation of the field. His poetic form is, as Fig. 4.1 details, located outside the consecrated zone of the field, but it is also an example of playing the field very well: rap is heterodoxical both within the poetry field and in society more generally, and this underscores his own (valued) heterodoxy. He is not only a spoken-word artist: his poems also work successfully in published form because he has high-level literary capacity (his novel Here come the dogs was long listed for the Miles Franklin Award in 2015). Moreover, from the start, he possessed social capital associated with being the child of an arts journalist and a poet, and with educational credentials perhaps more in keeping with lyric poets than (the popular image of) rap poets. In this, he is an exemplar of all those poets in the study who have achieved field-specific capital and consecration; though they did not all begin with family connections, they all found their way early in the field, built and maintained strong poetry networks, achieved high levels of education, and learned to operate on a global stage.

The field study probed the development of poetic habitus, in part by asking poets about when they first recognised that there was something different about poetry from other language forms. Nearly all remembered the precise moment when they were captivated by the form and realised a sense of belonging. For most of the poets, this occurred sometime between primary school and university, and they describe it in passionate terms: "I completely fell in love with [famous poet]"; "[famous poet] excited me"; "I still remember the first time I heard [famous poet], and that was like a bell tolling in my head"; and "it felt like a kind of beseeching of something, a kind of an attempt to draw beauty closer". They also, frequently, remembered the very poem that switched them on, and then recited lines from it to the interviewer. What they recall too is being stimulated to write their own work, and then receiving recognition for their early efforts: winning a school prize for poetry, being published in a local paper, or simply being assured by their teacher or other mentor that they do have "it".

These first-encounter stories are indications of the ways in which their habitus was formed. Their own backgrounds are variable: some poets were raised by bibliophiles and artists, whose parents recited poetry to them; others grew up in bookless homes and went to impoverished schools; and quite a number were introduced to poetry at school—not through the curriculum, but through an inspiring teacher who switched them on to reading and then writing the form.

A significantly shared characteristic among poets who have achieved high levels of symbolic capital is that they are persistent. Poetry is a long-haul game. Though an occasional young poet splashes onto the scene and achieves real attention—U.K.'s Kate Tempest, Australia's Omar Musa—for most poets, it is a long, slow haul. In this sample of poets, the ages range from 33 to 86, but the highly successful poets have a median age of 65. They have been making their work and working their field, usually, since childhood or, at the latest, university, and have persisted in the face of the very minor rewards available to any poet. And the overwhelming story told by the poets we interviewed was that their lives as poets seem both gift and inevitability: what else could they do, given this "calling", but write poetry?[4]

Conclusion

Field theory does not produce formal finished work, but it provides tools for investigation, ways of seeing and understanding, and the flexibility to recognise, accommodate, and account for changes. This emerged in this field study of contemporary poetry, because in some ways the field has changed significantly since Bourdieu's account. Some changes were extraordinary in terms of their effect on the field and on the habitus of its agents: for instance, what followed the gaining of autonomy by the art world and drove them inward on themselves. Other changes, equally consequential, are external in origin: for example, the emergence of digital technology: the presence of cheap and easily used digital cameras and recorders; the availability of accessible production and publication software; and the built-in audiences provided by social media. These have made everyone potentially an artist, potentially participants of this field, which has led to new legitimising practices, an increasing permeability between the avant-garde and the popular, and with it the intrusion into the public domain of poetic work that once remained firmly in the private sphere.

What has not changed, with respect to field studies, is that field and habitus remain intertwined. An individual's habitus directs them to enter a field and then is formed in and by the field/s in which they take up a position. The field is, in return, inflected and changed by the field-specific operations of those agents; it is, therefore, relational and dynamic, "a field of forces" that is also a "field of struggles" (Bourdieu 1983, p. 312). The field study of poetry confirmed some things that the investigators—themselves poets and insiders—believed they knew: that economic returns are rare, that a long and sustained effort matters. But it also inverted others: for instance, the enduring importance of networks of support and rivalry to achieve recognition and consecration, rather than luck or native skill being the necessary ingredient. And it showed too the importance of early recognition of young people who have been captivated by poetry, and helping them build the confidence, technical capacity, and social capital that will help them build towards success in the field.

Finally, what field theory offers researchers is a careful, reflexive, and comprehensive approach to investigation, analysis, and interpretation; and one that, by attending closely to relational aspects, rejects dualisms in favour of building understandings of the complexity that is associated with all social actions and interactions.

NOTES

1. Michael Grenfell diagrams this in his *Pierre Bourdieu: Education and training* (London: Bloomsbury, 2007), p. 248.
2. Available at http://www.publishersweekly.com/pw/by-topic/international/international-book-news/article/67224-the-world-s-57-largest-book-publishers-2015.html.
3. A recent study by cultural economist David Throsby shows that AUD 4000 is the average annual income for poets from their writing (Throsby et al. 2015, p. 21).
4. Most poets also write prose fiction, nonfiction, plays, children's literature, journalism, or scholarly work.

Acknowledgements The research for this chapter was supported by the ARC Discovery project "Understanding creative excellence: A case study in poetry" (DP130100402).

REFERENCES

Becker, H. S. (1982). *Art worlds.* Berkeley: University of California Press.
Becker, H. S., Faulkner, R. R., & Kirshenblatt-Gimblett, B. (Eds.). (2006). *Art from start to finish: Jazz, painting, and other improvisations.* Chicago: University of Chicago Press.
Bourdieu, P. (1983). The field of cultural production: Or, the economic world reversed. *Poetics, 12,* 311–356.
Bourdieu, P. (1984). *Distinction: A social critique of the judgement of taste* (R. Nice, Trans.). London: Routledge.
Bourdieu, P. (1987). What makes a social class? On the theoretical and practical existence of groups. (L. Wacquant & D. Young, Trans.). *Berkeley Journal of Sociology, 32*(1), 1–18.
Bourdieu, P. (1991). *Language and symbolic power* (G. Raymond & M. Adamson, Trans.). Cambridge: Polity.
Bourdieu, P. (1993a). *Sociology in question* (R. Nice, Trans.). London: Sage.
Bourdieu, P. (1993b). *The field of cultural production: Essays on art and literature.* Cambridge: Polity.
Bourdieu, P. (1996). *The rules of art: Genesis and structure of the literary field* (S. Emanuel, Trans.). Stanford: Stanford University Press.
Bourdieu, P. (2010). *Sociology is a martial art: Political writings by Pierre Bourdieu* (P. P. Ferguson, R. Nice, & L. Wacquant, Trans.). New York: The New Press.
Bourdieu, P., & Haacke, H. (1995). *Free exchange.* Cambridge: Polity.

Bourdieu, P., & Wacquant, L. (1992). *An invitation to reflexive sociology.* Cambridge: Polity.

Cohen, P. (2005). The occasions of poetry: Some reflections on the 'social' in poetry. Presentation for the ESRC seminar methods in dialogue, Cambridge, May. Retrieved from http://philcohenworks.com/the-occasions-of-poetry.

de la Fuente, E. (2007). The 'New Sociology of Art': Putting art back into social science approaches to the arts. *Cultural Sociology, 1*(3), 409–425.

Graña, C. (1989). *Meaning and authenticity: Further essays on the sociology of art.* New Brunswick: Transaction Press.

Grenfell, M., & Hardy, C. (2007). *Art rules.* Oxford: Berg Publishers.

Hanquinet, L., & Savage, M. (Eds.). (2016). *The Routledge international handbook of sociology of culture and art.* London: Routledge.

Inglis, D., & Hughson, J. (Eds.). (2005). *The sociology of art: Ways of seeing.* London: Palgrave.

Katz, S. (2006). Foreword. In H. S. Becker, R. R. Faulkner, & B. Kirshenblatt-Gimblett (Eds.), *Art from start to finish: Jazz, painting, and other improvisations* (pp. ix–xi). Chicago: University of Chicago Press.

Lahire, B. (2010). The double life of writers (Gwendolyn Wells, Trans.). *New Literary History, 41*(2), 443–465.

MacLeish, A. (1985). *Collected poems 1917–1982.* Boston: Houghton Mifflin.

Throsby, D., Zwar, J., & Longden, T. (2015). *Book authors and their changing circumstances: Survey method and results.* Sydney: Macquarie University.

Ward, J. P. (1981). *Poetry and the sociological idea.* Brighton: Harvester Press.

Wolff, J. (1981). *The social production of art.* London: Macmillan.

Wolff, K. H. (1986). Exploring relations between surrender-and-catch and poetry, sociology, evil. *Human Studies, 9,* 347–364.

Zolberg, V. (1990). *Constructing a sociology of the arts.* Cambridge: Cambridge University Press.

CHAPTER 5

Academic Literacy Support: Challenging the Logic of Practice

Jacqueline Widin

INTRODUCTION

Levels of students' academic literacy are key points of differentiation and distinction in Australian higher education (HE) institutions, the assessment of which demarcates the student body. Academic literacy is sometimes described as a set of instrumental skills which some students possess, and those deemed not to possess it are characterised through various 'deficit' discourses as lacking in this cultural capital. These 'deficit' discourses have been used to describe the very students that Australian universities are driven to attract through priorities of internationalisation and widening participation, underpinned by financial imperatives. Universities are practised in the processes of legitimation—how students are or become recognised as legitimate participants through their accumulations of cultural or academic capital (academic capital captures the subtle distinctions of academic skills and knowledge valued in students by the HE field and logically translated into academic attainment). The HE field is made up of a system of power lines

J. Widin (✉)
University of Technology Sydney, Ultimo, Australia

© The Author(s) 2018   67
J. Albright et al. (eds.), *Bourdieu's Field Theory and the Social Sciences*,
https://doi.org/10.1007/978-981-10-5385-6_5

which delineates the social space and is in an intense period of hysteresis (Bourdieu 1990), that is, there are ruptures between academic habitus and the current social contexts. This occurs when a newcomer enters the field or when the field changes conditions. In the HE field, the logic of practice is undergoing profound change through universities' pursuit of government funding and private income, contested notions of a 'traditional student' and 'newcomers', increasing diversity, and so-called attempts to democratise the field. Yet, what does all this mean for the orthodoxy of academic work? A central concern of this chapter is how the university provides ways for the newcomers to learn the rules of the game.

This chapter examines the practice of academic literacy support within the HE field; it shows how Bourdieu's field analysis brings to light the processes of acculturation or, some might say, assimilation that take place within the support units. The focus is on three sites of academic literacy support within an Australian university (hereafter known as Metro University), and this chapter gives an account of current struggles as this university adopts strategies to attract and retain different groups of students. The three different sites are as follows: a centre for Indigenous student education, an English and study skills programme for international students, and a discipline-specific academic literacy subject in a master's degree. In particular, this chapter explores the way the university's academic literacy services orient themselves to the particular needs of the students and the practices of differentiation which occur. Academic literacy services most often sit on the margins of HE institutions and are conceived of and implemented as a one-size-fits-all fix for those students seeking to lack the cultural capital required by the academy. The purpose of this chapter is to show, through the lens of Bourdieu's field theory, that the field is complex and that students enter the field with different accumulations of capital. These accumulations of capital may or may not be legitimated, the students may be given 'false hope' (Bourdieu 1984), or they may take up effective strategies to navigate the unfamiliar territory.

This chapter draws on a larger study (Widin et al. 2014) which examined the way academic literacy services provide a pathway or access to the university, and how they enable (or not) students to accumulate the cultural capital (sometimes referred to academic or linguistic capital) to succeed in HE. Specifically, it was concerned with the ways that academic literacy services are often regarded as a curative or remedial type of service for students who are 'deficit' in the skills needed to complete university work or pass in their courses. The study was also interested in what students perceive as what they need to know, what lecturers need to know about the students, and the relationships that are formed in the acquisition of new knowledge and skills. Using Bourdieu's field analysis, the study firstly examined HE's relationships with and within the field of power; it offered a detailed description of the research participants, as inhabitants of these fields, and examined the relationship between cultural and academic capital and habitus, the struggles encountered, and the positions and trajectories of individuals within the field, before considering the scope for changing the established logic of practice.

The researcher, who is from the field of adult and language education, worked from within Bourdieu's (1984, 1988, 1990, 1998) explanatory devices of field, capital and habitus, to analyse and understand HE issues and power relations in the local and global contexts. Bourdieu's analytical framework allows for a multilayered investigation, highlighting complexities and contradictions, within both the field of university education and the broader social context, the field of power. Bourdieu's work is of particular interest in examining the HE context because much of his research has considered his own academic culture as part of a wider intellectual field (e.g. Bourdieu 1988). Bourdieu emphasises the necessity for researchers to investigate their own social space to break with the taken-for-granted practices and thereby provide the means to understand and perhaps even change the logic of practice (Bourdieu 1988).

The Field of Power/Field of Practice

The university field is both dominating and dominated within the broader field of power, and it is itself a markedly differentiated field. The case studies examined here exemplify the stratifications and differentiations, and the complexity of the power relations within and surrounding the field. A central feature is the way the field is shaped by and shapes government policy and corresponding national and international interests. This study provides an opportunity to look closely at the types of capital and legitimation processes that are operationalised. While the case studies yielded rich data about the dynamics/power relations in the HE context, this chapter is limited to describing how by using field theory it is possible to examine the struggles and tensions between the espoused and enacted values of the academy by illuminating the struggles of students and academic staff to accumulate the legitimated academic capital, and what, if any, possibilities there might be for change.

The case study site, Metro University, is located in fields inhabited by powerful national and international institutions; the relations of power between the field of HE and the broader field of power are represented by government departments, institutions such as government ministries, Australian aid agencies, Australian foreign relations, international aid and finance organisations, and universities inside and outside. At particular points in time, the field of HE has occupied a more dominant position and more assertively shaped the policies which govern, in this particular focus, the strategies students undertake to accumulate capital/become legitimate students. At other times, the political field has dominated and imposed conditions on universities—more often with respect to funding arrangements. The following sections explore the relationship between the field of power and the field of HE to further contextualise the logic of practice in the case study sites.

Tensions in the HE Field

The Australian HE field is highly differentiated, although all universities are under pressure to increase their income through external sources and there is great competition amongst them to attract international students and implement widening participation (though in the latter case, without incurring additional costs). It is apparent that the research intensive Great Eight universities—the 'sandstone' universities (as opposed to the 'redbrick')—are the more desired destinations for overseas students (Norton and Cherastidtham 2015). The focus in this case is on the increasing reliance of University Metro on the enrolment of international students and the widening of participation (Gale and Parker 2013). Although Bourdieu's research was carried out prior to the intense and volatile globalisation of the late twentieth and early twenty-first centuries and, in some eyes, is nation bound (Marginson 2008), his analytical framework provides great insight into the dynamics of domination and subjugation in the national and international fields of HE.

The enrolment of international students is critically important for the financial survival of Australian universities, a key source of economic capital. The bulk of Australian university income is derived from full-fee-paying international students, and international education is Australia's third largest export after coal (Dodd 2016). In 2015, Australian universities earned over $12 billion from student fees. This does not seem excessive at first. However, Australia earned more than $19 billion from international students, both on and offshore, spending not just on fees, but also on food, transport, accommodation, living costs, and entertainment (Dodd 2016).

Along with the full-fee-paying students, Australian governments have a long history of providing different types of scholarships through its aid programmes: up until 2015, the Australian government had increased the number of HE scholarships it offered in the Asia–Pacific region (O'Reagan 2014). These too are lucrative for the Australian economy (Phelan 1998). The Australian government has also revived the Colombo Plan, which essentially carries out colonial objectives with scholarships as the core of its programme (Marginson 2008).

The above statistics show that universities invest heavily in the struggle to maintain their dominant positions in the international field. Key questions to consider are as follows: Where is this investment made? Is it an investment in the students? Is their entry into a pre-established field made any smoother or easier? Is it an investment in staff to increase skills and knowledge about working in an internationalised setting? The same questions need to be asked about widening the participation of Indigenous students. Australian universities' attempts to increase Indigenous student enrolments sit within the widening participation portfolio, the goals of which are for students of low socio-economic status backgrounds to become 20% of the HE student body by 2020, including an increase in Australian Indigenous students by 2.5% (Gale and Parker 2013).

Legitimate Language: Academic Literacy Within the University

The notion of academic literacy is far from straightforward; the term is used widely within the HE sector and seems to imply there is a single form of legitimated literacy that requires a systematic approach to 'fixing the academic literacy' of those students who do not display or match the set requirements of the field. Legitimated language and/or literacy are almost always upheld by the powerful figures in the university and the external markets for accreditation that they bring together. Student attributes are often spoken about in terms of levels of literacy. Great concern is raised about literacy standards, and in Bourdieu's terms, knowledge of 'standard' (English) academic literacy allows students to better play the game of academic work. Academic literacy programmes in themselves are often felt to be 'marginalised' or 'isolated' from mainstream courses and curriculum programmes (Helmer 2013).

Academic literacy is approached from a variety of beliefs about literacy—on the one hand as an instrumental skill, and on the other from the perspective of literacy as a social practice. The research approach in this project took the latter view; as a social practice, literacy as an activity cannot be understood in isolation from the political, sociocultural, and historical context in which it occurs (Street 1995; Baynham 1995). The academic literacy practices of students are acquired and learnt, most usually through successful schooling. This accumulated cultural capital—in the forms of legitimated language and literacy (Bourdieu 1982; Bourdieu and Wacquant 1992)—grants advantage to those who possess it. Power and easy passage through one's academic study derive from the ability to participate in the valued language and literacy practices. Working with a field analysis, it is possible to map the positions of those who are more powerful, those who hold the most cultural (and economic) capital and determine the literacies that are recognised as valuable, those who hold resources which will ensure success, and those whose academic literacy does not comply or fulfil the set criteria.

Academic literacy support services may be seen as a part of a process to 'democratise' the field by providing access to the valued literacies. However, the striving towards uniformity and abiding by the rules of the game result in the services providing a gatekeeping role, making sure that students are acculturated into how 'things are done here'. Academic language did not escape Bourdieu's prescient observations of university power relations; his astute pronouncement that the attempts to democratise or broadening student enrolment 'will need to be matched by a deliberate effort to rationalize techniques of communication' (Bourdieu et al. 1994, p. 9) describes the role of the academic literacy support unit.

Capital in the HE Field

Academic work takes place in a global context and is bounded by the rhetoric of 'partnership and collaboration' and the espoused recognition of the students' attributes and previous qualifications. One might assume that the cultural (linguistic) and social capital accumulated by bilingual and/or bicultural students would place these agents in a less subordinated position in the field. But as was revealed in this research, this is not the case. The participants' mother tongue (L1) was not valued or afforded status as a form of legitimate capital in the field, and the dominant language, English, was validated (Skutnabb and Kangas 2000, 2008). The value of one's cultural (linguistic) capital is far greater if you are a native speaker of English. This then accumulates a greater amount of symbolic capital, which, for those in dominant positions, usually converts to economic capital. However, the language market is not a binary; within English language, as it operates in Australia, there are differentiations, with some forms of English stigmatised and not accumulating the same amount of capital as, for example, a highly schooled form of English language.

Symbolic violence runs through this whole discussion of Metro University's work and perhaps most strongly in discussing the core motive of the university's quest for an increase in international student enrolments and in Indigenous student participation. The foundation of international education valorises Australian universities while it delegitimises (or invalidates) the students' home country qualifications. It is here that one is able to see clearly the relations in the field as they pertain to HE, in particular how one of the main goals of the university—to replace existing behaviour in the field—is realised.

A highly contested area of the HE field is where participants are engaged in struggle over the scarce intellectual resources in the field, that is, legitimacy in terms of voice and participation, intellectual and academic credibility, economic stakes, and educational resources. A key issue is the ways in which intellectual or knowledge capital, or in Bourdieu's (1992) terms, symbolic capital, is accumulated. Bourdieu argued that because legitimate knowledge in the different fields is determined in relation to the dominant conception or ruling ideas/theories at any moment in a field (which is dominated by symbolic capital), on average it is unlikely that the international and/or Indigenous students' (localised) knowledge or practices can change the structure of those dominant practices and legitimate knowledge (Bourdieu and Eagleton 1992, p. 119). If we think about the nature of the symbolic capital in the fields, is it possible for a range of 'knowledges' to equally accumulate the relevant capital needed to create change or give recognition to Indigenous practices? In his conversation with Terry Eagleton, Bourdieu was discussing the rise of 'rap' music and its impact on the field of popular culture, and whether it would gain an orthodox position. This analysis is relevant to the dynamics of the HE field and the ways in which legitimacy is bestowed on certain knowledge ('native speaker' of English) and practices (approaches to disciplines, Western corporate organisations' modes of work).

Bourdieu's notion of interest (also referred to as *illusio*) underpins this examination of university work and academic literacy support services. Bourdieu looked deeply into what agents do in a field, what activities they are involved in, where they are positioned, and how well they carry out what they do. Pivotal to this examination is the question about what interests the agents may have in doing what they do (Bourdieu 1998). For Bourdieu, interest is to 'be there', to participate, and to admit that the game is worth playing and that the stakes created in and through the fact of playing are worth pursuing; it is to recognise the game and to recognise its stakes (Bourdieu 1982, p. 180). The metaphor of the 'game' is a way Bourdieu spoke about the dynamics and relationships in a field and 'having a feel for the game is having the game under one's skin; it is to master in a practical way the future of the game; it is to have a sense of the history of the game' (Swartz 1997, p. 80).

Why is it important to ask the question about what interest an agent has in doing what they do? On the one hand, an agent's interest may seem obvious and not worth probing into, yet on the other hand, a deeper investigation of the practices or actions of the agent may reveal that 'everything is not as it seems'. What is important is the fact that what happens in the 'game' matters to those who are engaged in the game. There may be multiple 'interests' at stake, and it is also the case that some 'interests' dominate others.

Universities are shown to hold a multidimensional position in the field and represent a myriad of interests. The institutions themselves are not unitary entities; the students (a highly differentiated body) are distinct from university staff; and the lecturing staff are distinct from faculty management, which is distinct again from the university management. Also, within the universities, there are private entrepreneurial centres and organisations which deliver pathway programmes to allow students to accumulate the requisite cultural capital. Australian universities' quest for economic capital coupled with the increasing demand for English language on an international scale provides fertile conditions for the continued diversification of the HE field. The practices inherent in university work are governed by the dominant ideas and theories of the time, theories that most often conserve, not challenge, the current practices in the field, and in so doing protect the dominant positions of the dominant groups. The academic literacy services maintain the doxa (the commonly held beliefs) of the HE field.

There are of course contradictions. University lecturers and tutors in this study engaged in struggles to attempt to democratise the field. In Bourdieu's terms, this is an attempt to redistribute resources and to address the symbolic violence underlying all teaching practice. The lecturers drew not only on their own professional resources (capital) to support the learners but also, as one lecturer explained, on her social and linguistic capital and other cultural resources to connect with and give benefit to the learners. This lecturer was multilingual and had experience working in countries other than Australia. Another lecturer actively drew out the resources the learners brought with them and facilitated the redistribution of these resources into the classroom.

It was clear from this study that lecturer–student relationships are critical in an academic literacy setting context where the purpose is helping students learn and perform effectively in their disciplines (Chanock 2007). The relational aspect of teaching and learning was highlighted by the students interviewed for this research, and in many cases, given higher value than attention to English language itself, the students wanting to learn more than English language. Yet, the practices of academic literacy support are premised on the teaching of reading and writing skills to the level deemed necessary by the dominant group. Writing classes in the dominant academic genres, presentation skills, editing skills, grammar, and vocabulary feature in the array of classes and individual sessions offered in the literacy support centres.

Through examining the capitals students held when they entered into the HE field and their strategies to accumulate new capital, it is possible to identify the underlying dynamics of the field. Here, the notion of habitus is highly relevant, particularly in cases where students and staff, both sitting in the margins of the field, feel uneasy for not fitting into the orthodoxy of HE. This points to the symbolic violence played out in the field, where some agents, in this case 'newcomers', feel ignored or silenced and engage in struggles to try to break through the gatekeeping role of academic practices, heavily defended by those who wish to maintain the orthodoxy of the field.

One of the participants in the Indigenous education support centre reported her discomfort in returning to study after a 20-year break. Alice had entered the HE field with social and cultural capital; she held a significant position in her Indigenous community and had a lifetime of learning. In the HE field, Alice generally felt unable to understand the 'rules of the game' and comprehend the academic readings, the assignment task questions, and how the readings and the assignments related to each other. She felt close to dropping out. Her course involved math subjects and even in the support centre felt the symbolic violence of the tutor standing over her and correcting her mistakes; she felt intimidated. Her work with the literacy lecturer was qualitatively different, and through this academic relationship, she was able to see a way into the texts, identify and highlight the relevant parts, and generally take up some agency with them. Through her interaction with the tutor, she was able to gain some understanding of the 'rules' and to develop dispositions which enabled her to keep going. Alice highly valued the support centre. She felt it offered her a safe space in the HE field, and she drew social capital from her involvement in the centre through its resources and the social relationships she developed there. She was able to access study skills and discussion groups, tutorial support in all areas of study, and equipment such as computers, all which contributed to her developing a 'feel for the game'.

Yasmin, an international student, did not identify language or writing as a key problem, but rather talked more generally about an issue to do with her particular education and social background. She was unfamiliar with the approach to learning, and she expressed her dissatisfaction with the teaching and learning approach in the academic literacy support class. She felt that the focus on language was of little use to her and that the lecturer's lack of knowledge about her background and what she did know was detrimental to her learning 'the rules of the game'. She was quite distressed about the way the lecturer proceeded with the classes without first checking if they were of use to the students; she felt de-legitimated when the students were grouped together and the class focused on 'fixing' the students' writing problems. Her most positive experience was in a specialist discipline subject where the lecturer was able to recognise what she needed to know in order to undertake the tasks. She felt that the lecturer validated and legitimated her abilities and showed her the 'way things are done around here'.

A pivotal struggle in these case studies is around who defines the value of the capital one holds. But the nature of what constitutes 'capital' varies depending on the logic of practice in the field in which one is operating. The notion of completion of degree or bestowing of an academic award is not necessarily indicative of success in the academic field; it is more telling to consider the capitals that the students accrue and how well they hold their value and their transferability to other fields. For example, a Ph.D holds some weight in the field of HE but considerably less in others where it might be of no particular value and not constitute a form of capital at all. With those rules of the game oriented in favour of the most dominant players in any field, what we are seeing in the HE field are the struggles of the less well-positioned players to secure legitimacy in a particular field. The students in this study had the economic capital to enter the field, through full fees, aid funding, or government support (widening participation), yet they were in a subordinate position.

While cultural capital is potentially distinct from and not always convertible to economic capital, in this study, the students' aims were to increase their economic opportunities. In general, the effort to convert one's specific cultural capital through symbolic capital to economic capital may be either fruitless exercise or very rewarding, depending on the field in which an individual is operating and the portfolio of valued capitals that they have at their disposal. An obvious example from the research into internationalisation activities and widening participation is the cultural capital the 'newcomers' hold in their previous qualifications. Australian universities contest the cultural capital imbued in students' previous qualifications awarded by universities outside Australia. As an example of what Bourdieu describes as symbolic violence, the Australian universities, as the more dominant voices in the field, privilege Australian qualifications over those from other countries (although there is a hierarchy of stigmatisation), and in turn, the 'newcomers' legitimate or comply with this judgement by seeking out these Australian qualifications and rewarding them above others.

The universities invalidate newcomers' previous qualifications in order for the cultural capital held by the Australian institutions to be more highly valued (or validated) when converted into economic capital.

Conclusion

Bourdieu's field theory provided a way to position certain practices in the HE field and shows that everything is not as it seems. The academic literacy services are a feature of the HE field and may appear as a benign provision of assistance. However, using field analysis, one can see how they operate to bolster the legitimated language of the university, as determined by powerful actors in the field. Students experience these services in different ways according to how and with what capital they enter the HE field. The 'traditional' students entering the field with accumulations of cultural capital through successful schooling experiences (particularly if in English) and other attributes have an advantageous position within the field and will easily accumulate the valued resources. As Bourdieu (1986) observed, 'capital begets capital'.

From another perspective, field theory brings to light possibilities for change in the HE field. It is in a period of transition, and the international student market and the pressure to increase a diversified local student body is bringing about a hysteresis effect (Bourdieu 1990); the old academic habitus may no longer fit. The question still remains: Will the field accommodate moves towards democratisation?

References

Baynham, M. (1995). *Literacy practices: Investigating literacy in social context.* London: Longman.

Bourdieu, P. (1982). *Language and symbolic power.* Cambridge, MA: Harvard University Press.

Bourdieu, P. (1984). *Distinction.* Cambridge, MA: Harvard University Press.

Bourdieu, P. (1986). The forms of capital. In J. Richardson (Ed.), *Handbook of theory and research for the sociology of education* (pp. 241–258). New York: Greenwood.

Bourdieu, P. (1988). *Homo academicus.* Stanford, CA: Stanford University Press.

Bourdieu, P. (1990). *The logic of practice* (R. Nice, Trans.). Oxford: Polity Press.

Bourdieu, P. (1992). Thinking about limits. *Theory, Culture and Society, 9,* 37–49.

Bourdieu, P. (1998). *Practical reason.* London: Polity Press.

Bourdieu, P., & Eagleton, T. (1992). Doxa and Common Life. *New Left Review, no., 199,* 111–121.

Bourdieu, P., Passeron, J.-C., & Saint Martin, M. (1994). *Academic discourse.* Cambridge, UK: Polity.

Bourdieu, P., & Wacquant, L. J. D. (1992). *An invitation to reflexive sociology.* Chicago: University of Chicago Press.

Chanock, K. (2007). What academic language and learning advisers bring to the scholarship of teaching and learning: Problems and possibilities for dialogue with the disciplines. *Higher Education Research and Development, 26*(3), 269–280. doi:10.1080/07294360701494294.

Dodd, T. (2016). Education revenue soars to become Australia's $20 billion export. *Australian Financial Review*. Retrieved from http://www.afr.com/news/policy/education/education-revenue-soars-to-become-australias-20-billion-export-20160203-gmke3k.

Helmer, K. A. (2013). Critical English for academic purposes: Building on learner, teacher, and program strengths. *Journal of English for Academic Purposes, 12,* 273–287.

Gale, T., & Parker, S. (2013). *Widening participation in Australia in higher education*. Leicester: Higher Education Funding Council for England; CFE Research.

Marginson, S. (2008). Global field and global imagining: Bourdieu and worldwide higher education. *British Journal of Sociology of Education, 29*(3), 303–315.

Norton, A., & Cherastidtham, I. (2015). *University fees: What students pay in deregulated markets*, Grattan Institute Background Paper. Melbourne: Grattan Institute.

O'Reagan, S. V. (2014). *Government cuts scholarships to students from Latin America, Caribbean*. SBS. Retrieved from http://www.sbs.com.au/news/article/2014/04/10/government-cuts-scholarships-students-latin-america-caribbean.

Phelan, L., & Hill, D. (1998). *To whose benefit? Australian education aid to Papua New Guinea*. Sydney: AID Watch.

Skutnabb-Kangas, T. (2000). Linguistic human rights and teachers of English. In J. K. Hall & W. G. Eggington (Eds.), *The sociopolitics of English language teaching* (pp. 22–45). Bristol: Multilingual Matters.

Sknutnabb-Kangas, T. (2008). *Language education and (violations of) human rights*. Keynote address presented at Linguistic Human Rights Symposium. Retrieved from http://www.linguistic-rights.org.

Street, B. V. (1995). *Social literacies: Critical approaches to literacy development, ethnography, and education*. London: Longman.

Swartz, D. (1997). *Culture and power: The sociology of Pierre Bourdieu*. Chicago: University of Chicago Press.

Universities Australia. (nd). *A smarter Australia: An agenda for Australian Higher Education, 2013–2016*. Retrieved from http://www.spre.com.au/download/UniversitiesAustraliaBenefitsPublished.pdf.

Widin, J., Kelly, A., & Pyke, A. (2014). *Academic literacy in diverse tertiary contexts*. Unpublished project report: HERDSA.

CHAPTER 6

Transformations of the Danish Field of Welfare Work: Shifting Forms of Dominated Capital

Jan Thorhauge Frederiksen

INTRODUCTION

Bourdieu's field analysis allows the researcher to delineate a specific *terroir* of the social world, while at the same time requiring the researcher to break with ideas—his own, and those that obtain in the field—about the order and organization of that part of the social world. In this chapter, I examine the feasibility of understanding *welfare work* as a field. Welfare work is the work done, at the behest of a welfare state, by a number of welfare professionals. These professions represent a historical and institutional division of labor and different knowledge-based forms of practice.

Employing social fields to understand welfare work means departing from these common understandings. The professional division of labor, the set of welfare professions, and their distinctive knowledge bases represent one current position in a long and complex power struggle.

J.T. Frederiksen (✉)
Department of Education, University of Copenhagen, Copenhagen, Denmark

© The Author(s) 2018
J. Albright et al. (eds.), *Bourdieu's Field Theory and the Social Sciences*,
https://doi.org/10.1007/978-981-10-5385-6_6

Understanding welfare work as a field is nothing more than making this struggle—rather than its current, provisional outcome—the object of research. To examine welfare work as a field entails a break with conventional theories of professions. Instead of a set of well-defined professions, one must instead examine the professionalization of welfare work as an empirical historical phenomenon: Both the divisions between professions and their relative positions are to be examined as the historical product of a struggle. What separates a teacher from a social educator is nothing more than the specific course of their professionalization struggle—a power struggle over the institutionalization of childhood and socialization.

This chapter uses an empirical case—a study of the recruitment to welfare work in Denmark. I study all graduates from 52 forms of professional training related to welfare institutions. From the social origins of two such cohorts, I construct the cross-sections of newcomers into welfare work at two points in time. This shows how the recruitment to the field of welfare work has changed in the intervening years—what forms of capital structure the two sets of newcomers? The new aspects of this approach are twofold: Neither the longitudinal comparison of cross-sections of a field nor the examination of many welfare professions as a social field has been used before. While both are logical extensions of methods already in common use, they both come with complications and theoretical caveats, which I discuss along the way.

This chapter will initially discuss Bourdieu's notion of field and relationships between fields and time. I then describe how these ideas can be applied to welfare work and demonstrate in a study of Danish welfare work as a field how successive geometric data analyses can describe historical structural changes. These changes and their relation to the professional division of labor demonstrate the strength of both the notion of field as applied to here and the methods used to examine the field of welfare work.

SOCIAL FIELDS

Bourdieu's field concept presumes that in certain parts of social space ordering principles exist that do not exist elsewhere. What makes up a field is not the agents, nor the institutions, but the common principles to which they adhere: the logic of the field. The academic field is not limited to universities and the researchers they employ; the academic field encompasses all those agents who act in accordance with the logic of the academic field—the academic *nomos*, as it were. The nomos is the fundamental principles of vision and division within the field. The nomos orders the social world, in ways which, to the agents within the field, appear to be objective and self-evident. In his analysis of the structure and origin of the field of religion, Bourdieu argues that in order to understand a symbolic system, one must not only understand how the system *symbolically orders* perceptions and practices, as would Durkheim, but also understand how the division of symbolic competence and labor contributes to legitimizing a particular *social order*, as would Weber (Bourdieu 1991a). This allows the sociologist to examine the homologous correspondence between the symbolic order and the social order (Bourdieu and de Saint Martin 1976). Bourdieu, citing Engels, exemplifies this with the field of law: Only once the practice of law has become autonomous from both economy and religion does it become possible to produce a discourse of law, which appears to rely solely on principles of law, and thus ignore that these principles in fact express homologies with the economic power relations (Bourdieu 1991a, p. 39, note 12).

The field is *also* exactly those agents whose practice is oriented by the nomos of the field in question. So, an employee of a university is an agent of the academic field only in so far as he or she orients her practice in accordance with the nomos of the academic field. There may be a multitude of such orientations available—being a researcher might, for instance, mean taking part in the formalized hierarchies of universities and accumulating merits within that institution—but it may also mean engaging with students and grassroots movements, and taking part in public and political debates. Such conservative(orthodox) or reformist(heterodox) academic practices correspond with dominant and dominated positions within the field (Bourdieu 1991b).

Social Fields and Time

Social fields are in constant motion, the agents making up the field struggling about the above principles of vision and division. Yet to some extent, they are also relatively stable; big changes do not occur overnight. This is because social fields incorporate their own temporal structure in their logic. In Bourdieu's study of the French academic field (Bourdieu 1988, p. 88 f.), he shows how the field incorporates the temporal structure of an academic career. Agents within the academic field can observe connections between position, academic power, and age or seniority.

Waiting is an important part of dominant orthodox academic strategy; conversely, changing position too soon, or belatedly, characterizes heterodox positions. The way positions of power are obtained reproduces hierarchies of authority and career expectations. The structure of the field serves a temporal *template* for the agents within the field. This is only possible because of the relative autonomy of the field; the temporal structure of the field is embedded in the categories of perception within the field, so that the structure of said field presents itself as natural and self-evident to its agents (Bourdieu 1991a, p. 16).

However, since fields in fact do change, the agents' ability to predict changes in the field and position themselves with strategical adequacy is also important. In his study on higher education, Bourdieu highlights this *"sense of placement, and intuition about the structure and the dynamics of a field that enables agents to anticipate its future"* (Bourdieu 1996, p. 219), which is dependent on the origin of the agents:

> One of the principal advantages enjoyed by bourgeois adolescents could well be their ability to move rapidly into newly opened courses of study, which are often initially both easier and more profitable. The network of social, familial, and academic connections give them access to the information they need to shore up their practical intuition of the value of the different institutions, channels and diplomas, information that is absolutely essential for discovering the channels that are at once new and promising, the placements that are risky and productive, in time. (Bourdieu 1996, p. 218)

Bourdieu occasionally terms this *informational capital* (Bourdieu 1996, p. 423; Broady 1998).

While fields are the product of ongoing symbolic struggles, their structure only changes slowly, and the hierarchies of power within the fields change even slower—if at all—because the agents who are at the pinnacle of that hierarchy are also the ones best equipped to anticipate the changes and act accordingly. This means that to study changes over time in a field, one must study long timespans and be wary of interpreting superficial changes as indicative of structural changes. Since the terms by which agents within a field describe and understand themselves are part and parcel of the struggle within that very field, they may well be a guise under which the existing structures are being reproduced and are thus also a suspect avenue of analysis.

Welfare Professions and a Field of Welfare Work

Most studies of welfare examine either welfare policy, tracing either the effects of specific reforms, or the history of specific institutions (Hjort 2008). The merit of such studies none withstanding, they risk misinterpreting changes in how the factions of the field enunciate their positions for changes within the structure of the field, as their analyses take off from the language of the field itself.

Furthermore, the welfare professionals who embody welfare institutions are partially absent from these welfare studies, as welfare institutions and policymakers are seen as agents in their own rights. This risk glossing over differences contained within the population of welfare professionals, as well as similarities between different groups of professionals (Carlhed 2011; Saks 2012; Brante et al. 2015).

The approach of this chapter seems feasible exactly because of its ability to explore such similarities and differences, from outside the logic of welfare work.

Recruitment to Welfare Work

The social origins of the welfare worker population have rarely been studied as one. Most are concerned with specific professions. An exception is (Thomsen et al. 2013) who examine the degree of selectivity of teacher, social educator, social worker, and nurse training. This study shows that the selectivity of these four professions differs, with the teachers being the most selective and the social educators the least. These differences indicate a status hierarchy between these professions. The degree of selectivity is shown to be more or less stable when compared to Danish higher education in general. A larger and more comprehensive study on Swedish professions comes to similar conclusions.

Previous studies on larger welfare professions have shown that familiarity with welfare work, from unskilled employment, or from parents working in welfare, makes a difference in training as a welfare worker (Frederiksen 2010, 2013a; Reimer and Dorf 2013). This aspect of the recruitment has been termed welfare capital (Frederiksen 2010)

The notion that welfare professions could be studied together as a coherent field of welfare work has only been explored to a limited degree. Carlhed (Carlhed 2011) argues that professionalization—the process of obtaining status as a profession—is a struggle of establishing what constitutes capital within a given field, and thus that determining what functions as capital must be part of any analysis of professional work. Brodersen examines the forms of capital organizing welfare professions in 1955, 1975, and 2005 (Brodersen 2009). Through the analysis of union journals, Brodersen shows how the articulation of welfare practice alternates between a position close to the client and a position closer to state and administration, or what Bourdieu terms the left and right hand of the state. Brodersen hypothesizes specific forms of capital related to these two poles.

Following these studies, economic capital and cultural capital are important factors in recruitment to welfare work, but field-specific forms of capital also contribute. I will thus be constructing the field of welfare work as a field structure by different forms of capital—cultural, economic, and welfare capital.

METHODS

I construct the field of welfare work as a space of welfare professional agents through two multiple correspondence analyses. This form of analysis shares the idea of relationism with the theory of social fields, which implies that welfare professions are characterized not by substantial attributes of their work or knowledge, as in sociology of professions. Rather, they obtain their characteristics from their position within the field for welfare work, relative to other professions. Multiple correspondence analyses incorporate this notion by constructing a cloud of points from the individuals within the population being analyzed, the position between points representing their similarity. Thus, geometric data analysis can represent welfare worker cohorts as relational spaces of positions. The relative positions can then be explored in two-dimensional planar projections, "mapping out" individuals and modalities in relation to each other and thus providing partial representations of the structure of the field, as seen in several works of Bourdieu (Bourdieu 1988, 1996).[1]

RESEARCH QUESTION

The research question posed by this chapter is whether the structure of the Danish field of welfare work has changed over time and what can be gained by examining welfare work as a field, rather than as professions. I will not be examining these questions by testing hypotheses formally, for several reasons. Most importantly, the entire idea of a social field is to embrace numerous diverse aspects of the social world in a skein of relations and explore what relations bear importance. Formal hypothesis tests require the researcher to decide upon a limited set of free variables and to specify the relationships hypothesized between these; in other words, the field must be specified before testing. To avoid this, Bourdieu was instrumental in the development of geometric data analysis. In my case, the data contain the entire population of students recruited to welfare work in the 2 years selected. Formal testing ensures that findings about the sample at hand are not produced by interpreting miniscule variations and random artefacts. However, there is no larger population in this case. This is the entire population, and the analysis is purely descriptive. So, any variation is fair game for sociological interpretation. The research questions are instead evaluated by comparing the two spatial constructs and their properties: What contributes to each construct, to what extent, and what differs?

ANALYSIS

Data, Population, and Operationalization

The population analyzed are all members recruited to these professions in the years between 1990 and 2010: teachers, social workers, physiotherapists, occupational therapists, social educators, nurses, librarians, police officers, and others ($n = 30.581$, a total of all analyses). I

Table 6.1 Cohorts by profession

Profession	1990	2010
Psychomotor therapist		0,33
Librarian	0,98	1,41
Bioanalyst	9,55	2,73
Dietician	1,66	2,18
Occupational therapist	1,59	2,08
Physiotherapist	2,32	2,85
Teacher	11,00	12,59
Police constable	3,49	2,15
Socialworker	2,50	4,15
Midwife	0,43	0,82
Social educator	20,96	19,82
Social educ. assistant	0,85	1,35
Social/nurse assistant	23,81	36,17
Nurse	20,88	11,66
Total	**100**	**100**
n	11,008	19,573

construct two spaces of welfare worker capital structure from register data on the capital portfolios of these individuals, encompassing inherited forms of capital. These data are obtained from Statistics Denmark and are population-wide comprehensive data as reported by public institutions. Since there are great changes in professional training, one way in which the welfare field visibly changes is the number of individuals recruited to welfare work. As can be seen in Table 6.1, this number in fact doubles between the 2 years studied. Another possible indicator for structural changes is the distribution of individuals between professions when comparing the cohorts. Table 6.1 shows this distribution of professional training at an aggregated level.

CONSTRUCTION OF THE TWO SPACES

The construction of a field of welfare work is based on three different forms of inherited capital. The first is economic capital, which is represented in the data by income, and social benefits, for both the welfare workers and their parents.

Cultural capital can be central to the differentiated educational pathways within welfare professions (Frederiksen 2013b). This study examines two forms of cultural capital: educational capital and welfare capital. The former is represented by education of the welfare workers parent. Welfare capital concerns familiarity with welfare work. It is represented by the line of work of the welfare workers' parents. Areas of work and education have been aggregated at high levels. However, all areas of work conceivably related to welfare work have been kept separate from non-welfare areas, making welfare capital visible as separate modalities. All modalities with a frequency below 2.5% are put as passive in the analysis, which means that they do not contribute to the variance of the space constructed (le Roux and Rouanet 2009).

These forms of capital constitute the active questions of the multiple correspondence analyses conducted. Thus, the analysis constructs the space of welfare workers based almost entirely on inherited capital.[2] Since the two populations consist of recently enrolled students, we may assume that the capital accumulated throughout the student's own life trajectory will be limited.

Within the space of these analyses, supplementary data can be projected. The only supplementary variable discussed here is the profession of the welfare workers.

RESULTS OF THE MULTIPLE CORRESPONDENCE ANALYSES

The modified eigenvalues and the modified rates of variance according to Benzecri's formula (Benzecrí 1992, p. 412) provide a measure of quality for the spaces constructed. For both spaces, the first axis explains a large amount of variance, 44 and 62%, respectively. The second axes both explain a further 21 and 17%, bringing the total variance explained by the first two dimensions to 65% for the space of 1990 and 80% for the space of 2010. The third axis of the space of 1990 explains a further 15%, whereas the third axis of 2010 only explains 5%. In total, more than 80% of the variance of the spaces constructed are explained by the first three axes of each space.

In this chapter, I will only discuss the interpretation of the first two dimensions of either space, but I will draw attention to the difference in the distribution of the eigenvalues within the two spaces: The fact that a greater amount of variance is explainable by fewer dimensions in 2010 indicates differences between the structure of the two spaces constructed.[3]

INTERPRETATIONS OF THE AXES

My interpretations of the axes use the method of contribution of modalities (le Roux and Rouanet 1998), examining shared properties of modalities contributing above average at first one, then the other end of the axes, and finally, examining how to describe the opposition between the two poles. The axes can be seen in Figs. 6.2 and 6.4.

The first axis of both spaces describes differences in capital volume: At the negative ends, we find lower-income modalities, having retired from work and having completed only primary school. Opposed to these the contributing modalities are being in employment, short/medium/education, above average income modalities, and working in teaching and social work. Thus, modalities of relatively high educational levels, higher income, and being employed are opposed to lower income, lower education, and unemployment.

The first axis of the two spaces is quite similar, with the exception that the first axis of 1990 associates fathers working in farming, self-employed fathers, and mothers who are co-working spouses with low capital volume. These modalities are absent on the first axis of the 2010 space.

Looking at the second axes for both spaces, they include several modalities that also contributed to the first axes, meaning that the second axis specifies oppositions that are subsumed by the first axis. In the 1990 space, the second axis separates the previously discussed farmers (at the positive pole) from the retirees and unemployed at the negative pole. The farmers are also on this axis associated with high income. Thus, the two axes in the 1990 space must be interpreted together. They describe a triangular relationship between employment, self-employed farmers, and the medium educated parents.

The second axis of the 2010 space contains, at the negative pole, all modalities of above average education as well as some indicating fathers working in welfare. At the positive pole are fathers working in farming, construction, and manufacturing, as well as having vocational training and medium income. This axis shows an opposition to educational capital volume and the areas of work associated with such education. To some extent, there is an opposition here between above economic capital (average income) and educational capital.

Summing up, the space of 1990 is structured by a dimension of capital volume and a dimension of employment versus self-employed, whereas the space of 2010 is structured by first a dimension of capital volume and then an opposition between welfare and educational capital versus economic capital.

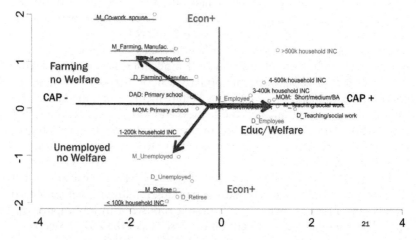

Fig. 6.1   Cloud of modalities 1990

Figure 6.1 below plots the cloud of modalities of the 1990 spaces, and Fig. 6.2 shows the cloud of individuals of this space.[4] The individuals disperse in a triangular shape, which indicates that the two dimensions correlate with some extent. From the positions of the modalities in Fig. 6.3, I interpret this correlation as the second axis specifying the first—specifically, the pole of low capital volume on the axis is separated into unemployed and farmers/self-employed.

Figure 6.3 below plots the cloud of modalities of the 2010 space. Similarly, the clouds of individuals, populating the space of 2010, are shown in Fig. 6.4. As is immediately apparent from both figures, there is a distinct parabolic shape to the dispersion of both individuals and modalities. This is an artifact of visual analysis of categorical data known as the Guttman effect.[5] In sociological terms, this means that the two axes cannot be interpreted separately. They are related, albeit in a non-linear way. Thus, in this space capital volume (axis 1) cannot be disentangled from capital composition (axis 2).

Summing up, there are several differences between the two spaces: The space of welfare workers recruited in 1990 is structured by two oppositions both of which relate to employment and income, and farming and self-employed parents contribute strongly to both axes. The first axis describes differences in capital volume, and the second axis describes the aspect of economic capital, into low- and high-income origins. This results in a triangular cloud of individuals (Fig. 6.1).

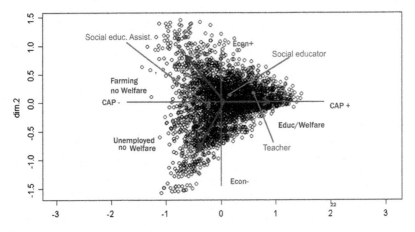

Fig. 6.2   Cloud of individuals, 1990

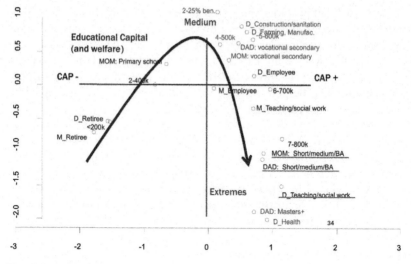

Fig. 6.3   Cloud of modalities, 2010

This is not the case in 2010. While employment does factor in the first axis, this cannot be interpreted without relating to the second axis, where welfare capital and educational capital occupy a pole of their own. The cloud of modalities (Fig. 6.2) clearly shows the parabola starting at the lower left quadrant of little capital volume, progressing through the upper quadrants where vocational training and medium income modalities are situated, and then descending to the lower right quadrant, where high educational, welfare, and economic capital are situated. In other words, the opposition from 1990 between different low capital origins has in 2010 given way to a strong relationship between welfare, educational, and economic capital.

Finally, I have plotted three of the professions into both spaces. In Figs. 6.1 and 6.3, the modality points for three professions (teachers, social educators, and social educator assistants) are shown. These three professions relate to each other in a semi-hierarchical way; teachers possess a higher status and are more selective than social educators, who possess a higher status and more selective form of training than social educator assistants (Frederiksen 2014; Thomsen et al. 2013). A similar order exists in the division of labor between the three professions as well. Their positions in the two order them along the lines of increasing capital volume. While this is not conclusive, the fact that both hierarchies of

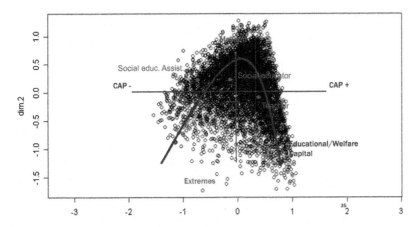

Fig. 6.4 Cloud of individuals 2010

status and division of labor to some extent appear to be ordered along the axial directions of increased capital does indicate that the structure of the space and that of welfare work are related.

DISCUSSION

The analyses above show that the structures of the two spaces differ. While education was tied up with overall capital volume in the space of 1990, in 2010, it contributes strongly to the second axis on its own. And while income and employment in 2010 contribute strongly to the first axis, these contributed more to the second axis in 1990. This I interpret to show that cultural capital, in the forms of educational and welfare capital, has become more important in the field of welfare work in the time between 1990 and 2010 and contributes to structuring the space on their own. This answers the first research question, whether the structure of the Danish field of welfare work has changed over time. The second—what can be gained by examining welfare work as a field, rather than as professions—is not as such answered by the geometric data analyses. But the relations between forms of capital, professions, and the field may now be examined from the spaces. Plotting the three professions in the clouds of individuals indicates that the field approach allows for complicated exploration of the relationships between forms of professional training, as well as the social origins of recruits. This indicates that the professional welfare work is indeed affected by the structures shown in this analysis, and further exploration of the field of welfare work seems a fruitful avenue of research.

There are limitations to this approach: The individuals from whom the spaces were constructed are the cohorts of welfare workers. The field obviously consists of workers from many cohorts, with varying seniority, and a workplace hierarchy. These dimensions are absent in my analyses, and so are data on forms of capital accumulated by the welfare workers themselves, as well as potential field-specific forms of capital, such as managerial positions, further education, and specialization. Constructing the field from only inherited forms of capital means that parental social origin obtains primacy in the analysis. This is not necessarily a problem, but it does mean that this analysis cannot examine other possibly important social differences. Unskilled labor and voluntary work also elude this analysis completely.

Conclusion: The Field as a Tool for Studying Welfare Professions

The field concept allowed me to compare professions in an analysis that is sensitized to relations between positions in social space. This enabled me to locate the positions of various professions and interpret them as expressions of recruitment, and as possibly homologous to hierarchies of the workplace, and of general professional status. This is a major advantage over traditional professional theories, which are limited to, e.g., the perceived status of various professions in the population as the axis of comparison. This method of relating professions to each does not mean that one must abandon other typical salient topic in the study of professions; both measures of autonomy, monopoly, and social closure may be projected into the spaces thus constructed.

The field notion requires a break with the preconceptions of the field itself, and this means that assuming, e.g., that some occupation or other is a profession is counterproductive. However, these preconceptions may be put into the analysis, and their meaning to the agents of the fields can then be related to the other structures of the field. To name a few: Institutions, legal relationships, union membership, informal training, seniority in work, and various levels of managerial positions may be examined, in order to compare their position and relations in the field— their social meaning to their presumed meaning.

The analyses conducted here also attempt to examine longitudinal changes within the framework of geometric data analysis. Longitudinal comparisons are purely analytical in this methodology, and as such, the comparison takes place outside of the geometrical constructions. Geometric data analysis does in fact allow for more strictly statistical comparative operations, such as supplementary individuals or class analysis (le Roux and Rouanet 2009), which could be applied to this situation. However, while this would allow for a geometrical quantification of the comparison, I think such approaches suffer from other weaknesses: They are limited to two cohorts at a time, and they blur an otherwise very clear cutline between sociological and statistical interpretation. The presented methodology maintains the visual interpretative force of correspondence analysis, and I am potentially able to conduct comparisons of many cohorts (or waves of surveying, etc.).

This use of the field notion, and the specific analytical application, opens many possibilities for the study of professions and of welfare work, and hopefully, this chapter will encourage further research in this direction. The field analysis introduces a distance to what may seem pertinent within the field and allowed me to take a different look at long-held convictions about this area of study, and indeed the entire concept of a profession. Field analysis allows the study of professions to engage with murky delineations between occupations and understand them as ongoing political and historical struggles, rather than a predictable process—professionalization—with a fixed, theoretical outcome.

NOTES

1. For a more comprehensive introduction to geometric data analysis, the reader is referred to (le Roux and Rouanet 2009; Lebaron 2010).
2. It should be noted that the active questions that construct this space potentially may correlate; this is a common occurrence for work area, education, and income. This is in part offset by using household income, and aggregating especially education and work at a high level, so that doctors and nurses are in the same area of work, yet at different levels of education and income. Any correlation thus stems from social relations above individual level (e.g., marriages) rather than a fixed relationship between income, education, and area of work.
3. For reasons of space conservation, the exact eigenvalues and contributions of modalities and questions have been omitted from this chapter. They may be found online at [https://goo.gl/sfhkby].

4. In the four Figs. 6.1, 6.2, 6.3, 6.4, the first axis and all modalities contributing above average to it are red, whereas the second axis and its contributing modalities are green. Modalities contributing to both axes are red and underlined in green. The polar interpretations of the axes are shown as well, in the same color scheme. Finally, the total interpretation of the structure of the two spaces is shown with purple arrows and text.

5. The Guttman effect is produced by banding in the data table and represents a nonlinear dependency between the two axes (le Roux and Rouanet 2004, p. 220)—a pseudoscale. In the case of the cloud of individuals, the individual points cluster within the parabolic shape making what is known as a filled-out horseshoe. This shape is a geometrical effect of the binary indicator matrix, where the errors, respectively the Guttmann pseudoscale, are projected inside the horseshoe (Murakami 2012).

REFERENCES

Benzecrí, J. P. (1992). *Correspondence analysis handbook.* New York: Dekker.

Bourdieu, P. (1988). *Homo Academicus.* Cambridge, Polity Press.

Bourdieu, P. (1991a). Genesis and structure of the religious field. *Comparative Social Research, 13,* 1–44, Emerald Publishing Group.

Bourdieu, P. (1991b). *Language and symbolic power.* Harvard University Press.

Bourdieu, P. (1996). *The state nobility: Elite schools in the field of power.* Cambridge: Polity Press. doi:http://doi.org/10.2307/2655468.

Bourdieu, P., & de Saint Martin, M. (1976). Anatomie du goût. *Actes de La Recherche En Sciences Sociales, 2*(5), 2–81.

Brante, T., Johnson, E., Olofsson, G., & Svensson, L. (2015). *Professionerna i kundskapssamhället.* Malmö: Liber.

Broady, D. (1998). Kapitalbegrebet som uddannelsessociologisk værktøj. In Bjerg, J. (red.): Pædagogik – en grundbog til et fag. Copenhagen. Hans Reitzels Forlag.

Brodersen, M. (2009). Fra profession til felt for velfærdsarbejde. *Tidsskrift for Arbejdsliv.*

Carlhed, C. (2011). Fält, habitus och kapital som kompletterande redskap i professionsforskning. Socialvetenskaplig tidskrift. nr 4: 2011, 283–300.

Frederiksen, J. T. (2010). *Between practice and profesion. The relationship between students' social biographies, educational strategies, and the demands of the specially structured program for social educator training. Educational studies.* Forskerskolen i Livslang Læring, Roskilde Universitetscenter, Roskilde.

Frederiksen, J. T. (2013a). Quelling dissent with democracy. *Journal of Social Education,* (24).

Frederiksen, J. T. (2013b). Velfærdsprofessionernes vidensproduktion: Praktiker-industri og praktiker-monopol. *Dansk Paedagogisk Tidsskrift,* (2), 51–61.

Frederiksen, J. T. (2014). Trawling for students. In F. Lebaron & M. Grenfell (Eds.), *Bourdieu and data analysis*. Bern, Peter Lang.

Hjort, K. (2008). Farvelfærdsstat—skal vi sælge velfærden for at beholde den? In *Demokratiseringen af den offentlige sektor*. Roskilde, Roskilde Universitetsforlag.

le Roux, B., & Rouanet, H. (1998). Interpreting axes in multiple correspondence analysis: The method of the contributions of points and deviations. In J. Blasius & M. Greenacre (Eds.), *Visualisation of categorical data*. San Diego.

le Roux, B., & Rouanet, H. (2004). *Geometric data analysis: From correspondence analysis to structured data analysis*. Boston: Dordrecht.

le Roux, B., & Rouanet, H. (2009). *Multiple correspondence analysis: 163* (Vol. 1). London: SAGE.

Lebaron, F. (2010). L' analyse géométrique des données dans un programme de recherche sociologique : Le cas de la sociologie de Bourdieu. *Noûs, 102*–109.

Murakami, T. (2012). A geometrical interpretation of the horseshoe effect in multiple correspondence analysis of binary data. In W. Gaul, A. Geyer-Schultz, L. Schmidt-Thieme, & J. Kunze (Eds.), *Challenges at the interface of data analysis, computer science and optimization*. Springer.

Reimer, D., & Dorf, H. (2013). Teacher recruitment in context: Differences between Danish and Finnish beginning teacher education students. *Scandinavian Journal of Educational Research, 58*(6), 659–677. doi:http://doi.org/10.1080/00313831.2013.821088.

Saks, M. (2012, June). Defining a profession: The role of knowledge and expertise. *Professions and Professionalism*. http://doi.org/10.7577/pp.v2i1.151.

Thomsen, J. P., Dencker, S., & Pedersen, T. M. (2013). Hvem læser på velfærdsprofessionsuddannelserne? -ændringer i rekrutteringsmønstre de sidste 25 år. *Dansk Sociologi, 24*(3).

CHAPTER 7

Breaking from the Field: Participant Observation and Bourdieu's *Participant Objectivation*

Emma E. Rowe

INTRODUCTION

In this chapter, I will explore participant observation as a method within the academy, through a framework of Bourdieu's field theory. This methodology is of interest to Bourdieu, who refers to it as '*participant objectivation*' and 'the highest form of the sociological art' (Bourdieu 1992, p. 259). Despite Bourdieu's enduring interest in ethnographic fieldwork and *participant objectivation,* over many decades of his work (1988, 2003; Bourdieu and Wacquant 1992), there has been relatively little take-up or exploration of how he practises fieldwork, especially in comparison with the attention paid to many of his other contributions. Certainly, if compared to Bourdieu's (1986) *Forms of Capital,* the concept of *participant objectivation* remains under-developed and under-explored in the broader scope of social sciences. Goodman (2003) points to this, 'it is somewhat surprising that his work has remained largely outside the purview of the literature attentive to the political and ethical

E.E. Rowe (✉)
Deakin University, Geelong, VIC, Australia

© The Author(s) 2018
J. Albright et al. (eds.), *Bourdieu's Field Theory and the Social Sciences,*
https://doi.org/10.1007/978-981-10-5385-6_7

responsibilities of ethnographic representation' (p. 782). In the widely circulated *Handbook of Ethnography* (2001), for example—which tends to be widely endorsed for graduate students—Bourdieu's fieldwork has little influence. In this handbook, Emerson et al. (2001) describe participant observation as a method that establishes

> ... a place in some natural setting on a relatively long-term basis in order to investigate, experience and represent social life and social processes that occur in that setting... [This] comprises one core activity in ethnographic fieldwork. (p. 352)

In these accounts, the sociologist participates in the very research space they are observing and becomes a 'kind of member of the observed group' (Robson 2002, p. 314) by sharing life experiences and learning the group's social conventions and habits. A membership would imply a sense of belonging and acceptance within the research space. Bourdieu presents a radically contrasting account of participant observation, as distinct from the 'natural setting' and orderly process that ethnographic texts depict. In *An Invitation to Reflexive Sociology,* Bourdieu (1992) writes,

> What I have called *participant objectivation* (and which is not to be mistaken for participant observation) is no doubt the most difficult exercise of all because it requires a break with the deepest and most unconscious adherences and adhesions. (1992, p. 253, emphasis in original)

Bourdieu continually emphasizes the difficulty of *participant objectivation,* for it requires 'objectivation'. *Objectivation* (as distinct from observation) requires the break and disruption of unconscious knowledge and latent assumptions, the objectification of the researcher, as opposed to the objectification of the participants. I will now briefly turn to how this is reflected in his work, before expanding on three central concepts—the notions of objectivity for the sociologist, 'objectivation' and epistemic reflexivity. The central motif is the critique of power and the (in)visible mechanics of power which are produced, structured and constructed within the research field.

BOURDIEU'S PARTICIPANT OBJECTIVATION IN THE FIELD

For Bourdieu, participant objectivation is ethically precarious and fundamentally political. This is demonstrated throughout his work. Bourdieu continually sought to inhabit and excavate particular social worlds, of which were inherently interested in the construction of cultural and social modes of meaning—traditions, rituals and customs—not as a singular tradition or ritual, but as operative and dependent upon a system and structure which gives it value (Bourdieu, 1977). He immersed himself in landscapes and social worlds experiencing significant political and economic upheaval. For example, Bourdieu conducted fieldwork in Kabylia during the Algerian War, which he draws from in *Outline of a Theory of Practice* (1977). In this work, he critiques social customs, strategies and social 'games' such as marriage. He studied the 'exotic' and the 'familiar' (Wacquant 2004, p. 389), by returning to his native Béarn in south-western rural France in the late 1950s and 1960s (see, Bourdieu 2004, 2008). In *Homo Academicus* (1988), he conducts a sociological analysis of the academic world, looking to trap the 'supreme classifier among classifiers, in the net of his own classifications' (xi). Bourdieu identifies each of these studies—the Kabyle research, the Béarn society (also, *Homo Academicus*)—as instructive in how he thinks about ethnographic fieldwork and 'objectivation' (Bourdieu, 2003). Indeed, his fieldwork is critical for how it shapes his leading theoretical and methodological contributions, including the concepts of habitus and field.

Bourdieu does not extend upon *participant objectivation* in *Homo Academicus*, but rather contends it was the methodological aim in *The Practice of Reflexive Sociology (The Paris Workshop)* (1992). It is debatable why he did not focus on *participant objectivation* in this text, but clearly, Bourdieu became more interested in this method over time. Indeed, he dedicated his Huxley Memorial Lecture in 2002 to *participant objectivation* in order to illuminate this

> technique, a method, or, more modestly, a "device" that has helped me immensely throughout my experience as a researcher: what I call "participant objectivation". I do mean participant "objectivation" and not "observation" (Bourdieu 2003, p. 281).

This method is at the crux of Bourdieu's sociological practice, by accentuating his critique of persistent academic dualisms—objectivity versus subjectivity; positivist versus interpretivist; and legitimate knowledge versus illegitimate knowledge. This is drawn out by Bourdieu (1989), when asked to characterize the theoretical principles that guide his research: 'If I had to characterize my work in two words, that is, as is the fashion these days, to label it, I would speak of *constructivist structuralism* or of *structuralist constructivism*' (p. 14, emphasis in original). These concepts gesture towards significant methodological concerns for Bourdieu that undergird his field theory—the internalized and externalized structures and constructions of power; the rules and divisions between science and positivism; and the authorization of knowledge.

THE TENSIONS AND PRESCRIPTIONS WITHIN THE FIELD

This chapter is influenced by my own research as a participant observer within the field of education, engaged as both an academic and participant observer within ongoing activist groups for public education. Starting in 2011 as a graduate student, I participated as a researcher–activist within long-term activist groups lobbying the government in Melbourne, Australia. The inner-city lobby groups were demanding a brand new government-funded public high school in their immediate locale (see, Rowe 2014, 2015, 2017). The campaigners graciously granted me permission to participate in their campaigns, and over the course of 18 months, I attended all of their meetings and events, armed with my notepad and pen. I selected participant observation for its ability to 'get inside' and *become* a campaigner, privy to their discourse, action and motivations (Emerson et al. 2001). I found the methodology to be provocative as habitus, not only for the internalized ethical dilemmas that it raised, but also as a method within the *Bourdieusian field*. Practising participant observation within the academy raises barriers and provocations. From inside and within the field, participant observation is ethically contentious and epistemologically contested.

From the start of my study, ethics approval was problematic and required several modifications. As Tope et al. (2005) write, it is 'increasingly difficult' to acquire ethical permission to conduct participant observation,

> University institutional review boards … in recent years [have] made it increasingly difficult for projects based on participant observation to

receive human subject's clearance. Our conclusions caution against bureaucratic and legalistic curtailments of embedded field observation. (p. 471)

Participant observation is contentious for the method in which it produces knowledge. This is reasonable given the researcher interaction and participation within the research space. Certainly, participant observation retains a contentious history within the academy, evoking a series of ethical restraints and dilemmas (Becker 1958; Calvey 2008; Ellis 1984, 1995; Hinsley 1983). This is illuminated by the controversial work of Carolyn Ellis (1984, 1995), in her covert study of fishing communities, or James Patrick (1973), in his 'undercover' study of street gangs. Gans (1999) criticizes the subjective and introverted uptake of participant observation, particularly when associated under a broad umbrella of 'ethnography' and 'autoethnography'.

When it came time to publish, increasingly, I found that participant observation as a method was problematic for peer reviewers. Peer reviewers baulked at publishing data about educational activists, particularly when it involved participant observation. The pseudonyms of the activists were a point of concern. One reviewer recommended that the pseudonyms be significantly extended to protect the 'vulnerable' campaigners. On the other hand, another academic (superior in the hierarchy) advised me to remove the pseudonyms from the study altogether. He told me the study would have little value or merit if the pseudonyms were to remain.

Arguably, the practice of participant observation within the academy constitutes a struggle, and there are methodological prescriptions and rules for how it is to produce valid, legitimate knowledge. Like all methods, participant observation requires knowledge of the *field*—the rules that govern and sanction how participant observation be ethically practised and contribute 'valid' knowledge. Bourdieu (1992) argues that the sociologist and their instruments function within and via 'objectively hierarchized fields' (p. 257) to legitimize their knowledge. For Bourdieu, failing to pushback and critique this *field* is a critical omission.

Taking up Bourdieu's *participant objectivation* has the potential to advance field theory by illuminating the academy as a contentious and 'bounded' Bourdieusian field. This is further explained by Grenfell and James (2004):

Any *field* is also 'bounded', and there is that which is included in it and that which is excluded. If we regard educational research as a *field*, as a "configuration of relations", then it is constituted by all that is methodologically possibly within it; in other words, its topography amounts to the range of research activity and the principles that guide it. (p. 510, emphasis in original)

There are many principles guiding participant observation and justifiably so. An underpinning ethical guideline stipulates that fieldwork will be carried out with informed consent, at all times. But there is constant slippage between covert and overt participant observation (Calvey 2008; Li 2008). In her research regarding female gamblers, Li (2008) first participates as a 'participant observer'. Through her regular conversations with women—often casual, unplanned conversations—she finds herself frequently collecting 'data' from uninformed and non-consenting participants. Li adapts her method and level of involvement, yet also finds that women are less inclined to speak with her.

In similarity, as a participant observer within an ongoing activist group, I found that overt and covert observation was, at times, messy and thorny—and not as clear cut as I would have hoped (Ceglowski 2000). In the beginning, the working party graciously granted informed consent for participant observation, enabling me to record field notes at all meetings and events. Initially, the Working Party President introduced me at a meeting and explained the study. This was helpful, in terms of facilitating informed consent from many of the individuals involved. My ethics permission form also required that I do not record any data without receiving informed consent.

Over the course of the following 18 months, I interviewed many campaigners and attended monthly meetings and events as a participant observer (see, Rowe 2017). I often overheard conversations between campaigners—that perhaps they did not want me to hear—and I saw documents that were sometimes withheld from me. I overheard criticisms about the campaigns and those people involved, and I was slow to reach for my pen and paper. As Vaughan (2004) writes, in regard to her own experience as a participant observer, 'the imperative for me to produce a victory narrative about [the school] was quite strong' (p. 393).

The monthly meetings were held in the local pub. At times, only a small group attended of eight or nine people, whereas at other times—particularly during the local government elections—the groups were larger, with between 20 and 30 people in attendance. The campaigns collected quite generous donations from businesses, such as banks, real estate agents and pharmacies. Councillors who were bidding for local government election would attend and speak to the group, handing out pamphlets and urging their commitment to the group. Many individuals arrived late into the meetings and left early. This does not foreclose the opportunity to acquire informed consent, but it does make it problematic and slippery. Participant observation within a research space is dynamic, changeable and unpredictable—perhaps this is what makes the research meaningful and replete with 'contradictions [and] tensions' (Bourdieu 2003, p. 292).

BREAKING FROM THE FIELD

Bourdieu's fieldwork pushes towards a critique of different nodes of power that are instrumental and mechanical in the spaces we research. By immersing ourselves into pre-designed or pre-selected research spaces as participant observers, this necessitates a self-critical gaze. *Participant objectivation* seeks to fundamentally destabilize and disrupt the scholar's 'quasi-divine viewpoint' (Bourdieu 1992, p. 254) of the superior, all-knowing sociologist. Bourdieu (1992) explicates this further:

> Objectivation of the relation of the sociologist to his or her object is, as we can clearly see in this case, the necessary condition of the break with propensity to invest in her object which is no doubt at the root of her 'interest' in the object. One must in a sense renounce the use of science... (p. 259)

According to Bourdieu, reflexivity requires a critical break or rupture of unconscious knowledge, but it also asks for the academic researcher to re-examine the purposes behind their research, or the self-invested interests that impose 'blind spots indicative of her/his own vested interests' (1992, p. 259). In many ways, the researcher needs to turn the gaze back on their selves, but not for 'narcissistic entertainment' (2003, p. 286) and neither to achieve scientific authority. Rather, to engage with and critique power dynamics and relations, or the '*structuring structures*' (habitus) and 'configuration of relations' (field) that are simultaneously instructive and prescriptive.

The viewpoint I construct, as a participant observer within the academy, is 'not simply the expression of an individual viewpoint' (Kenway and McLeod 2004, p. 529) but is representative of a particular field, that is, the collective rules and unconscious dispositions and structures of an organization. Bourdieu (1992) argues that because sociologists function inside of the academic field and acquire forms of legitimization within this field, the sociologist believes they are able to achieve a type of 'impartial' interpretation. This impartiality is thereby 'imposed' upon the research participants as a type of 'objective', omnipotent knowledge (p. 257). All observers are dually playing the game (intricately involved in the construction of data) whilst observing the game, whether this is acknowledged or not.

This captures how participant observation becomes epistemologically contested within the academic *field*. The means in which it contributes knowledge is questioned on the grounds of 'objectivity' and 'neutrality'. Bourdieu (1992) expresses uneasiness towards claims of objectivity:

> I thus experienced in a particularly acute manner what was implicated in the claim to adopt the stance of the impartial observer, at once ubiquitous and invisible because dissimulated behind the absolute impersonality of research procedures, and thus capable of taking up a quasi-divine viewpoint...(p. 254)

In his work, Bourdieu engages with the epistemic dualism of the known and the unknown—the objective and the subjective—and constantly provokes it. By immersing himself in the distant Algeria and the familiar Béarn, he juxtaposes the exotic with the familiar, 'the near and the far' (Reed-Danahay 2005, p. 69). His engagement and immersion into the familiar are particularly demonstrated in *Homo Academicus*, and Bourdieu (2003) contends that this research is the most 'scandalous' of all his work, 'the most controversial... despite its extreme concern for objectivity' (p. 283). His work is scandalous in that he challenges the long-standing intellectual debate between anthropologists and ethnologists (e.g. Durkheim 1982) that an ethnographer requires unfamiliar surroundings to truly be objective (Reed-Danahay 2005; Stocking 1983). Bourdieu 'overturns the undiscussed presumption ... that one must necessarily be socially distant and culturally different from those whom one studies in order to carry out valid participant observation' (Wacquant 2004, p. 395). Bourdieu recommends epistemic reflexivity as a methodological and theoretical intervention.

EPISTEMIC REFLEXIVITY

Bourdieu describes epistemic reflexivity as a systematic, analytical method, rather than an introspective moment (Bourdieu and Wacquant 1992). He describes reflexivity as a 'deliberate and methodical exercise' (2003, p. 289), an exercise that is brought to the fore and demanded by *participant objectivation*. The sociologist needs to break from their disinterested gaze and objectify their own epistemological space. Bourdieu (2003) argues that social experience must be *'previously subjected to sociological critique'* (p. 288, emphasis in original). He extends upon this by discussing his fieldwork in Kabylia, writing that 'I was constantly drawing on my experience of the Béarn society of my childhood, both to understand the practices that I was observing and to defend myself' (p. 288). As a participant observer, we draw on our own experiences and our own point of view, to construct and make meaning of our observation. It is the participant observer who 'constructs the space of points of view' (Bourdieu 1992, p. 254). Regardless of whether fieldwork consists of participatory or non-participatory observation, the researcher's perspective and gaze are central to the selection of data (which notes have been recorded in the field and how they have been recorded); the analysis of data; and how data are compiled, selected and constructed into narrative. Fundamentally, the meaning is constructed and produced *by* the researcher.

Even though Bourdieu calls for the sociologist to 'renounce the use of science', he is not calling for a laissez-faire approach. This is what Bourdieu (1992) calls a *'double truth*, objective and subjective, which constitutes the whole truth of the social world' (p. 255, emphasis in original). Grenfell and James (2003) describe this position as an 'attempted synthesis of subjectivism and objectivism' (p. 157). Bourdieu employs both a positivist and an interpretivist lens at different points in time, and he utilizes quantitative and qualitative data, perhaps ironically at times, such as the utilization of percentages, statistics and calculations in *Distinction*. Wacquant (1992) critiques this as a double reading or a 'set of double-focus analytic lenses that capitalize on the epistemic virtues of each reading while skirting the vices of both' (p. 7).

Bourdieu's method borrows from both sides of the methodological fence, and the fence itself—the division between the two—is critically damaging:

I am profoundly convinced that this scientifically damaging division must be overthrown and abolished; but also, as you will have seen, because it was a way of exorcising the painful schism, never entirely overcome, between two parts of myself, and the contradictions or tensions that it introduces into my scientific practice and perhaps into my whole life. (Bourdieu 2003, p. 292)

The positivist and interpretivist methodological division functions as a type of field—a configuration of relations that impose determinations and rules—but also as a habitus that overlaps and distinguishes between the ethically tasteful and epistemologically fashionable. Yet, the methodological tension and structural divisiveness do not call for abandonment of processes and practice (Bourdieu 2003), more so it operates as a double truth and antinomy.

For Bourdieu, *participant objectivation* accentuates the crux of this 'painful schism'. It is neither observation nor participant observation, and nor is it positivism or interpretivism. He explains that a sociologist need not 'have to choose' between being an observer ('who remains as remote from himself as from his object') and a participant observer ('a necessarily fictitious immersion in a foreign milieu') (Bourdieu 2003, p. 282). *Participant objectivation* combines subjectivity and objectivity; it is participant and observer; and it does this by exploring:

> ... not the 'lived experience' of the knowing subject but the social conditions of possibility—and therefore the effects and limits—of that experience, and, more precisely, of the act of objectivation itself. It aims at objectivizing the subjective relation to the object which, far from leading to a relativistic and more-or-less anti-scientific subjectivism, is one of the conditions of genuine scientific objectivity (Bourdieu 2001). (Bourdieu 2003, p. 282)

Recognizing the 'act of objectivation' (and therefore, the rationale in why Bourdieu refers to this method as participant objectivation) is to struggle with the crux of Bourdieu's field theory. Rather than denying the inherent subjectivity in our research—from selecting the research space, the participants and what we publish—we must recognize how we are complicit within the field, our role as researcher, and also how we are complicit in objectifying the field and the participants. As scholars, as observers, interviewers and participant observers, we are objectifying the participants as 'data', rationalizing and representing. It is crucial to acknowledge this in order to strive for greater consciousness and scales of objectivity in producing knowledge.

CONCLUDING DISCUSSION

In this chapter, I have focused on *participant objectivation* as a lens to critique Bourdieu's field theory within the social sciences. Bourdieu's *participant objectivation* reveals formative 'thinking tools' (Bourdieu and Wacquant 1989, p. 50) for the sociologist, in its attempt to break from the *field* and struggle with modes of relational and structural power.

I argued that Bourdieu's *participant objectivation* illuminates persistent academic dualisms, related to objectivity and subjectivity, positivism and interpretivism. His work captures the importance of the critical gaze, not simply applied to the participants, but by objectifying ourselves within the research practice. Critiquing the *field* means critiquing the methodology and the structures in which we produce knowledge and claim objectivity and truth within the academy.

Kenway and McLeod (2004) argue that Bourdieu 'overstates the distinctiveness of his project of reflexivity' (p. 529), and positivism is presented as 'monolithic and simple' (p. 529). Whilst Bourdieu's method may have shortcomings in the way it identifies and deals with positivism, exploring his fieldwork is arguably useful for a greater understanding of his theoretical and methodological contributions. Bourdieu calls for epistemic reflexivity and consciousness as an analytical and methodological approach to sociological knowledge. It advocates for ethnographers to incur and provoke personal discomfort in their research space. By entering into and living in locations which Bourdieu describes as foreign and faraway, but also the research spaces he 'knew without knowing' (2002, p. 10), Bourdieu opens up the possibility for ethnographers to reconfigure the rules of the field. However, this ultimately requires a critical engagement and critique of our structural dispositions. *Participant objectivation* calls for objectification of the sociologist and a complete rupture or break from their ontological and epistemological space. I use the term 'space' in this instance to emphasize Bourdieu's 'spaces of point of view' (1992). When it comes to *participant objectivation*, the sociologist immerses themselves within a pre-constructed space of interaction and 'wields a form of domination' (Bourdieu and Wacquant 1992, p. 253).

The space is critical in constructing and structuring the relations and the dispositions, the field and the habitus.

Bourdieu's ethnography represents methodological multiplicity and fusion, as opposed to compartmentalization and epistemological dualities. There is a systematic approach to how Bourdieu practises epistemic reflexivity (Grenfell and James 2003), and this is where Bourdieu's scientific underpinnings are accentuated. His concepts of habitus and field are useful in thinking about the rules and methodological injunctions that govern how participant observation is legitimized and validated. Bourdieu's fieldwork enables a reconfiguration of the power dynamics and domination of the sociologist in spaces of observation.

References

Atkinson, P., Coffey, A., Delamont, S., Lofland, J., & Lofland, L. (Eds.). (2001). *Handbook of Ethnography*. London: Sage.

Becker, H. S. (1958). Problems of interference and proof in participant observation. *American Sociological Review, 23,* 652–660.

Bourdieu, P. (1977). *Outline of a theory of practice* (R. Nice, Trans.). Cambridge: Cambridge University Press.

Bourdieu, P. (1986). Forms of Capital. In J. Richardson (Ed.), *Handbook of theory and research for the sociology of education* (pp. 46–58). New York: Greenwood Press.

Bourdieu, P. (1988). *Homo Academicus* (P. Collier, Trans.). Oxford: Polity Press.

Bourdieu, P. (1989). Social space and symbolic power. *Sociological Theory, 7*(1), 14–25.

Bourdieu, P. (1992). The Practice of Reflexive Sociology (The Paris Workshop) *An Invitation to Reflexive Sociology (with Loic Wacquant)* (pp. 217–261). Chicago: University of Chicago Press.

Bourdieu, P. (2002). *Le Bal des célibataires: Crise de la société paysanne en Béarn.* Paris: Points Seuil.

Bourdieu, P. (2003). Participant objectivation. *The Journal of the Royal Anthropological Institute, 9*(2), 281–294. doi:10.2307/3134650.

Bourdieu, P. (2004). The peasant and his body. *Ethnography, 5*(4), 579–599.

Bourdieu, P. (2008). *The bachelor's ball: The crisis of peasant society in Béarn.* Cambridge: Polity.

Bourdieu, P., & Wacquant, L. (1989). Towards a reflexive sociology. A workshop with Pierre Bourdieu. *Sociological Theory, 7*(1), 26–63.

Bourdieu, P., & Wacquant, L. (1992). *An invitation to reflexive sociology.* Chicago: University of Chicago Press.

Calvey, D. (2008). The art and politics of Covert research: Doing 'Situated Ethics' in the field. *Sociology, 42*(5), 905–918.

Ceglowski, D. (2000). Research as Relationship. *Qualitative Inquiry, 6*(1), 88–103.

Durkheim, E. (1982). *Rules of sociological method* (S. Lukes Ed.). New York: Free Press.

Ellis, C. (1984). Community organization and family structure in two fishing communities. *Journal of Marriage & Family, 46,* 515–526. doi:10.2307/352594.

Ellis, C. (1995). Emotional and ethical quagmires in returning to the field. *Journal of Contemporary Ethnography, 24*(1), 68–98.

Emerson, R., Fretz, R., & Shaw, L. (2001). Participant observation and fieldnotes. In P. Atkinson, A. Coffey, S. Delamont, J. Lofland, & L. Lofland (Eds.), *Handbook of ethnography* (pp. 352–369). London: Sage.

Gans, H. J. (1999). Participant Observation in the era of "ethnography". *Journal of Contemporary Ethnography, 28*(5), 540–548.

Goodman, J. E. (2003). The proverbial Bourdieu: Habitus and the politics of representation in the ethnography of Kabylia. *American Anthropologist, 105*(4), 782–793.

Grenfell, M., & James, D. (2003). *Bourdieu and education: Acts of Practical Theory (with Hodkinson, P., Reay, D. and Robbins, D.).* London & New York: Taylor & Francis.

Grenfell, M., & James, D. (2004). Change in the field—changing the field: Bourdieu and the methodological practice of educational research. *British Journal of Sociology of Education, 25*(4), 507–523.

Hinsley, C. (1983). Ethnographic charisma and scientific routine: Cushing and Fewkes in the American Southwest. In G. W. Stocking (Ed.), *Observers observed: Essays in ethnographic fieldwork* (pp. 1879–1893). Madison: University of Wisconsin Press.

Kenway, J., & McLeod, J. (2004). Bourdieu's reflexive sociology and 'spaces of points of view': Whose reflexivity, which perspective? *British Journal of Sociology of Education, 25*(4), 525–544.

Li, J. (2008). Ethical challenges in participant observation: A reflection on ethnographic fieldwork. *The Qualitative Report, 13*(1), 100–115.

Patrick, J. (1973). *A Glasgow gang observed.* London: Eyre Methuen.

Reed-Danahay, D. (2005). *Locating Bourdieu.* Indiana: Indiana University Press.

Robson, C. (2002). *Real world research* (2nd ed.). Oxford: Blackwell.

Rowe, E. E. (2014). The discourse of public education: An urban campaign for a local public high school in Melbourne, Victoria. *Discourse: Studies in the Cultural Politics of Education, 35*(1), 116–128. doi:10.1080/01596306.2012.739471.

Rowe, E. E. (2015). Theorising geo-identity and David Harvey's space: School choices of the geographically bound middle-class. *Critical Studies in Education, 56*(3), 285–300.

Rowe, E. E. (2017). *Middle-class school choice in urban spaces: The economics of public schooling and globalized education reform.* New York & Milton Park: Routledge.

Stocking, G. W. (1983). *Observers observed: Essays on ethnographic fieldwork.* Madison: University of Wisconsin Press.

Tope, D., Chamberlain, L. J., Crowley, M., & Hodson, R. (2005). The benefits of being there: Evidence from the literature on work. *Journal of Contemporary Ethnography, 34*(4), 470–493.

Vaughan, K. (2004). Total eclipse of the heart? Theoretical and ethical implications of doing post-structural ethnographic research. *Discourse: Studies in the Cultural Politics of Education, 25*(3), 389–403.

Wacquant, L. (1992). Toward a social praxeology: The structure and logic of Bourdieu's sociology. In P. Bourdieu & L. Wacquant (Eds.), *An invitation to reflexive sociology.* Chicago: The University of Chicago Press.

Wacquant, L. (2004). Following Pierre Bourdieu into the field. *Ethnography, 5*(4), 387–414.

PART II

Positionality, Struggle and Legitimation

The chapters in Part 2 of the book are linked through their use of Bourdieu's concepts of struggle, legitimacy/illegitimacy and positioning, which themselves are interrelated. The chapters are all based on areas of practice close to the authors own field of practice and explore dynamics of the fields that illustrate the value of Bourdieu's field theory to their study. The chapters address the application of field theory in diverse areas: the private English language sector, journalism, academic development within the tertiary field, surfing and cultural production, and using Bourdieu's heuristic devices identify how the conflicts, positioning and strategies of legitimation/delegitimation occur. The authors share premises about the elements and dimensions of field analysis, the key ones being:

1. Fields are arenas of struggle for control over valued resources—over the definition of what are to be considered the most valued resources—struggle for legitimation—for the right to monopolise the exercise of 'symbolic violence';
2. Fields are structured spaces of dominant and subordinate positions based on types and amounts of capital;
3. Fields impose specific forms of struggle on actors, and actors believe that the struggle is worth pursuing in the first place, i.e. 'worth the candle' (Nash, 1999 p.175); in Bourdieu's terms the doxa, a tacit agreement on the stakes of struggle between opposing agents and all agents have an interest in the field, it is worth preserving.
4. Relative autonomy of fields.

Field analysis directs the researcher's attention to a level of analysis capable of revealing the integrating logic of competition between opposing viewpoints, to seek out sources of conflict in the field, relate this struggle to the broader areas, that is, the field of power and look for underlying shared assumptions by opposing parties.

The field is an area of struggle for legitimation. Much of Bourdieu's research has been in the cultural studies and education fields, most often focussing on issues of equity, access and the process by which ideas, language and so on are legitimated (Bourdieu 1989). Bourdieu's field analysis of the position of teachers, for example, is one where differences in ideas are viewed as strategies in a struggle for intellectual recognition. In Bourdieu's terms, legitimation of ideas or position comes about through:

(a)   understanding the rules of the game (embodiment of the dispositions)
(b)   accumulating the relevant types of capital.

Using another example from the education field, in the case of tertiary education, the ideas held by those in dominant positions usually become legitimated by the field and struggles ensure the maintenance or change in these ideas. Participation in a field requires buying into its legitimacy, embodying the stakes of the field, at some level. The struggles that characterise field are those carried out by agents pursuing strategies of succession usually armed with capital that will challenge those in the most powerful positions and through the recognised signs of success that the university offers, for example, prestigious external and internal research grants and promotion, the successor's ideas become the legitimate ideas:

the university field is, like any other field, the locus of a struggle to determine the conditions and the criteria of legitimate membership and legitimate hierarchy, that is, to determine which properties are pertinent, effective and liable to function as capital so as to generate the specific profits guaranteed by the field (Bourdieu 1984:6).

Legitimisation, the domination by the established way of thinking, is most often carried out in a tacit way. A premise present in the chapters in Part 2 is that the governing principles or, in Bourdieu's terms, regularities of any field of activity are never fully articulated, never made fully explicit. This is particularly pertinent in the chapters as they look at relations in the various fields where agents clearly have different priorities and interests or illusio, beliefs in the worth of the game.

Struggles in the fields are a focus of the chapters in this section of the book; in Chap. 8, Jonathon Crichton conducts a multilayered analysis of the struggles apparent in the private English language teaching field and the positioning of teachers, at the centre level; the three-way struggles are depicted as between the managers–teachers–students. The application of field analysis allows Crichton to identify the contradictory position of the centres and the impact on the professional lives of teachers. Situated towards the economic axis within the field of power, the commercial centre pursues strategies, which subordinate teachers' social and cultural capital vis-à-vis economic capital. The entrepreneurial venture is legitimated.

Mason et al's Chap. 9 examines field struggle in journalism education where an education program called Aboriginal Community Engagement (ACE), established to foster collaboration between journalism students and indigenous people to tell stories that are not generally told. ACE is a heterodox attempt to influence orthodox journalistic practices and norms inside and outside universities. Orthodox practices legitimise competition, not cooperation, ACE actors found themselves in conflict with other field actors and positions over the perceptions and practices by which participating students produced their stories. This conflict represented the struggle for recognition and legitimacy that went against the prevailing understanding of what constitutes and is acceptable in, the sub-field of student journalism at our university.

Gibson and Moore's Chap. 10 locates struggles in the field of cultural production, the focus here is on what is often typically described as the conflict between 'fringe' and 'mainstream' productions. Through the application of Bourdieu's field theory, the authors adopt the terms 'field of restricted production' and 'field of extensive production'. The renaming of the fields allows the author's more analytical scope and ability to critique normative perspectives on the different areas of cultural production. For example, they are able to examine how the problem with 'exceptionalism' in relation to 'fringe', Bourdieu's field analysis is helpful in seeing how the struggle for the power to impose the dominant notion or style of cultural production takes place. In this chapter, we see a much more nuanced discussion of the movement and fluidity of the field, rather than depicting the 'fringe' in romantic terms.

In Chapter 11, Katrina Waite conducted an insider study of her role as an academic developer, she charts how she came to Bourdieu and how heuristic devices such as participant observation and field analysis provided the framework for her to analyse her position as a researcher and work colleague and the impact of this reflexive analysis on her analytical and representational choices. Her chapter has a focus on positioning, within the higher education academic field, and in particular, within the academic development field, there are various positions in relation to academic capital. She situates herself, from a positioning of low-academic capital within the academic field; her research had allowed her to make strategic moves. Her chapter is a critical account of insider research and the value of reflexive sociology.

In Chapter 12, lisahunter explores the logics of practice found in empirical work of an ongoing ethnography of female involvement in the surfing field she examines the legitimisation and positioning practices within surfing to challenge the potential superficiality of such empowerment and equity celebrations. In the chapter, lisahunter argues that a doxa underpinned by (colonial) patriarchy is responsible for illusio, misrecognition and symbolic violence, ultimately providing the superficial perception of participation equity for and of females. In her analysis, she constructs a historical field of surfing ranging from early Hawaiian surfing practices, how women have been variously positioned over time, through to pre-colonisation, colonisation and post-colonialisation. She introduces concepts such as patriocolonial to further illuminate the subordination of women in surfing and various events in the surfing field exercise symbolic violence to further subordinate women's positioning.

The application of Bourdieu's field analysis in the above chapters highlights struggles for legitimation and strategies of dominance and subordination in the social spaces under research. The authors strive to 'reveal that which is hidden', and their analyses rest on a shared understanding that fields are not static, boundaries shift and the logic of practice is challenged or sustained.

REFERENCES

Bourdieu, P. (1984). *Distinction: A Social Critique of the Judgement of Taste.* (Nice, R. trans.). Cambridge: Harvard University Press.

Bourdieu, P. (1989). *Language and Symbolic Power* (Raymond, G. and Adamson, M. trans.). Cambridge: Polity Press.

Nash, R. (1999). Bourdieu, 'Habitus', and Educational Research: Is It All Worth the Candle? *British Journal of Sociology of Education*, 20(2), 175–187

CHAPTER 8

Framing a "Community of Consumption": Field Theory, Multi-perspectival Discourse Analysis and the Commercialization of Teaching

Jonathan Crichton

INTRODUCTION

This chapter focuses on how field theory contributed to a study (Crichton 2010) that examined how the commercialization of education affects the professional lives of English language teachers. Two quotes evoke the focus of the study and the relevance of Bourdieu's work. The first comes from the journal of a teacher who took part in the study:

> The image the school gives, what actually happens and what a student expects are all pulling at each other. In the middle is the teacher. I nearly decided to leave the industry that afternoon. I know that it was impossible to keep all my students happy, teach them in a way I felt was worthwhile and that they were also satisfied with. I am always aware of the fact that students must be kept happy or they'll complain... I feel that I have to

J. Crichton (✉)
University of South Australia, Adelaide, South Australia, Australia

© The Author(s) 2018   117
J. Albright et al. (eds.), *Bourdieu's Field Theory and the Social Sciences*,
https://doi.org/10.1007/978-981-10-5385-6_8

be all things to all people, a magician. That afternoon I wondered what course of action I should take and how I should teach – was I a good/bad teacher, what stance should I take. How should I be? I couldn't come up with a solution. So I give them what they want. (Teacher A).

Here, the teacher voices the struggle that permeates and thwarts her working life: caught between economic pressures on her college to survive in the international market in education and her understanding of her professional accountabilities as a teacher, she finds herself torn between contradictory representations of herself—obliged on the one hand to meet the expectations of students qua clients and on the other to teach according to the principles of pedagogy. The second quote comes from Bourdieu (1985):

> There has to be a break with the objectivism that goes hand-in-hand with intellectualism, and that leads one to ignore the symbolic struggles of which the different fields are the site, where what is at stake is the very representation of the social world and, in particular, the hierarchy within each of the fields and among the different fields. (p. 723)

This quote anticipates the pertinence of and the challenge set by field theory for research that would seek to explain the experience of people who find themselves positioned in this way. This chapter explores how the implications of this challenge were addressed in a particular case. Specifically, this chapter explains how the ontological framing provided by field theory brought into relevance Bourdieu's account of the "unification of the market" (1991), motivated the development of a multi-perspectival approach to discourse analysis (Candlin and Crichton 2013, 2011b; Crichton 2004, 2010), and informed the notion of "community of consumption" that was developed to explain the findings.

Field Theory as Theoretical Framing

The link to field theory and the theoretical starting point for the study was Bourdieu's (1991) account of the "unification of the market", a process in which social values and interests are subordinated to the market economy, leading to what Bourdieu (1998, p. 95) calls the "a programme of methodological destruction of collectives." This opened connections between my own experience of working first as a teacher and later as a manager in a sector of education in which I had been employed for over 10 years, to the lives of those teachers who participated in the study and to major themes in the literature.

Central was Bourdieu's account of "social capital" (1986), the source of shared social values, interests and mutual commitment among members of groups such as families, unions, and professions. Bourdieu has argued that neoliberal policies and associated discourses entrench the dominance of economic capital over forms on which such groups depend through the "structural violence of unemployment, of insecure employment, and of the fear provoked by the threat of losing employment" (Bourdieu 1998, p. 98). Those subject to this violence are endemically cut off from their own pasts, futures and each other by the need to compete against each other in the struggle for dwindling security. Unable to unite and with their collective social capital diminished, they are assigned a position in the social space that complies with and aspires to capital associated with the economic field and those whose groups whose interests this serves, a process which further empowers the market to determine and reduce their conditions. Set within Bourdieu's account of social space, those caught up in the unification of the market exemplify how:

> agents and groups of agents are thus defined by their relative positions within that space. Each of them is assigned to a position or a precise class of neighboring positions (i.e., a particular region in this space) and one cannot really – even if one can in thought – occupy two opposite regions of the space. Inasmuch as the properties selected to construct this space are active properties, one can also describe it as a field of forces, i.e., as a set of objective power relations that impose themselves on all who enter the field and that are irreducible to the intentions of the individual agents or even to the direct interactions among the agents. (Bourdieu 1985, p. 724)

Foreshadowed here is a potentially "divided or even torn habitus" (Bourdieu and Wacquant 1992, p. 127) that may result from such contradictory positioning within the social space and the fact that sources of such positioning—the "field of forces"—will typically lie beyond the horizons of those affected. In elaborating this potential, the study drew on Bourdieu's (1990, 1994) account of "habitus" as dispositions reflexively related to the social space. It is the interplay between the forms of capital a person brings to a field in the form of habitus—their "assets"—and the distribution of capital within the field and how it is valued by others which determines a person's capacity to accumulate further capital. A key stake in these struggles is "common sense" representations of the social world, which include people's sense of what it is possible for them to aspire to. As a consequence, "classes and other antagonistic social collectives are continually engaged in a struggle to impose the definition of the world that is most congruent with their particular interests" (Wacquant 1992).

The study explored the potential for such struggle arising from contradictory positioning in the context of the private English language teaching sector in Australia. The sector typifies market-oriented educational organizations that compete for survival in a global market for educational goods and services. Over the last 20 years, its growth has paralleled the growth of export education at all levels, promoted by private and public sector organizations through a wide range of strategies, including marketing initiatives, cooperation with other sectors such as government and tourism, and the cultivation of international agent networks and links with overseas institutions and governments.

Beyond the specific context of the study, the framing enabled by field theory resonated with the potential for conflict between economic and educational interests that has been noted in the literature (e.g., Brown and Carasso 2013; Hill and Kumar 2009; John and Fanghanei 2015; Kenway and Bullen 2001; Marginson and van der Wende 2007; Stromquist 2002). The thematic connection here is that the economic field and that associated with education are ultimately mutually incompatible, the endgame being that the capital associated with the economic field subordinates that associated with education, which becomes defined solely by its economic utility—reducing students to repositories of measurable skills, education to training for work, reformulating teaching to reflect market imperatives, and translating the purposes of education into the language of the market (Apple 1996; Giroux 1999). This trend has been described, for example, by Grant (2009, p. vii) as a process by which "the learning process becomes almost entirely instrumental", and the associated loss of professional standing among those involved in teaching has been widely noted (McCowan 2009; Morrow 2006; Naidoo and Jamieson 2006).

MOTIVATING REFLEXIVITY: FIELD THEORY AND MULTI-PERSPECTIVAL DISCOURSE ANALYSIS

The methodological challenge posed by field theory for the design of the study is summarized in Bourdieu's (1991) critique of the "language as an object of contemplation rather than an instrument of action and power" (p. 38) and the resulting "illusion of linguistic communism" (p. 43).

The force of the challenge lies in its linking the particular forms and uses of language through the habitus to the positioning of the habitus within—and the reproduction of—the "linguistic market" as a "system of specific sanctions and censorships" (p. 38). Language on this account is "linguistic capital" which together with the other forms of capital are "like trumps in a game of cards, are powers which define the chances of profit in a given field" (Bourdieu 1994, p. 112). The upshot is that the linguistic capital of the highest value is, and is ipse facto taken for granted as, the authoritatively appropriate "legitimate language" (Bourdieu 1991, p. 43) within the given field.

This sets a twofold challenge: How to explain any instance of language use by participants and the researcher as reflexively implicated within the given field and how to enable the boundaries and relationships among relevant fields to become visible. The former points to Bourdieu's account of the "object of research", in which he cautions "us to resist by all means available our primary inclination to think the social world in a substantialist manner"; rather "one must think relationally" (Bourdieu and Wacquant 1992, p. 228). The latter points back to the need for a reflexive and relational approach to research because "the question of the limits of a field ... is always a stake in the field itself and therefore admits of no a priori answer ... thus the boundaries of the field can only be determined by empirical investigation" (Bourdieu and Wacquant 1992, p. 100).

In relation to studies of professional discourse, Candlin (2006) has characterized this challenge as one of "authentication," in particular how discourse analytical studies can adequately reflect the nature of the sites in which they are conducted, and—crucially—how this adequacy is to be warranted from the point of view of participants. The challenge this poses is to explain instances of language not as if they have "lives of their own" (Cicourel 2007, p. 736) but as part of people's understandings and activities of daily life that are set within more complex social and organizational contexts. As Cicourel (1992) explains:

> Verbal interaction is related to the task in hand. Language and other social practices are interdependent. Knowing something about the ethnographic setting, the perception of, and characteristics attributed to, others, and broader and local organisational conditions becomes imperative for an understanding of linguistic and non-linguistic aspects of communicative events. (p. 294)

This is in the first instance not a methodological issue focused on choosing among paradigms but a matter of working through the answers to ontological, epistemological, and methodological questions of how to select and harmonize different data sets and their associated methods of analysis into an integrated account (Candlin and Crichton 2014). Specifically:

- Ontologically, how we are to understand the nature of the site, including the evolving reciprocity of relationships among researchers, participants, language, and the local and broader contexts in which it is used (Candlin 1997; Cicourel 1992; Duranti and Goodwin 1992).
- Epistemologically, how we are to understand the worlds of participants, acknowledging the perspectives of analysts and the research participants themselves (Sarangi 2007; Sarangi and Candlin 2001) so as to establish the relevance of the research in a way accountable to these different perspectives (Candlin 2006).
- Methodologically, how we are to translate the responses to these ontological and epistemological questions into a research design, including methods and techniques of data collection and analysis, so as to achieve an accountable program of research (Candlin and Crichton 2011a).

No single methodology, however, well-grounded and finely applied, will be able to match the demands of such a program. Rather, it requires the integration of multiple methodologies, and acknowledgment of their own distinct discourses, in seeking to make visible the reflexive relations between the different perspectives that may be relevant. Such an approach is captured in Fig. 8.1.

The approach brings together theoretical and research traditions from linguistics and sociology within five "perspectives"—the analyst, the participants, the semiotic, the social practice, and the social/institution. Each of the circles represents these as distinctive but mutually implicating analytical perspectives on the discursive practices under scrutiny. The overlaps between them highlight the reflexive and interdiscursive nature of the research and practice envisaged. Different researchers with distinct interests, research purposes, understandings of the research context, and research backgrounds will operationalize the approach in different ways, giving different weightings to these perspectives. Researchers and

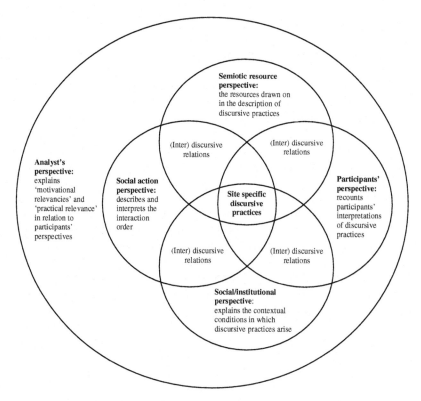

Fig. 8.1 Multi-perspectival approach (Candlin and Crichton 2011b; Crichton 2004, 2010)

participants will be brought together in different modes of collaboration depending on their relationship to and interest in the particular site.

The analyst's perspective identifies her guiding assumptions and interests, her motivational relevancies (Sarangi and Candlin 2001), and her evolving understanding of the practical relevance of the research to the participants (Roberts and Sarangi 1999). Counterpointing this perspective, the participants' perspective aims to recount participants' interpretations of what it is that is going on specifically in relation to their interpretations of discursive practices. This meets the need to understand the world as they see it, understanding its meaning in terms of the meanings it has for each participant, as "forged out of what he perceives, interprets, and judges" (Blumer 1966, p. 542). It invokes, for example, narrative research as a means by which this perspective can be explored. However, because people's experience of the social world is typically naturalized and taken for granted (Garfinkel 1967), the further three perspectives are needed.

The semiotic perspective focuses on describing the resources drawn upon by participants to create meaning in interaction. It invokes a range of linguistically orientated analytical resources to be potentially drawn upon in relation to the data. However, because these resources tend to foreground structural features of language (Linell 2001), there is the need to capture broader social relations in combination with the other perspectives.

The social practice perspective focuses on interpreting how people contribute to social practices by participating in interaction and suggests methodologies associated with symbolic interactionism (Blumer 1969; Goffman 1959, 1981) and ethnomethodology (Garfinkel 1967). However, because these methodologies do not offer a means of exploring interaction as situated within the wider social context (Layder 2005; Mouzelis 2008), the social/institutional perspective is required.

The social/institutional perspective explains the institutional and broader social/historical conditions—the "already established character" of social practices which cannot be deduced only from how participants experience and engage in these practices (Layder 1993). It invokes social-theoretical resources, in this case field theory, that explain the interaction of individual lives in relation to larger-scale social processes, resources and conditions, including their associated affordances and inequalities, and how these are produced and change over time; in other words, how the social world has "an ongoing life that is identifiable apart from specific instances of situated activity" (Layder 1993, p. 90).

Depending on which direction the researcher takes here, there will be different answers to questions that are central to the research agenda, including how methodological as well as ontological reflexivity is understood and acknowledged within the design and research process.

THE DYNAMICS OF A FIELD: A COMMUNITY OF CONSUMPTION

The design of study drew on this approach to investigate the discourses which shape teachers' abilities to maintain their standards of professional practice.

In operationalizing the analyst's perspective in relation to that of participants, my symbolic capital as the analyst brought within the focus of the study through thematic analysis of my autobiographical narratives of experience of working as a teacher and manager in relation to those of the participants, to the design of study, and to the social-theoretical account of commercialization developed throughout the study.

The other perspectives that were operationalized drew on five data sets. The participants' perspective drew on critical incident journals kept by teachers; the social resource perspective on promotional brochures produced by colleges; and the social/institutional perspective on published data: the sector newsletter, regulations of the industry regulatory authority, and teacher training materials.

The study took as its perspectival entry point a systemic functional analysis (Halliday 1985) of the promotional brochures produced by a sample of ten privately run English language colleges in Australia. The analysis focused on discovering patterns of "transitivity," the aspect of grammar which serves "as a means of representing patterns of experience" (Halliday 1985, p. 101). Brochures were chosen because they are used to promote a construction of the colleges and the service they offer that will compete with other providers in attracting members of target groups to convert to the role of clients (Cook 2001). This requires that courses, teachers, and students, and how they participate in processes of teaching and learning, be represented in a saleable way. The analysis of the brochures was therefore an opportunity to explore and to generate an account of these constructions of products, participants, and the relationships between them.

The aim was to compare these constructions in the brochures with how teachers themselves represented their own work, as evidenced in journals that participating teachers at each of the colleges kept. These journals and their narrative analysis (Riessman 2008) operationalized the participants' perspective. The point of the comparison was to discover whether the comparison provided evidence of dissonance—and therefore the potential for "symbolic struggle" (Bourdieu 1985, p. 723)—between the representations of teaching the promotional brochures and teachers' representations of their own practices. The reason for thinking that there could be was that the pressure on organizations to package, promote and sell English language teaching and learning does not stop at their brochures but, textualized as the "legitimate language" (Bourdieu 1991, p. 43), extends to all aspects of the students' experience. The teacher is thereby included in the marketing chain, obliged to deliver on the representations of teaching and learning established for the "student" qua "client."

As well as providing the theoretical framing and methodological orientation of study, field theory informed the social/institutional perspective. This enabled the study to go beyond the description and interpretation of data to provide an explanation of why, in the struggle over how teachers' practices are to be understood and the purposes they are to serve, it is capital associated with the economic field which dominates and how in this process teachers reflexively contribute to the reproduction of their own disadvantage qua teachers. More specifically, the findings provide an account of the "dynamics of a field" which:

> lie in the form of its structure and, in particular, in the distance, the gaps, the asymmetries between the various specific forces that confront each other. The forces that are active in the field – and thus selected by the analysist as pertinent because they produce the most relevant differences – are those that define the specific capital. (Bourdieu and Wacquant 1992, p. 101)

Viewed in this way, it becomes possible to explain the relevant difference between the three groups as resulting from how each group is positioned in relation to each other such that they form and reproduce a "community of consumption" (Crichton 2010, p. 183). Within this community appear as inevitable and natural the risks that confront and define each group's "specific capital", and through which their fates are interlocked as each group reflexively reproduces the community by seeking to reduce the risks that threaten their particular capital and thereby increasing the risks for the others. For teachers, there is the risk of losing their profession, for managers the risk of losing market share, and for students the risk of losing the education they have purchased. In this process groups, exemplified in the study by teachers and students, who aspire to but lack the habitus to access the forms of capital of value within the economic field are thereby caught in a cycle of disadvantage in which the value of their habitus is reduced as those with the greatest economic capital come to dominate the market.

As foreshadowed by field theory, this account of the community of consumption is better understood not as involving the conflict between "groups"—as if the meanings of "teachers," "students," and "managers" were set in advance of the study and immune from its inception, process, and findings. Rather, as the study showed, these meanings are precisely what was at stake among those involved. Rather than conflict or domination among groups, Bourdieu argues that one can

> speak of the field of power ... the relations of force that obtain between the social positions which guarantee their occupants a quantum of social force, or of capital, such that they are able to enter into struggles over the monopoly of power, or which struggles over the legitimate form of power are a crucial dimension. (Bourdieu and Wacquant 1992, pp. 229–230)

This framing of the community of consumption as a field of force resonated with the relationships that emerged between the analyses of data sets. My own narratives of working as a teacher and manager and their relation to those of participants evinced my struggles over these meanings as evidence of a "divided or even torn habitus" (Bourdieu and Wacquant 1992, p. 127) and the impossibility of reconciling contradictory positioning in the social space (Bourdieu 1985, p. 724).

For their part, the teachers' accounts of their work in their journals provided evidence that their social capital, in the form of professional expertise, was subordinated to economic capital in three-way struggles between managers, teachers, and students. In these struggles, the teachers represented their authority qua teachers to be contested by or invisible to both managers and students.

This three-way interplay of tension emerged most clearly in the data in practices of evaluation and appraisal, in which managers, teachers, and students were mutually implicated in struggles over how "teaching" was to be practiced and understood. Here, the capital assets (Bourdieu 1994) held by teachers in virtue of their membership of a profession are devalued and learning constructed as inevitable for students, at the same time—and contradictorily—positioning teachers as responsible for this learning. In this process, the social capital of teachers and of students—respectively, their expertise and their ability to learn—is subordinated to serve economic interests, creating for them a "divided or even torn habitus" (Bourdieu and Wacquant 1992, p. 127) and designating the structure of the community of consumption as a "hierarchy within each of the fields and among the different fields" (Bourdieu 1985, p. 723). The community of consumption thereby represents a form of symbolic violence (Bourdieu 1991) that operates to redefine capital associated with "teaching" and "learning" in terms of the economic field.

CONCLUSION

The study illustrates both the importance of addressing the challenge posed by field theory to discourse analytical research and its value in motivating reflexively orientated, relationally focused approaches, exemplified here by multi-perspectival discourse analysis. Moreover, key to the interpretation and explanation of the findings was the potential for field theory to operationalize the social-institutional perspective such that field theory itself—as a representation by the researcher—could be reflexively warranted against participants' representations of themselves in relation to the site of the research. Beyond the boundaries of the site of the research, field theory enabled the positioning of those involved—including researcher and participants—to be understood against those larger-scale social and historical processes associated with the "unification of the market" (Bourdieu 1991). Underlying this unification—and made visible as an object of research through the application of field theory—was the community of consumption as instantiating and reproducing the "methodological destruction of collectives" (Bourdieu 1998, p. 95).

REFERENCES

Apple, M. W. (1996). *Cultural politics and education*. Buckingham: Open University Press.

Blumer, H. (1966). Sociological implications of the thought of G.H. Mead. *American Journal of Sociology, 71*, 535–544.

Blumer, H. (1969). *Symbolic interactionism: Perspective and method*. Englewood Cliffs: Prentice-Hall.

Bourdieu, P. (1985). The social space and the genesis of groups. *Theory and Society, 14*(6), 723–744.

Bourdieu, P. (1986). The forms of capital. In J. G. Richardson (Ed.), *Handbook of theory and research for the sociology of education* (pp. 241–258). Westport: Greenwood Press.

Bourdieu, P. (1990). *The logic of practice* (R. Nice, Trans.). Stanford: Stanford University Press.

Bourdieu, P. (1991). *Language and symbolic power* (G. Raymond & M. Adamson, Trans.). Cambridge: Polity Press.

Bourdieu, P. (1994). Structures, habitus and practices. In A. Giddens, D. Held, D. Hubert, D. Seymour, & J. Thompson (Eds.), *The Polity reader in social theory* (pp. 95–110). Cambridge: Polity Press.

Bourdieu, P. (1998). *Acts of resistance: Against the new myths of our time* (R. Nice, Trans.). Cambridge: Polity Press.

Bourdieu, P., & Wacquant, L. J. D. (1992). *An invitation to reflexive sociology*. Cambridge: Polity Press.

Brown, R., & Carasso, H. (2013). *Everything for sale? The marketisation of UK higher education*. London: Routledge.

Candlin, C. N. (1997). General editor's preface. In B. L. Gunnarsson, P. Linell, & B. Nordberg (Eds.), *The construction of professional discourse* (pp. viii–xiv). London: Longman.

Candlin, C. N. (2006). Accounting for interdiscursivity: Challenges to professional expertise. In M. Gotti & D. Giannone (Eds.), *New trends in specialized discourse analysis* (pp. 21–45). Bern: Peter Lang.

Candlin, C. N., & Crichton, J. (2011a). Introduction. In C. N. Candlin & J. Crichton (Eds.), *Discourses of deficit* (pp. 1–22). Basingstoke: Palgrave Macmillan.

Candlin, C. N., & Crichton, J. (Eds.). (2011b). *Discourses of deficit*. Basingstoke: Palgrave Macmillan.

Candlin, C. N., & Crichton, J. (2013). From ontology to methodology: Exploring the discursive landscape of trust. In C. N. Candlin & J. Crichton (Eds.), *Discourses of trust* (pp. 1–18). Basingstoke: Palgrave Macmillan.

Candlin, C. N., & Crichton, J. (2014). *Beyond mixed methods: Warranting multi-perspectival research in applied linguistics*. Paper presented at the American Association of Applied Linguistics Conference, Portland.

Cicourel, A. V. (1992). The interpenetration of communicative contexts: Examples from medical encounters. In A. Duranti & C. Goodwin (Eds.), *Rethinking context: Language as an interactive phenomenon* (pp. 291–310). Cambridge: Cambridge University Press.

Cicourel, A. V. (2007). A personal, retrospective view of ecological validity. *Text & Talk, 27*(5/6), 735–759.

Cook, G. (2001). *The discourse of advertising* (2nd ed.). London: Routledge.

Crichton, J. (2004). *Issues of interdiscursivity in the commercialisation of professional practice: The case of English language teaching*. Unpublished doctoral thesis, Macquarie University, Sydney.

Crichton, J. (2010). *The discourse of commercialization*. Basingstoke: Palgrave Macmillan.

Duranti, A., & Goodwin, C. (1992). Rethinking context: An introduction. In A. Duranti & C. Goodwin (Eds.), *Rethinking context: Language as an interactive phenomenon* (pp. 1–42). Cambridge: Cambridge University Press.

Garfinkel, H. (1967). *Studies in ethnomethodology*. Englewood Cliffs: Prentice-Hall.

Giroux, H. A. (1999). Schools for sale: Public education, corporate culture, and the citizen-consumer. *The Educational Forum, 63*(2), 140–149.

Goffman, E. (1959). *The presentation of self in everyday life*. New York: Doubleday Anchor.

Goffman, E. (1981). *Forms of talk*. Oxford: Blackwell.

Grant, N. (2009). Foreword. In D. Hill (Ed.), *Global neoliberalism and education and its consequences* (pp. vii–xvii). New York: Routledge.

Halliday, M. A. K. (1985). *An introduction to functional grammar*. London: Edward Arnold.

Hill, D., & Kumar, R. (Eds.). (2009). *Global neoliberalism and education and its consequences*. New York: Routledge.

John, P., & Fanghanei, J. (Eds.). (2015). *Dimensions of marketisation in higher education*. London: Routledge.

Kenway, J., & Bullen, E. (2001). *Consuming children: Education—entertainment—advertising*. Buckingham: Open University Press.

Layder, D. (1993). *New strategies in social research*. Cambridge: Polity Press.

Layder, D. (2005). *Understanding social theory* (2nd ed.). Thousand Oaks, CA: Sage.

Linell, P. (2001). Dynamics of discourse or stability of structure: Sociolinguistics and the legacy of linguistics. In N. Coupland, S. Sarangi, & C. N. Candlin (Eds.), *Sociolinguistics and social theory* (pp. 107–126). London: Longman.

Marginson, S., & van der Wende, M. (2007). To rank or to be ranked: The impact of global rankings in higher education. *Journal of Studies in International Education, 11*(3/4), 306–329.

McCowan, T. (2009). Higher education and the profit incentive. In D. Hill (Ed.), *Global neoliberalism and education and its consequences* (pp. 54–72). New York: Routledge.

Morrow, R. A. (2006). Critical theory, globalization, and higher education: Political economy and the cul-de-sac of the postmodern turn. In C. A. Torres & R. Rhoads (Eds.), *The university, the state and the market: The political economy of globalization in the Americas* (pp. xvii–xxxiii). Stanford: Stanford University Press.

Mouzelis, N. (2008). *Modern and postmodern social theorizing: Bridging the divide*. Cambridge: Cambridge University Press.

Naidoo, R., & Jamieson, I. (2006). Empowering participants or corroding learning? Towards a research agenda on the impact of student consumerism in higher education. In H. Lauder, P. Brown, J.-A. Dillabough, & A. H. Halsey (Eds.), *Education, globalization and social change* (pp. 875–884). Oxford: Oxford University Press.

Riessman, C. K. (2008). *Narrative methods for the human sciences*. Thousand Oaks: Sage.

Roberts, C., & Sarangi, S. (1999). Hybridity in gatekeeping discourse: Issues of practical relevance for the researcher. In S. Sarangi & C. Roberts (Eds.), *Talk, work and institutional order: Discourse in medical, mediation and management settings* (pp. 473–504). Berlin: Mouton de Gruyter.

Sarangi, S. (2007). Editorial. The anatomy of interpretation: Coming to terms with the analyst's paradox in professional discourse studies. *Text & Talk, 27*(5/6), 567–584.

Sarangi, S., & Candlin, C. N. (2001). 'Motivational relevancies': Some methodological reflections on social theoretical and sociolinguistic practice. In N. Coupland, S. Sarangi, & C. N. Candlin (Eds.), *Sociolinguistics and social theory* (pp. 350–387). Harlow: Longman.

Stromquist, N. P. (2002). *Education in a globalized world: The connectivity of economic power, technology, and knowledge.* Lanham: Rowman & Littlefield.

Wacquant, L. J. D. (1992). Toward a social praxeology: The structure and logic of Bourdieu's sociology. In P. Bourdieu & L. J. D. Wacquant (Eds.), *An invitation to reflexive sociology* (pp. 1–60). Cambridge: Polity Press.

CHAPTER 9

Reshaping the Field from the Outside in: Aboriginal People and Student Journalists Working Together

Bonita Mason, Chris Thomson, Dawn Bennett and Michelle Johnston

This chapter examines field struggle in an education program called Aboriginal Community Engagement (ACE), established to foster collaboration between journalism students and people long marginalised by a field that valorises arm's-length practice (Thomson et al. 2016). We put Bourdieu's concept of field to work (Bourdieu and Wacquant 1992, p. 96) as conceptual, analytical and explanatory tool, and employ related concepts in Bourdieu's theory of practice to identify and examine the power relations, positions and other field contexts, structures and dynamics enacted and made evident through ACE and the symbolic challenge it represented to orthodox journalism education. These concepts include capital, habitus, homology, orthodoxy and heterodoxy, misrecognition and symbolic violence (Bourdieu and Wacquant 1992; Swartz 1997).

B. Mason (✉) · C. Thomson · D. Bennett · M. Johnston
Curtin University, Whadjuk Noongar Country, Perth, WA, Australia

J. Albright et al. (eds.), *Bourdieu's Field Theory and the Social Sciences*,
https://doi.org/10.1007/978-981-10-5385-6_9

133

The study aims to "construct a double object" (Bourdieu, in Bourdieu and Wacquant 1992, p. 67). The first object is field analysis: context, field logics and rules, positions, subjects and objects, all in relation to one another. The second is a "deeper object: the reflexive return entailed in objectivizing one's own universe", which includes institutions that "claim objectivity and universality for [their] ... own objectivations" (p. 67). This second object applies to our objectivations of journalism, journalism education and the university, and of others within it, and to our own interests in such objectivations (Bourdieu and Wacquant 1992, p. 68).

ACE is a heterodox attempt to influence orthodox journalistic practices and norms inside and outside universities. We work across fields marked by legitimised competition and less apparent and delegitimised cooperation to teach students the value of collaborating with Indigenous people to tell stories that are generally not told. Our intention is to contribute to change in the sub-field of journalism education, and the field of journalism practice, in the service of challenging broader cultural, economic and symbolic power relations between Australian Aboriginal and non-Aboriginal peoples: in part by producing reflexive, competent and confident Aboriginal affairs journalists.

We soon found ourselves in conflict with other field actors and positions over the perceptions and practices by which participating students produced their stories. This conflict represented struggle for recognition and legitimacy that went against the prevailing understanding of what constitutes, and is acceptable in, the sub-field of student journalism at our university. Bourdieu primarily saw fields as spatial and symbolic sites of struggle and competition between positions (Hallin 2005, pp. 234–235) and, in journalism, competition (for an exclusive story, for example) is highly valued. In ACE, we used collaboration and symbolic struggle as journalistic field strategies. The tensions between competition and collaboration, and between an orthodox news-first (and often only) approach and a more narrative style of journalistic storytelling, amounted to conflict over the "principles of vision and division" (Bourdieu 2005, p. 37) that define the boundaries of legitimate journalism.

This chapter represents a reflexive research and teaching journey in which field helped us understand conflict and its resolution. Bourdieu's concepts provide a language for and enable us to frame, analyse, understand and build upon symbolic struggle. We aim to explain and understand the symbolic struggle well enough to help free ourselves, our students and journalistic practice from some of its orthodox field constraints. We also seek to understand the individual context, and we challenge students and ourselves to be reflexive (Bourdieu and Wacquant 1992) practitioners, by which means we attempt to offer what Bourdieu does specifically for journalism (1998, p. 1): "a possibility of liberation, through a conscious effort, from the hold of ... [often hidden] mechanisms" on our practice. Bourdieu's field theory is central to this work; it provides a sufficiently complete and relational conceptual and methodological means to contextualise and structure our aims and activities.

The chapter begins by exploring how field theory provides context and framework to conceptualise, formulate and describe ACE's development and aims. We then turn to field theory as an analytical and explanatory tool as we locate ACE's overlapping field position within a larger network of structures, relations and practices, and describe how field theory informed the program's structure. We go on to identify actors' field positions, and describe a telling instance of symbolic struggle, coming to an understanding that the specific field struggle described operates at multiple levels—from ACE, via sub-field and field, to society—and that heterodox collaborative practices may function as a form of liberation in the journalistic field.

Working with Bourdieu 1: ACE—Context, Aims and Development

When ACE was developed in 2013, it was conceived as a direct if modest intervention in student journalism. One of the ACE founders—the authors of this chapter—had just completed a Ph.D. thesis that, along lines described in Mason (2012), advocated Bourdieu's theory of practice as a critically reflexive approach to journalism research and practice. A field approach, combined with action research and critical service learning (Johnston et al. 2016), informed ACE's aims, structure, field position and results.

By first using field theory to conceptualise and provide a language for our ambitions, we developed ACE with the desire to counter the misrecognition (Swartz 1997) perpetuated through orthodox journalistic practices, perspectives, norms and publications. Misrecognition—where cultural, political and economic interests are legitimised and appear as "unquestionable truth" (Calhoun and Wacquant 2002, p. 2)—is also evident in the unequal power relations between Aboriginal and non-Aboriginal peoples. The intention was to design a program of study, reflexive practice and cultural production that would develop critical self and social awareness in our students, and therefore avoid the imposition of pre-reflexive journalistic perceptions and practices in student journalism.

ACE would, therefore, need to offer habitus-transforming (Bourdieu and Wacquant 1992; Swartz 1997) knowledge and experiences, in the form of opportunities for secondary socialisation. Students needed to know and understand something of the histories and present-day circumstances of Australia's first peoples—in our case the Noongar people of south-western Australia—and to know and understand more about themselves in relation to those histories and circumstances.

Habitus—as a system of socialised dispositions, perceptions and actions, and as sense of the place of oneself and others in a field (Bourdieu 1989, p. 19)—structured our teaching practice and enabled us to track reflexive development. Potentially habitus-transforming activities included sessions with Noongar and other Indigenous elders, a field trip to a massacre site, and workshops on cross-cultural awareness and competency, sense of place (Thomson et al. 2015), and Bourdieu's reflexivity—which also structured student reflection (see Mason et al. 2016). Even more important was the students' collaboration with their Aboriginal community partners to produce works of journalism, set out in more detail below. Bourdieu's insight that the structures of habitus produce practice was at the centre of ACE's curriculum design, as is an understanding of the "ways in which particular professional practices produce certain sorts of texts ... particularly ... in the huge area of journalism beyond news" (Bacon 1999, p. 89).

To achieve ACE's aims, students needed to become critically reflexive journalists in three ways. At the level of the field, they needed to come to an understanding of the effects of patterns of coverage or an absence of coverage, the inclusion or exclusion of Aboriginal voices, their representation or misrepresentation, and of the relationship between media coverage and the life chances of Aboriginal people. Students needed to be able to conceptualise their position—its constraints and possibilities—in the journalistic field and the sub-field of student journalism within the university. At the level of their journalistic practices and perceptions of practice, they needed to avoid reproducing journalistic practices and publications that perpetuate the symbolic violence "exerted" through journalism (Bourdieu 2005, p. 29) against Indigenous people.

ACE's aims were contextualised by the understanding that unequal power relations as structures are produced and reproduced—or transformed—as homologies (Swartz 1997, p. 134), corresponding relations and positions, across fields. Consequences of the power relations between Aboriginal and non-Aboriginal Australians are evident in shorter life expectancies, and higher rates of child mortality, chronic illness and preventable diseases among Aboriginal people (Holland 2015), and in other indicators of social, cultural and economic domination. The profound inequality reflected in these circumstances spans overlapping medical, social and justice fields and is (mis)represented by and reproduced in and through journalism (see, e.g., Stoneham et al. 2014). Here the domination also becomes evident in "relations of symbolic power" (Bourdieu 1989, p. 21) that highlight the problems of representation, perspective, framing, absence, recognition and legitimacy. But domination and exclusion are rarely complete (Hall et al. 1978; Bourdieu 1989), and struggles within and across fields, over economic, cultural, social and symbolic position, are evident in Aboriginal history and present-day circumstances (see Thomson et al. 2015, pp. 143–145).

We developed ACE with the intention of taking part in a field struggle for position within the sub-field of student journalism, and through seeking recognition and legitimation—symbolic capital or power (Bourdieu 1989)—for ACE's journalistic practices. While the concept of field generally presupposes inequality and competition (Colvin et al. 2013), ACE is based on the idea that it is possible to collaborate to reduce inequality. We would use the cultural capital (Swartz 1997; Benson and Neveu 2005) of journalism, and our positions in a university, in favour of student journalism that was well-researched, accurate and truthful (including in its representation), engaging and thorough, primarily by including a greater number and range of Aboriginal voices.

While many of ACE's practices reflect cultural capital in the journalistic field, the pressures of round-the-clock, multi-platform news production and the dominating effects of economic capital often result in orthodox journalism that falls short of its own aims. As Champagne (2005, p. 51) points out: "The major contradiction within the operation of the journalistic field lies in the fact that the journalistic practices that best conform to journalists' ethical codes are very often simply not profitable". Our position in a university frees us from these constraints. We conceived of ACE as an attempt to elevate cultural capital over economic capital and we asked, as did Klinenberg (2005) in his study of US youth activists who sought to effect change in the journalistic field,

> whether and how exogenous pressures from subjects who are identified by the media can exert force on the journalistic field from below, and ... whether this form of heteronomy can help journalists to produce work that better meets their own criteria for excellence. (p. 175)

Overall, field theory is a contextual and conceptual framework that provides an understanding about how power, structure and practice are produced at individual, field and societal levels, and therefore how to work against symbolic domination through our teaching. In the small social realm in which we operate, ACE employs heterodox field strategies—such as privileging Indigenous stories and sources, and journalist-source and subject collaboration—and enters a field struggle to contribute to media coverage that avoids committing symbolic violence (Bourdieu 2005) against Aboriginal people and perpetuating unequal, status quo power relations, and exercises some measure of symbolic power. As students come to a reflexive understanding of their positions in the journalistic field, and of the social and political effects of their practice, both their practices and journalistic texts help redress relations of domination and inequality.

This section has shown how Bourdieu's framework can be employed to contextualise the development and aims of a project that shares his central concern with "how stratified social systems of hierarchy and domination persist and reproduce intergenerationally" (Swartz 1997, p. 6). In the following section, we turn to the concept of the journalistic field to situate ACE in a larger network of relations and practices.

Working with Bourdieu 2: ACE—Field Position, Power Relations and Symbolic Struggle

Field is employed here for its analytical and "explanatory power" (Klinenberg 2005, p. 174). Bourdieu (1998) argues that the concept of the journalistic field is essential to "grasp the explanatory mechanisms of journalistic practice" (p. 39). In order to understand what goes on in a media organisation—or a university media teaching and research project—Bourdieu writes one must take into account "everything ... [it]

owes to its location in a universe of objective relations between the different competing ... [interests]" (p. 39). Here we turn to ACE's location in such a "universe" by sketching ACE's field position, identifying
competing and cooperative interests and agents, and outlining a defining
moment in the symbolic struggle for legitimation.

Field Position

ACE contains its own field positions, networks, values and norms, practices and actors that are homologous to, in tension with and acted upon
by other fields. It is nested within and connects to the university education and research fields, the journalistic field, the small and specialist sub-field (Marchetti 2005) of Indigenous reporting, and to the field
occupied by Aboriginal community organisations in Noongar country.
Through publication, our students' stories also touch the fields their
community partners work in and that they write about: for example
Indigenous deaths in custody—justice and correctional fields; a young
Aboriginal woman's difficulty getting a boilermaking apprenticeship—
employment and anti-discrimination; healthy living programs; and young
Indigenous people breaking into the sport of surfing.

This network of relations is both hierarchical and lateral. ACE operates as a sub-sub-field of university-based specialised Indigenous affairs
journalism within the sub-field of journalism education at our university.
This sub-field has counterparts across Australian universities. University
and nation-wide learning and teaching structures, policies and programs
concerned with reconciliation and Indigenising the curriculum are also
relevant, but the most directly relevant fields to this study are the journalistic field and the journalism education sub-field at our university.
ACE's dominated position within the journalism education sub-field at
our university is homologous to that of Indigenous affairs journalism
within the journalistic field. It is also reminiscent of the "weakly autonomous" (Bourdieu 2005, p. 33) journalistic field's dominated position
within the field of power (Champagne 2005, p. 49).

As an attempt to re-make the world through changing practice
(Bourdieu 1989), we use field theory to understand ACE as a heterodox
(heretical) challenge to the conservative field orthodoxy (Swartz 1997)
in two ways: as a potential influence on orthodox practices and publication in the journalistic field; and as a potential influence on orthodox
practices and publication in the sub-field of journalism education—locally,

and more broadly through publication and conference presentations. Although, from the beginning, we conceived of ACE as symbolic struggle with orthodoxies within the journalistic field, we were less prepared for the symbolic struggle that emerged in the sub-field of student journalism at our own university. This is the set of positions, relations and practices that becomes the object for this part of our chapter. How these and other features and relations of ACE as a sub-sub-field come into play becomes clearer as we identify and describe actors and positions, and construct an object of and describe the sub-field symbolic struggle below.

Actors, Positions and Practices

Apart from ourselves, ACE students, and our Aboriginal partners, other important actors/positions taking part in this local symbolic struggle included a staff editor-in-chief and student editors of the university student journalism newspaper, *The Western Independent*, that the ACE students were writing for.

In 2013, the newspaper was produced through hierarchical structures, relations and practices that emulated local large-scale newspapers, including Perth's conservative daily newspaper, *The West Australian* and News Corporation's *Sunday Times*. For the student newspaper, students uploaded their stories onto the newspaper server; their stories were selected for publication, or not, by student editors, after which selected stories were allocated to student sub-editors who fact-checked and edited for structure, news style and grammar. ACE students could be asked to provide more information or more interview material. Stories could be further edited for focus and structure and then referred to the editor-in-chief for final editing. At any stage, the stories could be significantly changed by student editors who had little experience, but many of whom pre-reflexively accepted the newsroom's "game and its stakes" (Bourdieu and Wacquant 1992, p. 98). Many editorial changes improved stories, but some altered meaning and emphasis, and introduced mistakes that resulted in misrepresentation and inaccuracy. The stories could also be significantly edited by the editor-in-chief—who took overall responsibility for and exercised final control over what appeared in the paper—for news value, importance and other preferences, legal and/or ethical implications and other reasons.

In contrast, ACE was collaborative at every stage of the story production process, which began with connecting students to

Aboriginal community organisations. Each student was paired, alone or in groups, with one of Noongar Radio, cultural consultancy Kart Koort Wiern, Indigenous Community Education and Awareness (ICEA) and the Langford Aboriginal Association. Establishing a relationship of trust was the first priority, and story ideas emerged from the developing relationship. The resulting stories were produced collaboratively but retained accuracy, fairness and independence. Hence, they were *bona fide* journalistic stories expressing the cultural capital of journalism, and not that of the field of public relations.

Publication and Symbolic Struggle

The two ACE student journalists entangled in the field struggle were non-Aboriginal young women who were both actors and acted upon in the newsroom editorial process. They are identified here by pseudonyms. While Steph had come with some knowledge of and contact with Aboriginal people, Sophie had not.

Steph worked with the Langford Aboriginal Association. Together, they agreed she would research and write her story about the association's healthy eating, exercise and weight-loss program.

> The whole point of my article was to paint a picture of overweight Australians taking control over their weight and lifestyles ... I aimed to acknowledge the difficulties that the participants face in their weight-loss challenge. But, first and foremost, the goal was to capture the inspirational attitude of these women and what motivated them to change the lives of their families and themselves. (Steph)

Her draft story, sub-edited and refined with ACE lecturers—who were experienced professional journalists—was submitted for publication, and published under the headline "An exciting new Aboriginal twist to the biggest loser", which Steph later described as "borderline racist". She was similarly disappointed with the story's editing:

> Unfortunately, the *Western Independent* editors appear to have cut out many of the positive and inspiring quotes and focused heavily on the difficulties/negatives instead. In my opinion, this leads to an unfair and nauseatingly typical portrayal of Aboriginal women as lazy, and even insinuates poor parenting.

Apart from the negative and "typical" portrayal of Aboriginal women, the editing of Steph's draft feature story turned it into a more news-like story about Aboriginal "problems", repeating default, misrecognised narratives about Aboriginal people. Much anecdotal and/or descriptive material, however telling or relevant to the story's theme, was excised. The following material shown in italics, illustrating an important turning point in one of the interviewee's approaches to food and health, was also cut. The plain text remained in the story.

> Hansen says alarms bells have started ringing since she's noticed an increase in her grandchildren's weight.

> *"We went to the shop tonight and I thought, 'Right, we're going to prepare the meals and start eating really healthy'," she says.*

> *"We bought rock melon, I let [my grandchild] choose the fruit and then I let her have a chocolate and said, 'That's the only bad thing you're going to eat this week'. And so everything else is going to be healthy. She was quite pleased with that."*

> Hansen says she is going to use the skills she's learning throughout the program to encourage healthy lifestyles for her grandkids.

This cut and others, on the basis of a judgement that the material was insufficiently journalistic, reduced the story's power by dismantling its human connection and narrative arc. It diminished the voice of the Aboriginal source and hence a reader's ability to connect with her, weakening the journalism. Steph felt her story was no longer recognisably hers. She did not want to show it to her community partner or to future employers as part of her portfolio. Her and ACE's heterodox positions within the sub-field of student journalism were undermined by a dominant news-first mentality.

Sophie felt similarly disempowered when her edited story appeared in print. She was working with the ICEA reconciliation foundation. Her story profiled a young Bardi surfer from the One Arm Point community (2500 km north of Perth), to highlight an increase in young Aboriginal people surfing and its reconciliation potential. The story—about the ICEA Classic surfing competition at Perth's Cottesloe Beach—linked surfing with the millennia-long Bardi connection to the sea, and with reconciliation efforts between Aboriginal and non-Aboriginal peoples. It included verified facts, anecdotal and interview material that imparted a Bardi cultural perspective, and an interview with a Noongar surfer for whom Cottesloe Beach is special. It featured a deeper sense-of-place (Thomson et al. 2015) dimension: "According to the Town of Cottesloe's Indigenous records, the Cottesloe Beach area is an ancient ceremonial site known to the Nyoongar[1] people as Mudurup, meaning 'the land of yellow-finned whiting'" (Sophie).

The editing process removed contextual cultural information that made clear the distinction between the term Bardi—to represent the country and people of that part of north-western Australia—and One Arm Point as a community on Bardi country. For Sophie, these and other omissions introduced inaccuracies of representation and attribution that "completely ... [threw] the story out of context". The cuts diminished the presence of a Bardi cultural perspective in the story, and editing out the attribution of the Cottesloe surfer as a Noongar person was detrimental. "Without saying anything about who she is ... [we] don't even know that she is an Aboriginal person" (Sophie). In journalism, when a source is introduced, readers are usually told why that person appears in a story. Even in a single journalistic text, field position is important.

Neither student was consulted about the final shape of her story. At the time, Steph wrote:

> I do feel like the disturbing editing of our stories reveals [a] lack of consideration and sensitivity that Curtin journalism students have when it comes to race reporting. This is an issue that needs to be addressed.

The treatment of the ACE stories reflected a narrow view of journalism, rather than the range of narrative styles and approaches possible in journalistic storytelling. It imposed an orthodox hierarchy of sources: the more powerful the source, the higher up in the story they appear—for example, the Prime Minister, a corporate leader first; an Aboriginal person speaking from a community position last—their dominated position symbolically reproduced across fields. This particular news-first approach leached the story of alternative cultural perspectives, voices and characters.

After the newspaper was published, the ACE journalism lecturers met the paper's staff editor-in-chief to suggest a different approach to editing stories. The lecturers were told that the orthodox news-form, content and hierarchies-of-information version of journalism was not negotiable, and no change in editorial policy or approach would be considered. Although part of the journalism team at Curtin, we were positioned as external to the vision, structure and process of producing legitimised student journalism at the university. The editor-in-chief had used the symbolic power of his title and senior position to impose the "explicitly practical principles of vision and division" (Bourdieu 2005, p. 37) over what would be "recognised as legitimate categories of construction of the social world" (p. 37), and in how groups and interests would be defined—"who are the citizens and who are the foreigners" (p. 38).

This incident can be read as a misrecognised, and therefore more powerful (Bourdieu and Wacquant 1992, p. 167–8), deployment of symbolic violence. Because the students' bylines appeared alongside their edited newspaper stories, they seemed to be complicit in their published form. This was apparent in the students' dismay at the final shape of their stories, made less recognisable to them but appearing as though they were what each of them intended. ACE students were dominated by the editor-in-chief's field position—which embodied an orthodox news-focused view of journalism. Our positions as subordinate staff in a university hierarchy saw us become subject to institutional and coercive power. These objective power relations positioned us, and ACE, as the "foreigners".

The same applied to Aboriginal sources. We were told that they should be treated no differently to any other source, as if they occupied a position within the field of power, when in reality they struggle to attain a media voice from one of the most subordinated positions in Australian social space. This marginalisation of Indigenous voices by a student newspaper replicated their marginalised position in the Perth media (see Thomson et al. 2016). It also represented a microcosm of the struggle for symbolic capital that often expresses itself in competition between the economic capital imperatives of large media organisations and the cultural capital of Australian Indigenous peoples who, although they have the oldest continuing culture in the world, struggle to be heard on their own terms.

Although the symbolic struggle in ACE represents a microcosm of broader societal power relations across fields that are replicated through large-scale media, our collaborative approach meant that strategies of resistance were open to us and we had support.

Strategies, Capital/s and Support

Klinenberg (2005) identified field strategies employed by youth organisations, which included in-house media production that sidestepped large-scale media outlets. To meet our aim of more complete reporting that challenges prevailing stereotypes, and helps to legitimate Aboriginal voices and stories, we withheld subsequent stories from the newspaper. We employed our cultural and social capital to step around the limitations of the news-first logic by publishing instead on an existing website set up originally to showcase the work of students in an Online Journalism unit that one of us was coordinating. We have continued this practice and since developed a distinct ACE website where we also publish student work: https://www.communityyarns.com. In 2016, a story from this website was the only piece of student journalism from our university to be commended at the national student journalism awards.

ACE is now in its fifth year, and has garnered sufficient social and symbolic capital to strengthen its field position within the university outside of the journalism department. Working as a cross-disciplinary team gives us more relative power (Bourdieu 1998) than we would have as individuals. National policy frameworks that favour Indigenous perspectives in higher education (Bartleet et al. 2014) provide rationale and support for what we are doing and help counter local opposition, as does support from senior people in the university who understand that ACE helps the university meet broader societal and organisational objectives (Curtin University 2014). Curtin University's Centre for Aboriginal Studies has also been important in lending its cultural and social capital.

CONCLUSION

Field theory can be employed in many ways: to structure practice and analyse and describe it; and to demonstrate how perspectives and practice in one field may act upon another—ACE as heterodox actors in the sub-field of journalism education seeking to change practices in the journalistic field; the orthodoxy of the journalistic field acting through the journalism education sub-field to repel our challenge. While field and associated concepts have worked as a form of capital in ACE, through this analysis they have also helped us to appreciate ACE as symbolic field struggle, between orthodox practices and relations of competition and heterodox practices and relations of cooperation, at multiple levels. Field analysis has demonstrated that such heterodoxy can achieve more in journalistic field cultural capital terms than an orthodox adherence to arm's-length practice—shaping the field from the outside in.

NOTE

1. Noongar (mostly used throughout this chapter) and Nyoongar are just two ways to spell this word. Others include Nyungah and Nyungar.

REFERENCES

Bacon, W. (1999). What is a journalist in a university? *Media International Australia incorporating Culture and Policy, 90*, February, pp. 79–90.

Bartleet, B., Bennett, D., Marsh, K., Power A., & Sunderland, N. (2014). Reconciliation and transformation through mutual learning: Outlining a framework for arts-based service learning with Indigenous communities in Australia. *International Journal of Education and the Arts, 15*(8), 1–23. Retrieved July 13, 2017, from http://www.ijea.org/v15n8/.

Benson, R., & Neveu, E. (2005). *Bourdieu and the journalistic field*. Cambridge: Polity Press.

Bourdieu, P. (1989). Social space and symbolic power. *Sociological Theory, 7*(1), 12–25.

Bourdieu, P. (1998). *On television*. New York: The New Press.

Bourdieu, P. (2005). The political field, the social science field, and the journalistic field. In R. Benson & E. Neveu (Eds.), *Bourdieu and the journalistic field* (pp. 29–47). Cambridge: Polity Press.

Bourdieu, P., & Wacquant, L. (1992). *An invitation to reflexive sociology*. Cambridge: Polity Press.

Calhoun, C., & Wacquant, L. (2002). 'Everything is social' – In memoriam: Pierre Bourdieu (1930–2002). *Footnotes, 30*(2). Retrieved July 13, 2017, from http://www.asanet.org/sites/default/files/savvy/footnotes/feb02/fn5.html.

Champagne, P. (2005). The "double dependency": The journalistic field between politics and markets. In R. Benson & E. Neveu (Eds.), *Bourdieu and the journalistic field* (pp. 48–63). Cambridge: Polity Press.

Colvin, C., Fozdar, F., & Volet, S. (2013). Intercultural interactions of mono-cultural, mono-lingual local students in small group learning activities: A Bourdieusian analysis. *British Journal of Sociology of Education, 36*(3), 414–433.

Curtin University. (2014). *Curtin's reconciliation action plan 2014–2017: Stretching our vision and commitment*. Perth: Curtin University.

Hall, S., Critcher, C., Jefferson, T., Clarke, J., & Roberts, B. (1978). *Policing the crisis: Mugging, the state, and law and order*. London: Macmillan.

Hallin, D. C. (2005). Field theory, differentiation theory, and comparative media research. In R. Benson & E. Neveu (Eds.), *Bourdieu and the journalistic field* (pp. 224–243). Cambridge: Polity Press.

Holland, C. (2015, February). *Close the Gap: Progress and priorities report 2015*. Close the Gap Campaign Steering Committee, Human Rights Commission. Retrieved from: https://www.humanrights.gov.au/our-work/aboriginal-and-torres-strait-islander-social-justice/publications/close-gap-progress-and-0.

Johnston, M., Bennett, D., Mason, B., & Thomson, C. (2016). Finding common ground: combining participatory action research and critical service-learning to guide and manage projects with Aboriginal communities. In B.-L. Bartleet, D. Bennett, A. Power, & N. Sunderland (Eds.), *Engaging first peoples in arts-based service learning: Towards respectful and mutually beneficial educational practices* (pp. 51–70). New York: Springer.

Klinenberg, E. (2005). Channeling into the journalistic field: Youth activism and the media justice movement. In R. Benson & E. Neveu (Eds.), *Bourdieu and the journalistic field* (pp. 174–192). Cambridge: Polity Press.

Marchetti, D. (2005). Subfields of specialized journalism. In R. Benson & E. Neveu (Eds.), *Bourdieu and the journalistic field* (pp. 64–82). Cambridge: Polity Press.

Mason, B. (2012). "The girl in cell 4": Securing social inclusion through a journalist-source collaboration. *Media International Australia, 14*(2), 167–176.

Mason, B., Thomson, C., Bennett, D., & Johnston, M. (2016). Putting the 'love back in' to journalism: Transforming habitus in Aboriginal affairs student reporting. *Journal of Alternative and Community Media, 1*, 56–69.

Stoneham, M. J., Goodman, J., & Daube, M. (2014). The portrayal of Indigenous health in selected Australian media. *The International Indigenous Policy Journal, 5*(1), 1–13.

Swartz, D. (1997). *Culture and power—The sociology of Pierre Bourdieu*. Chicago: The University of Chicago Press.

Thomson, C., Bennett, D., Johnston, M., & Mason, B. (2015). Why the where matters: A sense of place imperative for teaching better Indigenous affairs reporting. *Pacific Journalism Review, 21*(2), 141–161.

Thomson, C., Mason, B., Bennett, D., & Johnston, M. (2016). Closing the arm's-length gap: Critical reflexivity in student Indigenous affairs journalism. *Australian Journalism Review, 38*(1), 59–71.

CHAPTER 10

Cultural Innovation on the Fringe— the Fields of 'Limited' and 'Extensive' Production

Mark Gibson and Tony Moore

INTRODUCTION

In this chapter, we will attempt to demonstrate how Bourdieu's field theory can be used productively as a way of thinking about exchanges between small, intimate settings for cultural production and large-scale media and cultural industries. In doing so, we will discuss some research we have undertaken for a project, *Fringe to Famous*, examining the crossover in Australia between fringe, independent and avant-garde cultural production and the 'mainstream'. Key examples include punk and postpunk music, television comedy, graphic design, short film and computer games. The chapter draws particularly on Bourdieu's (1993) discussion in the *Rules of Art* of the relation between the 'field of restricted production' and the 'field of extensive production'. While these terms were developed out of an analysis of nineteenth-century French literary

M. Gibson (✉) · T. Moore
School of Media, Film and Journalism, Monash University,
Melbourne, Australia

© The Author(s) 2018
J. Albright et al. (eds.), *Bourdieu's Field Theory and the Social Sciences*,
https://doi.org/10.1007/978-981-10-5385-6_10

149

production, Bourdieu's analysis works from the particular example to more abstract models, inviting comparison with other fields.

In *Fringe to Famous*, we have found four kinds of value in Bourdieu's field theory. Firstly, the focus on the *scale* of production offers a useful alternative to terms such as 'independent', 'fringe' and 'underground'. While the latter point to important qualities of small-scale production for audiences of peers, they carry romantic assumptions about authenticity and originality that have long been exposed to criticism. Bourdieu's approach offers a more neutral, analytical perspective that attends to the very real differences between the 'small' and the 'large' while avoiding the tendency to romanticism.

Secondly, Bourdieu's framework allows greater precision in analysing the exchanges between the two fields. It offers an alternative, in particular, to the heavily reductionist concept of 'selling out' which has tended to dominate discussion of movements from the 'fringe' to the 'mainstream'. Rather than conceiving the field of limited production as 'pure', unsullied by commerce, Bourdieu sees it simply as structured by its own particular forms of capital and value. This opens up a more complex picture in which 'symbolic values' are exchanged for 'economic values'. Bourdieu's analysis is in fact backed up by the candid remarks of even the most romantic of authors, such as Henry Murger (1930, p. xxix), who confessed of 'Bohemia proper' that 'they have made some sign of their presence in life ... they have 'got their names up', are known in the literary and artistic market; there is a sale at moderate prices it is true, but still a sale, for produce bearing their mark'.

Thirdly, Bourdieu's conceptualisation of the field of restricted production as 'the economy turned upside down' is valuable in understanding not just the ultimate economic value that can accrue to art created within an avant-garde field, but the value to bourgeois consumers of the romantic discourse promoted within that field about autonomy from market imperatives. Within our study of post-1980s cultural innovation, many artists who circulate between the two fields have brought to popular markets a sense of their 'independence' from commerce, an authenticity that appeals to a discerning national and global niche that is nevertheless large enough to be considered a mass market. Romantic tropes about artistic freedom hostile to commerce have a long history, but since the late 1960s, the performance by artists of an 'underground', 'alternative', 'fringe' or 'indie' identity has proven profitable in the market of extensive production for emerging forms of music, comedy, drama and other art forms, especially those with genuine avant-garde provenance.

Fourth, the approach facilitates a comparison between areas of cultural practice that are not usually considered within the same analysis. Among the cases we are considering in *Fringe to Famous*, music or television comedy is not often discussed with reference to examples from graphic design or computer games. Yet there is real value to be gained from a comparative frame. Analysis developed in relation to one case can often be illuminating as a starting point in approaching another. Identifying structural features cutting across different cases also offers practical benefits for the development of cultural policy, providing it with greater leverage and allowing it to overcome common tendencies to fragmentation and incoherence.

CULTURAL ANALYSIS AND 'THE FRINGE'

The 'fringes' of cultural production have always attracted disproportionate attention—and not without reason. They are usually the sites of greatest cultural innovation, where new forms and styles emerge, and are often also sites of political and social tension. In Bourdieu's examples from nineteenth-century Paris, the 'field of restricted production' was the zone from which writers such as Baudelaire and Flaubert developed French literary modernism and sought to puncture the pretension and vanities of the bourgeoisie (Bourdieu and Nice 1980a; Bourdieu and Ferguson 1988). Among the examples we have considered in *Fringe to Famous*, the best known internationally is perhaps the gothic post-punk music of Nick Cave, but there are numerous others, from the subversive comedy of television shows such as *The Chaser's War on Everything* and *Fast Forward* to the eschatological designs of surfwear label Mambo.[1]

Yet cultural analysis of the fringe has also always been problematic. The fringe has been routinely associated with exceptionalist claims. Its distinction from the 'mainstream' has removed it from frameworks of analysis that might render it explicable. Unlike the mainstream, it is suggested that the fringe cannot be understood with reference to the logic of commodity production within a market system. Unlike the mainstream, its cultural products cannot be reduced to variations on known and established forms transmitted from the past. Unlike the mainstream, it cannot be interpreted within a clear logic of social exchange, where, for example, an audience is 'pleased' and the artist gains recognition or other social rewards in return. The concepts that generally fill the vacuum of analysis here—'artistic inspiration', 'creativity', even 'innovation'—are not so much alternative forms of explanation as attempts to prevent explanation from gaining any real purchase.

The problems with such exceptionalism quickly become evident when fringe cultural production is studied in any detail. The romantic figure of the bohemian outsider who lives 'only for their art' rarely withstands close scrutiny. Actual historical individuals are enmeshed like everyone else in messy social relationships, often intense rivalries and determined efforts to build reputations and safeguard legacies. Their relation to the market is also more complex than a picture of simple 'refusal' would suggest. As many commentators have argued, there were many aspects of the cultural radicalism of the 1960s and 1970s that in fact meshed quite closely with the development of post-war consumer culture (Alomes 1983; Thornton 1996; Heath and Potter 2004). Its ethos of individual self-expression was consistent in many ways with the development of ideas of consumer choice and its values of authenticity and altruism opened new possibilities for commodification—from converted loft apartments to designer clothing and organic foods.

A second problem with exceptionalism is that it makes it difficult to attend to the fertile crossover between 'fringe' cultural production and the 'mainstream'. If the two sides are incommensurable, then little can be said about the relations between them. This problem can be found even in work that is otherwise excellent in its attention to fringe cultures. For example, cultural geographer Kate Shaw has provided some richly textured accounts of the radical 'indie' subcultures of inner Melbourne since the 1960s. For Shaw (2013), these subcultures are defined by their opposition to 'the dominant commercial culture': 'All contain elements of resistance, subversion, anti-establishment or anti-'art', deliberately defying reason or control' (p. 334). This perspective captures the uncompromising and adversarial nature of radical fringe cultures. However, any focus is lost at the point where they filter out and hybridise with the mainstream. This is the point, for Shaw, at which they cease to be of interest, entering a 'mass-produced, commercialised culture' (p. 335) about which nothing much more can be said. Yet a number of studies have demonstrated that in both the British and Australian cultural market of the mid-twentieth century, crossover between fringe and mass cultural production has contributed to a vibrant and innovative national popular culture (Frith and Horne 1987; Moore 2012).

A third problem of the exceptionalist perspective is that it offers little basis on which one might develop a cultural *policy*. It is clear that fringe cultures perform crucial functions within the wider cultural system. It would be reasonable to conclude that they should therefore be a central focus in any effort to develop, or provide support for, that system. If, however, there is no way of knowing or accounting for these cultures, we are left without a guide to practical action. This perhaps accounts for the tendency in cultural policy towards models of state paternalism. The area is marked by an arbitrariness and indifference to program evaluation that would not be accepted in any other policy area (Tabrett 2013).

THE STRUCTURE OF THE FIELD

For Bourdieu, the fringe—or, as he preferred, the sphere of limited production—is defined not simply by its difference from the mainstream, but also by its own internal structure and organisation. At the base of this approach is the concept of the 'field'. The concept is often glossed as a 'social space', but the meaning given to it by Bourdieu is also stronger than that, implying a relative autonomy from other spaces. He often used the analogy of a sports field. As Patricia Thompson (2014) expands in her explication of the concept:

> A football field is a boundaried site where a game is played. In order to play the game, players have set positions ... The game has specific rules which novice players must learn, together with basic skills, as they begin to play. What players can do, and where they can go during the game, depends on their field position. (p. 66)

The analogy captures the key elements of the concept: the field is a space of 'position-takings' in which social agents define their identities in relation to others; it is governed by social rules or conventions about the kinds of 'moves' that are allowable; and the possibilities of individual agents are determined by their positions within the field. But perhaps the most important for our purposes here is that the field is 'boundaried'; it is relatively autonomous and independent in its functioning from those around it.

The model applies particularly well to small, specialised spheres of cultural production self-consciously set apart from the mainstream. The paradigm for Bourdieu (Bourdieu and Johnson 1993) was symbolist poetry 'where the only audience aimed at is other producers' (p. 39), but many of the examples we have considered in *Fringe to Famous* also fit the profile clearly. They have emerged from small cultural spheres, including university student revues, pub music scenes, independent record labels, fanzines, art school friendship groups, cineaste circles and independent games festivals. While these spaces may not be as sharply distinguished from the mainstream as the nineteenth-century Parisian avant-garde, they have nevertheless been relatively bounded, with their own internal social structure and particular forms of value. They have also been characterised by a blurring between the roles of 'artist' and 'audience' and active involvement of the audience in shaping the cultural form.

A good example is the punk and post-punk inner-city music scene, where devoted audiences in small inner city 'gigs' were composed of fellow band members or others who contributed creatively to the DIY ethic and aesthetic surrounding the music by writing and publishing fanzines, operating record stores, booking venues, designing record covers, producing promotional video clips or assembling a subcultural style. This was a market of limited production composed of discriminating connoisseurs, a band bohemia literate in trends from abroad and the encouraging of risk, experimentation and transgression against dominant popular musical styles.

The close social bonds and intensity of experience of such scenes have often been romanticised. This then provokes reactions—iconoclastic attempts to puncture claims to artistic value or social worth. Neither perspective is particularly analytical. The former tends to rest on the aura of direct experience: to understand, you had to have 'been there'. The latter fastens on unattractive aspects of the scene—clannishness, pretention or lack of professionalism—in order simply to discount it. Both tend to close off any attempt at detailed understanding of how they actually work.

Bourdieu's approach offers a way of charting a path between these two extremes. It allows recognition of certain truths to 'insider' accounts of small fringe scenes. Participants in these scenes often make major investments of time and energy and expose themselves to considerable risks. They willingly enter a world defined by the rejection of known or established paths to social recognition and demonstrate a 'capacity to remain there over a long period without any economic compensation' (Bourdieu and Johnson 1993, p. 40). For Bourdieu, these are the facts that need to be acknowledged. At the same time, he refuses the romantic impulse merely to celebrate them as evidence of a dedication to 'art', as if the latter was innocent, pure, entirely removed from social interests or calculations. Recognition of the distinctness of cultural production—its involvement of genuinely different values—is not the *end* of sociological enquiry, but the *beginning*, leading us to examine the social interests in which it is inscribed.

For Bourdieu, the field of cultural production is a paradoxical one in which the 'loser wins' (Bourdieu and Johnson 1993, p. 39). But the paradox is only apparent. The loss (or appearance of loss) is only in the field of extensive production—the mainstream economy. It is a loss that establishes the autonomy of the agent as a specifically *cultural* agent, allowing them to play to 'win' within the cultural field. The general point is that the field of cultural production is structured, just like other fields, by competition for social advantage. It has its own stakes and its own economy of recognition and rewards. As Bourdieu and Johnson (1993) put it for the case of writing,

> The field of cultural production is the site of struggles in which what is at stake is the power to impose the dominant definition of the writer and therefore to delimit the population of those entitled to take part in the struggle to define the writer. (p. 42)

Bourdieu explored the role of innovation in the late nineteenth- and twentieth-century French art market structured by a succession of bohemias and avant-gardes parading specific cultural literacy that correspond to particular cultural products—whether a school of painting, style of writing or an emerging genre of music—and parts of the market (Bourdieu and Nice 1980b). The formation of a bohemian group called into being a style, a genre and a new position in the field. Individual and collective subjects are involved in competition and conflict over the accumulation and deployment of 'modalities of capital' (Bourdieu 1986). The field of cultural production is dynamic, continuously changing through conflicts for power. Bourdieu and Nice (1980b) discerned a cultural dialectic, a struggle between new and established cultural producers and their work, a clash of generations, which creates the field of cultural production and gives it an historical dimension: 'On the one side are the dominant figures, who want continuity, identity reproduction, on the other, the new comers, who seek discontinuity, difference, revolution' (p. 289).

Such jousts for position have a long history in the Australian cultural field. They were apparent, for example, in the clash in the 1880s between the bush-scape impressionists (later labelled the Heidelberg School) and Victorian classicists, the bitter stand off in the 1930s and 1940s between the now canonised impressionists and young marginalised modernists such as the Angry Penguins group, and the generational stoush in the late 1960s over sexually explicit and irreverent countercultural art and satire that provoked the disdain of high modernist commentators who lamented art's descent into superficiality, play and popularity (Moore 2012). And since the 1980s, 'culture wars' have erupted over the attitudes and practices of at least two new generations to postmodernism, censorship, feminism, popular culture, sexual and ethnic difference and new technology.

From the perspective of our study, it is significant that a younger generation of punk provocateurs in the late 1970s and early 1980s was (at the time) as hostile to the now established musical styles and iconography of the established 'alternative' hippy and blues music scenes that had arisen in the late 1960s and early 1970s, as they were of the more overtly top 40 teenage pop music promoted by commercial radio and the public broadcaster, notably the ABC's *Countdown*.

This conflict against an old guard for position on the field was voiced not only by musicians, but also pronounced in the music press and electronic media that had origins in the earlier 1970s countercultures. A powerful and articulate voice in favour of the new music was music writer Clinton Walker, himself ensconced in the punk scenes of Brisbane and Melbourne, who championed associates such as The Saints, The Birthday Party and the Go Betweens. Writing in various publications, Walker engaged in one of the strategies for 'position taking' Bourdieu identified as available to new players in the field of limited production— depicting established artists as obsolete, fake and out of touch with new aesthetic trends and modern life. In 1984, Walker declared that the 'great majority of Australian rock is utterly mediocre', whereas 'the Australian new wave was responsible for some of the finest music made anywhere in the late seventies, but it was oppressed by the ignorance and fear of the record companies, the media and (partly as a consequence) the public' (Walker 1984, pp. 5–6).

Likewise, the musicians pitted the autonomy of their creative practice against the compromise of established musical styles and performance that dominated both the fields of limited and extensive production in the late 1970s and early 1980s. For example, 'Go Between' Robert Foster lamented the failure of the commercial music industry to accept what was critically acclaimed in Europe: 'We'd written six lauded albums and the band was broke ... a mess we had brought on by trying to gain our freedom' (Forster 2006, p. 52).

This kind of analysis opens up a fertile program of research into small cultural scenes. From one perspective, this is a sociological program: How do these small scenes work? How do they structure social relations? What social rewards do they offer to those who participate in them? What rules must be followed in accumulating those rewards? But the investigation is more than an investigation into the peculiar social rituals of small cliques or groups who have chosen to define themselves in opposition to the mainstream. From another perspective, it is also a program of research into cultural value, such as might be undertaken by a music critic or art historian: How do position-takings within the field define new genres, styles or aesthetic sensibilities? How do creative innovations establish differences between schools or tendencies, marking out new spaces of possibilities? How do they make claims on artistic 'truth', 'beauty' or insight into the human condition?

In our research for *Fringe to Famous*, we have used this approach in an attempt to develop a granular understanding of the contribution of peers to cultural value. Peer groups in the field of cultural production act as intimate audiences enhancing what is produced through critical responses, formal reviews, promotion and publicity, providing production assistance or contributing to an act's look through subcultural style. At the centre of many successful cultural productions is a friendship group, often developed through shared interests or experiences in young adulthood, particularly in educational settings such as schools and universities. These relationships are collaborative, affirming the actions of members even where there is little prospect of, or desire for, external validation. At the same time they are competitive: they establish shared hierarchies of value against which individuals strive to excel. This dual aspect provides a basis for broadening out to wider penumbra of collaborators, contacts and participants, who are also motivated by cultural aspirations.

THE PERFORMANCE OF AUTONOMY

Bourdieu and Ferguson (1988) describe the market of restricted production as an 'upside-down economy where the artist could win in the symbolical arena only by losing in the economic one (at least in the short term) and vice versa' (p. 553). Cultural production marketed as art or avant-garde is a high-risk investment that can either lose value or 'rise to the status of cultural objects endowed with an economic value incommensurate with the value of the material components which go into producing them' (Bourdieu and Johnson 1993, p. 68). In this sense, anti-materialism can be shown to be economic (Bourdieu and Nice 1980b). By denying the primacy of profit and other aspects of the economy, artists can enhance the value of their cultural products with particular discriminating consumers, and over time some work may move from marginal, to cult and eventually classic status.

Our research has also revealed instances where artists moving from limited to extensive production have been able to leverage some real creative freedom, at least for a time. For example, within the ABC, tyro satirists *The Chaser* were initially shielded from editorial interference through the protection of experienced mentors and enablers committed to encouraging risk and experimentation. Andrew Denton, as head of Zapruder's other films, the company that initially produced *The Chaser* for the ABC, took up the task of dealing with the national broadcaster's 'non-essential dickheads'.[2] Later *The Chaser* formed their own company, negotiating arrangements that provided them with a degree of autonomy and greater rights in their own content.

For Bourdieu, examining the French cultural field in the nineteenth and twentieth century, this shift from fringe to famous was a gradual process. However, our post-1980s Australian study revealed an acceleration in the move from marginality to mainstream for some artists and their work, in some cases due to policy initiatives promoting media and cultural industries outreach into the curatorial spaces of the field of limited production, such as inner-city comedy performances and fringe arts festivals or the harnessing of participatory 'do it yourself' capacity of online digital technology. Another factor is the elevation to key gatekeeper and taste-maker positions of connoisseurs and artists who had cut their teeth in alternative creative scenes, styles and acts, and now act as cultural entrepreneurs circulating within public and commercial cultural industries working with new emerging talent from the fringe. Examples from our study include Courtney Gibson, Richard Fidler, and Andy Nehl, who, as public broadcasting commissioners and producers at the Australian Broadcasting Corporation and Special Broadcasting Service, engaged with new comedy styles from the festival and university revue circuit and in many ways conform to Bourdieu's notion of the 'cultural intermediary'.

A shift from fringe to famous in our study that accords more closely with the time frame in Bourdieu's own studies is the retrospective curation of once marginalised artists and artefacts into an Australian 'alternative' cannon. This has occurred, for example, via the ABC's *Rage*, or through the documentaries created by Paul Clarke, Richard Lowenstein and Mark Hartley, all one-time participants in inner city creative bohemias.[3]

HOMOLOGIES AND CAPITAL CONVERSIONS

The structural analysis of the field of cultural production provides a basis for identifying what Bourdieu calls 'homologies' between different fields. It offers theoretical terms that cut across the particularities of these fields, allowing comparisons between music and graphic design, television comedy and computer games. As Wang (2016, p. 355) suggests, there are four principles governing the oppositional structure of fields: the opposition between the dominant and dominated; the opposition between orthodoxy and heterodoxy; the opposition between economic and cultural capital; and the opposition between the autonomous and heteronomous poles of a field.

Our research has revealed common homologies between the fields of post-1980s Australian music, comedy, design and screen fiction. One is the catalytic role across music, comedy and scripted drama of the community radio sector, for example 4ZZZ and 3RRR, established by the Whitlam Labour Government in the mid-1970s to promote media diversity and participation, and the two public broadcasters, the ABC and SBS. The Australian Broadcasting Corporation was established in 1932 and fulfils the role of a national broadcaster of radio and television independent of the government of the day, similar to the BBC in the UK. The Special Broadcasting Service was inaugurated in 1980 by the Fraser Liberal-Country Party Government under the policy of multiculturalism to reflect the ethnic diversity of Australia, and from 1992 it was permitted to take advertising, signalling its evolution into an 'alternative' network akin to Britain's Channel 4.

Notable public broadcasting initiatives enabling movement between the markets of limited and extensive production across art forms include: the inauguration of youth station Double Jay in 1975; its extension by the Hawke Government from 1989 into a national FM youth network, providing an alternative media in regional Australia; the funding under Prime Minister Paul Keating's Creative Nation cultural policy in 1994 of SBS Independent, that explicitly commissioned emerging and experimental content from independent cultural producers; screen finance and mentoring initiatives at the state and federal level that targeted indigenous creative story tellers working across art forms, coupled with the establishment of indigenous program units at both public broadcasters and Film Australia; and funding for digital screen projects, including gaming. A whole of cultural field approach has enabled us to identify homologies that have explicit policy implications for what has met with success in the past four decades—homologies that may be able to inform future action.

Another homology is circulation between music, comedy, design and screen fiction of personnel with shared ethical and aesthetic touchstones, notably punk's broad-based cultural provocation. Mambo surfwear emerged from the merchandise racks of Sydney's Phantom Record store, and punk's aesthetic was directly incorporated into Mambo's designs— hardly surprising as the label's principal artist was Reg Mombassa (aka Chris O'Doherty), the guitarist from inoclastic 'new wave' band Mental As Anything. Likewise, punk's shock value and ironic view of capitalism inspired the comedy sensibility and style of several generations of comedians, as disparate as the *D-Generation* and *The Doug Anthony Allstars* in the 1980s and Jon Safran and *The Chaser* in the late 1990s and early 2000s.[4]

CONCLUSION

In this chapter, we have sought to demonstrate the value of Bourdieu for conceptualising a dynamic and innovative relationship between fringe and popular culture markets in Australia that is all too frequently ignored in academic and sectoral accounts of the arts and media, and is consequently de-emphasised in narratives about cultural policy, notwithstanding the impact that specific policies have had in bridging the two markets. Bourdieu's insights into the markets of limited and extensive production enable us to understand the value of small peer-based and participatory scenes, variously labelled underground, fringe, alternative, or indie; to understand the economy of that market shorn of romantic 'art for art' sake myths; to nevertheless appreciate the value to a discerning popular market of a discourse of autonomy from markets, where emerging practitioners compete with established players for authenticity; and to bring together in a cultural field areas of arts practice usually treated separately, noting connections between players and past policy impact across forms and genres, with implications for future evidence-based cultural policy.

For Bourdieu, the boundaries of the field of culture itself were at stake in struggles within the field of restricted production. Our study considers whether the boundaries in official bourgeois culture have been extended through transgression and experimentation. Applying field theory to the Australian cultural market, our research reveals artists emerging within the field of restricted production transgressing the boundaries between the popular and the avant-garde fields and infusing fringe art with the genres and forms of popular culture, and popular culture with critical values.

NOTES

1. In the mid-1980s, young graduates from the University of Melbourne with a background in both student revue and an inner-city cabaret comedy scene came together as the *Fast Forward* on the commercial 7 network. Akin to Britain's *Not the 9 O'Clock News* and US cable's *Saturday Night Live*, these programs moved beyond the standard political satire to parody the contemporary mediascape of advertising, current affairs and daytime chat shows, as well as television's own history. *The Chaser* began in the late 1990s as a weekly satirical newspaper produced by Charles Firth, Chris Taylor, Craig Reucassel, Julian Morrow, Chas Liciardello and Andrew Hansen, an ensemble that had come together in student revue and journalism at the University of Sydney, much as the Oz and Monty Python satirists had in the 1960s. Transferred to public radio and then a number of series for ABC television, the *Chaser's* style of satire provided a colourful carnivalesque antidote to the grey managerialism of the conservative Howard government era (1996–2007). To the present day, the *Chaser*, across print, radio, television, live performance and online, have entertained and provoked with their anarchic anti-authoritarianism, Dadaesque stunts, parody of media, and flirtation with obscenity and offences against good taste. Like Barry Humphries, the *Chaser* is interested in hypocrisy

and the abuse of power wherever they lurk: in politics, corporations, the public service, the media, celebrity culture, religion.

2. Andrew Denton pioneered groundbreaking live tonight shows in the late 1980s and 1990s that blended anarchic comedy with agenda-setting interviews and community outreach targeting emerging social movements and issues. Initially developed and broadcast on ABC television, Denton broadened these formats on the commercial ATN 7 network, before forming his own independent production company to develop, professionalise and commercialise emerging comedians and their ideas.

3. Clarke produced *Long Way to the Top* (2001) and *Mambo: Art Irritates Life* (2016) for the ABC; Lowenstein produced and directed *We're Living on Dog Food* (2009) and *Autoluminescent: Rowland S. Howard* (2011) for cinema release; Mark Hartley directed and wrote *Not Quite Hollywood: The Wild, Untold Story of Ozploitation* (2008).

4. Like *Fast Forward*, *D-Generation* was a mid-1980s ensemble sketch show on ABC TV composed of young graduates who emerged from the university revue and Melbourne comedy scene that included Rob Sitch, Jane Kennedy, Santo Cilauro and Tom Gleisner. After the success of a *Saturday Night Live* style *Late Show* in 1992–1993 on the ABC, the D-Gen principals became cultural entrepreneurs as Working Dog, producing *Frontline*, *Funky Squad* and *The Panel*, which in their different ways ironically mined the same pop cultural seam. The *Doug Anthony All Stars* were an all-singing, all-dancing threesome comprising Paul McDermott (the nasty one), Tim Ferguson (the good-looking one) and Richard Fidler (the nice one) that came to prominence in the mid-1980s at the Edinburgh Fringe Festival and ABC TV's live cabaret comedy-showcase *The Big Gig*. The transgressive trio from Canberra sang and pranced in harmony to lively original ditties outrageous for references to the flotsam and jetsam of trash culture. Jon Safran achieved national attention in 1996 filing regular short documentaries for ABC TV's outreach initiative, *Race Around the World*, that were notorious for disregard for cultural sensitivities (streaking naked at the Wailing Wall in Jerusalem, having a voodoo curse placed on an ex-girlfriend, inserting a Saddam Hussein doll on the route of Disneyland's *It's a Small World* ride. He made a cycle of confronting polemical documentaries for SBS, mainly in collaboration with punk-inspired filmmaker Richard Lowenstein, notably *John Safran vs God*, in which the eponymous storyteller endured partial crucifixion in the Philippines.

REFERENCES

Alomes, S. (1983). Cultural radicalism in the sixties. *Arena, 62,* 28–54.

Bourdieu, P. (1986). The forms of capital. In J. G. Richardson (Ed.), *Handbook of theory and research for the sociology of education* (pp. 241–258). New York: Greenwood Press.

Bourdieu, P., & Ferguson, P. P. (1988). Flaubert's point of view. *Critical Inquiry, 14*(3), 539–562.

Bourdieu, P. (1993). In R. Johnson (Ed.), *The field of cultural production: Essays on art and literature.* New York: Columbia University Press.

Bourdieu, P., & Nice, R. (1980a). The aristocracy of culture. *Media, Culture and Society, 2*(3), 225–254.

Bourdieu, P., & Nice, R. (1980b). The production of belief: Contribution to an economy of symbolic goods. *Media, Culture and Society, 2*(3), 261–293.

Foster, R. (2006). A true hipster. *The Monthly,* July, p. 52.

Frith, S., & Horne, H. (1987). *Art into pop.* London: Methuen.

Heath, J., & Potter, A. (2004). *Nation of rebels: Why counterculture became consumer culture.* New York: Harper Collins.

Moore, T. (2012). *Dancing with empty pockets – Australia's Bohemians.* Sydney: Murdoch Books.

Murger, H. (1930). Preface. *The Latin Quarter (Scénes de la Vie Bohème).* E. Marriage & J. Selwyn, (Trans.). London: Collins.

Shaw, K. (2013). Independent creative subcultures and why they matter. *International Journal of Cultural Policy, 19*(3), 333–352.

Tabrett, L. (2013). *It's culture stupid: Reflections of an arts bureaucrat.* Strawberry Hills, NSW: Currency House.

Thompson, P. (2014). Field. In Michael J. Grenfell (Ed.), *Pierre Bourdieu – Key concepts* (2nd ed., pp. 65–82). Abingdon: Routledge.

Thornton, S. (1996). *Club cultures: Music, media and subcultural capital.* Hanover, NH: University Press of New England.

Walker, C. (1984). *The next thing: Contemporary Australian rock.* Kenturst, NSW: Kangaroo Press.

Wang, Y. (2016). Homology and isomorphism: Bourdieu in conversation with new institutionalism. *The British Journal of Sociology, 67*(2), 348–370.

CHAPTER 11

Bourdieusian Reflexivity in Insider Research in Higher Education: Considering Participants as a Critical Audience

Katrina Waite

INTRODUCTION

In this chapter, I explore insider research within higher education from my perspective as a doctoral candidate who also holds a full-time academic position. I position doctoral education as a subfield of the higher education academic field and consider the homologies of these fields. This exploration uses concepts of Bourdieu's "participant objectivation" in relation to the social and career trajectories of myself as an insider doctoral researcher and as an academic and explains how this reflexivity of my positioning within these fields led to the development of a new methodological "gaze" or "metanoia". Bourdieu's concept of "illusio" or sense of the game within the field is explored as it relates to the parallel formation of a "habitus" as an academic and a researcher over time. The chapter makes reference to Bourdieu's "socio-analysis" of his representation of the French higher education field to his peers, and discusses how this analysis has informed my own research and its representation.

K. Waite (✉)
University of Technology Sydney, Sydney, Australia

© The Author(s) 2018   165
J. Albright et al. (eds.), *Bourdieu's Field Theory and the Social Sciences*,
https://doi.org/10.1007/978-981-10-5385-6_11

Following Bourdieu's example, this chapter takes a reflexive sociological analytic approach, to explain how my own positionings within the higher education field influenced methodological decisions and strategic moves within the field.

I develop an argument to demonstrate that insider research in the higher education field is a unique form of insider research and that certain discourses relating to the practice of doctoral education may be inappropriate, potentially self-sabotaging, and even wasteful in this context. The chapter addresses the construction of the object of research within an insider context and discusses the process which led to the selection of a new analytical lens.

In this chapter, field analysis is used to analyse my position as a researcher and work colleague, and the impact of this reflexive analysis on my analytical and representational choices.

The chapter is likely to be useful to doctoral students and other researchers who are considering undertaking an insider study, particularly those who are considering a study which involves research relating to the practice of their peers and colleagues—especially when those peers are academic researchers themselves. The chapter begins with a critical reflexive moment which dramatically changed the direction of my research.

A Critical Reflexive Moment

Midway through my doctoral candidature, I was working late to develop a single slide as the basis for my university's three-minute thesis competition. At this time, I had undertaken data collection, performed some analysis, and successfully presented my preliminary findings at an overseas conference. I am a confident presenter and can present an argument concisely when required. My findings were interesting and, to an extent, novel. Yet I can still recall the sudden unpleasant visceral feeling when I realised that I could not present these findings within my own university context as the audience was likely to consist of the participants in my insider study and, as I was an academic within the university, also my colleagues. This epiphany, or critical reflexive moment, led to a reconsideration of the purpose of my doctoral research, my methodology, and its eventual representation—a reconsideration which was informed by Bourdieu's concepts of field, habitus, and illusio.

Context of the Study

During my doctoral study, I was employed as an academic developer within the central teaching and learning division of an Australian university. At the time, it was not unusual for staff to be employed in these units as full-time academics without a doctorate. In my unit, I was expected to enrol and undertake research related to my work. My doctoral study was quasi-ethnographic and focused on the practice of academics in the review and development of a new undergraduate business degree curriculum. I was a member of the curriculum development team. My team members were aware that I was working on my doctorate, and an early outcome from my doctoral research, including a brief critical review of the literature on business and management education, was incorporated into the documentation. The curriculum review resulted in some significant changes to the structure of the degree course, the addition of an innovative subject for which the development team received a university citation, and significant changes to academic practice. These changes have been sustained, and on these objective measures, at least, the curriculum change project was successful.

Data Collection and Analysis ... the First Time

My involvement in the project provided rich data. As an insider, I had the benefits of an insider's understanding. When I undertook interviews with my team members, my existing relationships allowed me to explore their perspectives in depth, as is reasonable to expect in insider research and is reported by many insider researchers and insider-research methodologists (Brannick and Coghlan 2007; Labaree 2002; Mercer 2007; Trowler 2014).

I initially treated the data, including documents and interview transcripts, as texts. Aiming for "objectivity", I undertook critical discourse analysis (Fairclough 2013) to produce the findings I presented in an international conference and was intending to present at the three-minute thesis competition. As an "impartial" observer, and through what could be considered an assimilation of the "doxa" of research practice within the field, I aimed to present my research with an analytical "disinterestedness" (Bourdieu, in Grenfell and James 2004, Chap. 8, Sect. 3, para. 3). Not surprisingly, even though I aimed to present my participants respectfully, my representation had constructed my research perspective as if I held an observation point from outside the site of study, allowing me to take a somewhat critical and evaluative approach to my data.

I looked for "discourses evident and absent" within the data, with only a limited understanding that the identification of an absence of an expected discourse could be viewed as critical. What might not be evident to participants is that the reason for the absence was as much *my* contribution—or lack of contribution—as that of anyone else in the team. I had not found this issue problematic when I made the conference presentation overseas. It was only when I found myself in the position where I would be presenting to my participants that I was struck with the methodological implications of representation and audience within the higher education field. Around the same time, and before my thesis writing began in earnest, I began to read Bourdieu's work on "participant objectivation" within the field of research (Bourdieu and Wacquant 1992). In the same way that Bourdieu criticised his own approach to his ethnographic work in Algeria, I immediately recognised that "I had committed a kind of disloyalty by setting myself up as an observer of a game I was still playing" (Bourdieu and Wacquant 1992, p. 254).

Bourdieusian Methodological Insights

In contrast to other chapters, my study was not initiated as a Bourdieusian field analysis. Like many doctoral candidates in the humanities and social sciences, I explored many theoretical and methodological approaches before I encountered Bourdieu, and was in an advanced stage of my doctoral project, the process of writing and representation, before Bourdieusian concepts appeared relevant. But then I was particularly intrigued by this quote:

> People at their most personal are essentially the product of exigencies actually or potentially inscribed in the structure or, more precisely in the position occupied with this field. (Bourdieu, in Bourdieu and Wacquant 1992, p. 45)

For me, this was another critical reflexive moment. I immediately understood that within the field of research, I had assimilated these exigencies of doctoral research practice unconsciously and therefore unquestioningly. I then took it upon myself to explore the exigencies which were contributing to the formation of my academic "habitus", and of which I had until that point been relatively unaware, with the aim of developing a new form of representation.

Insider Doctoral Research as a Subfield of the Higher Education Field

Reflecting on my position within the field, I realised that doctoral education may be viewed as a subfield of the higher education academic field. "Field" and "habitus" are defined as

> a set of objective, historical relationships between positions anchored in certain forms of power (or capital), while habitus consists of a set of historical relationships "deposited" within individual bodies in the form of mental and corporeal schemata of perceptions, appreciation and action. (Bourdieu and Wacquant 1992, p. 16)

Bourdieu gives some sense of the competitive nature of a field with reference to the common understandings of those who inhabit the field. The sense of the game, or illusio, is defined as the "tacit recognition of the value of the stakes of the game and as practical mastery of its rules" (p. 117), and that a defining characteristic of a field is "the specific profits that are at stake in the field" (Bourdieu and Wacquant 1992, pp. 72–73). I make the assumption here that readers of this chapter will have some understanding of the higher education field, in fact they will "concur in their belief (doxa) in the game and its stakes" (Bourdieu and Wacquant 1992, p. 98), the beliefs which determine the legitimacy of the field.

I suggest that there are homologies between these two fields. In both fields, high-quality research and publications are valued and may be considered "profits" in the competitive game. These profits lead to academic employment, career progression, and recognition. Yet there are particular discourses specific to doctoral education which suggest that the stakes in these two fields are somewhat different.

Doctoral candidates enter this subfield with a relatively low level of academic capital. The logic of practice within this field relates to the development of academic capital, through the supervised research process.

As many doctoral candidates discover, a significant challenge is the creation of project boundaries. Supervisors, including mine, regularly remind students that the doctorate is a small contribution to knowledge. The dissertation should be designed to be read by an audience of two or three examiners—what I term the "limited audience" discourse. And we are also reminded "you are not going to change the world"—the "limited impact" discourse.

In contrast, other academic research is intended for a far wider audience, and there is an acceptance that the outcomes, especially if they are supported by significant funding and are undertaken by a team rather than an individual, may have significant impact.

In the early stages of my candidature, this supervisory guidance was useful in providing focus through the myriad of possible methodological and theoretical approaches. The admonition to "think small" made sense, but the three-minute thesis critical moment called these discourses into question.

In parallel to my doctoral study, I was engaged in my everyday work as an academic developer and began to understand that there were conflicts between my positioning with the doctoral research field and my work with other academics.

Within the higher education academic field, there are various positions in relation to academic capital. For this chapter, I have not attempted to undertake a detailed analysis of the field, but a brief outline is included for the purpose of situating my own positioning, assuming that readers share an understanding of the academic field.

Researchers who publish in high-ranked journals and who obtain high-value research grants would be generally viewed as embodying the highest level of academic capital. The value of this academic capital is reflected in institutional promotion and recruitment practices. Teaching and integrated academics would be considered to have a moderate level of academic capital and often work towards increasing their academic capital through their research.

However, in terms of academic capital, the role of the academic developer is problematic. Research on the role of the academic developer and academic development units highlights the tensions within the field (for example, Hall 2016; Holmes et al. 2012; Kensington-Miller et al. 2015). A significant theme within the literature is the conflict between the construction of academic development as either a non-academic professional support role or as an academic role which includes a research component. Academic development is often positioned on the periphery of the academic field, characterised by precarity, and liminality. In 2016, the Australian Government closed the Office for Learning and Teaching, the organisation which funded a significant proportion of the research undertaken by staff within academic development units, thus contributing further to questions regarding the academic nature of these units and their staff.

This low level of academic capital provides little power of influence within the sphere of work—the development of teaching and learning practices of academics. The effectiveness of academic developers relies strongly on the individual's success in developing positive relationships with the academics within faculties and may be either limited or enhanced by numerous exigencies of the field, and the positionings of the participants in relation to the field.

In that one critical reflexive moment, and holding a relatively peripheral position within the academic field, I realised that I was at risk of damaging the relationships that made my everyday work possible, possibly risking job security, and limiting the future possibilities which might be generated by my research. I could relate to Bourdieu's experience of "a cleft habitus inhabited by tensions and contradictions" (Bourdieu 2007, p. 100), and I knew that I needed to explore the issue of representation.

Insider researcher and methodologist Labaree (2002) discusses the "disengagement" stage of insider research. This is the point when the study is complete and the researcher withdraws from the site of research. He notes that in the case of insider research, there may be no noticeable withdrawal. Normal work carries on as usual, with the researcher now resuming the everyday role of colleague. Labaree considers this area of insider research problematic and unexplored. Some researchers note that they restrict access to the dissertation to the doctoral assessors only. Other higher education insider researchers note the problematic nature of disengagement and have made the decision not to share their findings with their participants or more senior people within the organisation due to potential negative consequences for the participants (Mercer 2007). However, within the higher education field, there is the added risk that academics are resourceful and, if interested, likely to track down a doctoral thesis.

Two recent anecdotal examples further point to a silencing of the outcomes of insider higher education research and limitations on its impact.

The first was my conversation with an editor of respected higher education research journal. We were speaking about a separate study I had undertaken which involved ethnographic observations of the practices of academics and students in classes. She stated that there are very few ethnographic papers on academic practice in higher education in her journal or others, and she would like to see more. In the other case, I was presenting a paper on my methodological approach at a research conference. I posed a question to the audience asking about their experiences of insider research in higher education. One audience member commented that she had undertaken insider research for her doctorate. When I probed further about the impact of sharing her outcomes with her participants she revealed, "I just hope they never read it".

Within my doctoral study, if I had adopted the advice of my supervisor I might have accepted that my dissertation could be critical, evaluative, and if contentious, remain confidential. But by this time, I had progressed to the stage of producing new knowledge and was developing my own academic capital. As my research was based on the practice of academics within my own workplace context and was producing findings which could have value to future higher education curriculum renewal projects, both in my own university and elsewhere, the "limited audience" approach seemed problematic, wasteful in fact.

Furthermore, as a curriculum researcher, I began to bring the findings of my doctoral research into my everyday work. As Lee and Boud (2009) suggest, doctorates produce both *objects* such as the knowledge produced in the dissertation, and *subjects*, the transformed researcher. In my case, when I engaged in my everyday academic development practice, I had become a more theoretically and research-informed higher education teaching, learning, and curriculum practitioner.

From a positioning of low academic capital within the academic field, my research had allowed me to make strategic moves. As a bearer of limited capital within the field, I saw little personal value in orienting myself "actively (either) toward the preservation of the distribution of capital". Rather, through new approaches, my strategic moves were "toward the subversion of this distribution" (Bourdieu and Wacquant 1992, p. 109).

This translation of as yet unpublished outcomes into the workplace resulted in the production of successful teaching and learning grant applications, the use of Bourdieu's "misrecognition" as the theoretical basis to support a professor on a successful national research grant, and influence on the curriculum practices of senior academics in relation to gender and diversity within collaborative projects. My engagement with curriculum theory influenced the university teachers' professional development program and resulted in invitations to present guest lectures and workshops in areas where my research was providing radical insights, at my university and others. As the nature of this impact was on curriculum, and this influenced the educational experience of students, it is not too much of a stretch to suggest that there was some "world-changing" occurring. All the same, as these outcomes challenge existing practices and are somewhat subversive, my influence is highly dependent on my relationship with individual innovative academics.

Participants as Audience in Insider Higher Education Research, Learning from Bourdieu

In the practice of my everyday work, I was also learning how to communicate aspects of my research within the field in which the research was undertaken. Occasionally, I would be surprised that my presentation alienated my colleagues. Regardless of the validity of the content, and that this concept was based on research undertaken within their own context, my presentation could generate an antagonistic and defensive response.

I was also learning how my research could have impact—the "so what?" question often asked of doctoral students. Yet, to make the impact that I viewed as valuable, choices in representation of the research were critical. The audience really mattered. These were my peers and, as university academics, a highly critical audience. Interestingly, Bourdieu himself comments: "No-one has ever completely extracted all the implications of the fact that the writer, the artist of even the scientist writes not only for a public, but for a public of equals who are also competitors" (Bourdieu 1985, pp. 18–19).

I was also challenged by Bourdieu's reflections, as an insider, on his own representation of his higher education research to his peers. In particular, there were two examples from his own experience: La lecon sur la lecon (Lecture on the lecture) (Bourdieu 1990, pp. 177–198) and *Homo academicus* (Bourdieu 1988).

In his "self-socio-analysis" Bourdieu (2007) reflected on the pain of presenting an analysis of the field to his peers. In 1982, he was accepted into the College de France, and as is normal practice, was required to present an inaugural lecture. He decided to make the topic of his lecture, the inaugural lecture itself.

> But I had underestimated the violence of what, in place of a simple ritual address, became a kind of 'intervention' in the artist's sense … I thus discovered, in the moment of doing this, that what had become for me a psychological solution constituted a challenge to the symbolic order, an affront to the dignity of the institution which demands that one keep silent about the arbitrariness of the institutional rite that is being performed. The public reading of that text which, written outside the situation, still had to be read as it stood, without modification, before the assembled body of masters, Claude Levi-Strauss, Georges Dumezil, Michel Foucault and others, was a terrible ordeal. (Bourdieu 2007, pp. 110–111)

To myself, as an outsider, the lecture is an interesting scholarly work, highlighting the practice of turning one's gaze upon one's own field. However, I have no investment in the French intellectual field of that time and am able to read the lecture without emotion or offence.

An earlier interview with Loic Wacquant (1989) directly addresses Bourdieu's anxiety and reluctance to publish the results of his extensive research in the field of French intellectuals, *Homo academicus*, which, although not described as such at the time, could be termed an insider study on the practice of academics. Bourdieu states:

> I have in mind here in particular some of the passages which separated me from some of my best friends. I have had—I think that this is not of merely anecdotal significance—very dramatic clashes with colleagues who perceived very accurately the violence of the objectivation but who saw a contradiction in the fact that I could objectivize without thinking of myself, while of course I was doing it all the while. (p. 3)

In further comments, he explains how the emotional response to the critique obscured that argument.

It was becoming increasingly clear to me that an objective analysis and representation does not lead to an objective and unemotional response when the recipient of that representation is an insider to the field. Bourdieu held high status and embodied significant academic capital within the French intellectual field, and although these outcomes may have produced a negative emotional experience, for him this was not career limiting. This is not the case for new doctoral graduates and researchers like myself.

An Issue of Practical Impact and the Development of a New Gaze—A "Metanoia"

More recently, Grenfell (2010), Grenfell and James (2004) discussed issues of representation and methodology in relation to educational research. Grenfell (2010) states that

> a critical perspective can lead to a kind of 'ghetto-isation', which neutralises the potential for this approach to effect changes, often by creating a kind of critical meta-language that isolates and marginalises the substantive insights arising from policy research in this area. (pp. 85–86)

They make the case for the development of a new "gaze" or "metanoia" in educational research.

In the subfield of rhetoric research, Haliliuc (2016) makes the case for critical ethnographic approaches, where the focus of research moves from an analysis of texts to researching as the recipient of rhetoric by exploring the experience as an audience member within the intended field of the communication. Although my current research does not venture here, this concept offers interesting possibilities for exploration within the insider higher education research field.

At the same time as I was reading methodology literature, my personal experience in my parallel roles as doctoral researcher and full-time academic raised issues relating to practical impact. While I sought a new analytic and representational approach, my developing understanding of the academic field, "deposited" in my developing academic habitus, provided an understanding of future career possibilities both within academic development and within doctoral education. Moreover, as I already hold an academic position, doctoral completion did not have the urgency that it may have had for other doctoral candidates. This provided the luxury of time to seek an analytical lens which had authenticity within the research context and could be used to present my research in a way which was affirming for the participants. I also saw the need for not only a respectful but, following Grenfell and James (1998) in some ways, also a complicit representation which makes clear that the individual academics are doing the best they can in relation to the object of social construction, in this case, a new curriculum.

I have, as Grenfell and James suggest, developed a new gaze or "metanoia", which takes into account my positioning, and my strategies in relation to my understanding of my positioning, within the field/s of research and the implications for influencing change in practice which must engage colleagues, academics and academic managers, and, as my work is in the field of higher education curriculum, university students.

A NEW ANALYTICAL LENS…WITH FILTERS

My methodological challenge was the development of an approach to my data which would minimise the possibility of inflicting symbolic violence on my participants and colleagues, albeit unintentionally, and that my respect for my participants and the relationships that were developed during the project could be affirmed and potentially celebrated.

I considered the various ideological positions underpinning the various subdisciplines within the business/management discipline and determined that any strongly Marxist lens was unlikely to appeal to a large number of business academics, particularly those teaching marketing and finance. It could even be considered a direct challenge to their academic habitus. Taking to heart Bourdieu's exhortation to methodological polytheism (Bourdieu and Wacquant 1992, p. 30), as explained in Everett (2002), I engaged with Levitas's (2013) "utopia as method" as an analytical lens. This approach aligned not only with ideological purposes of curriculum which were evident within the data, but also the processes used to collaboratively produce the new curriculum such as a series of retreats in an almost "utopian" location. While Levitas's theory is based on socialist theories of equity, the future focus of a utopian lens moves away from a critique of past institutional practices and has the power to appeal to "the better angels of our (or my participants') nature". This approach has allowed me to take a positive, rather than critical, approach to my data. Specifically, my research question has changed from a critical evaluative question on the practice of curriculum change to a more open question which explicitly incorporates purpose. Briefly stated, the question is "What can be learnt through this research that will be useful to participants and their peers in future curriculum projects?"

The work has become more theoretical and less reliant on the instance of the site of the research. In effect, the new lens has allowed me to alter my focus from an evaluative analysis of a specific case of curriculum change, which would be of little interest outside the context of study, to a more theoretical study on curriculum. My explicit methodological concerns about representation to an audience of my participants and higher education academics have created an argument for applying "filters"—rose coloured if you will—on the data analysis. Within the field of social relationships, there are reasons that some findings are excluded as their publication would serve no positive purpose for the participants and could pose a risk to my own reputation within the field.

As Grenfell and James (1998) state, "The issue at stake is not whether a particular method should be used. It is rather, the intention behind it, and the validity of the claims laid on it" (Chap. 9, Sect. 5, para. 3). They further state, "In contrast to the symbolic violence that Bourdieu claims can be done in the name of research, this form of researcher engagement amounts to a kind of 'intellectual love'" (para. 19), which, in the case of my study, is a warm collegial respect for my participants and colleagues.

CONCLUSION

I have presented in a socio-analytic analysis of the development of a methodological approach in a doctoral study which was informed by Bourdieusian concepts of participant objectivation, reflexive sociology, and field theory. I have used these concepts to address the potential representational challenges which emerged as a result of undertaking insider research on the practices of myself and my colleagues within the academic field. As I see it, the development of my research approach has been directly related to the conflicts between the expected practices of the subfield of doctoral study and my positioning within the academic field as a full-time academic developer. While my response to withdraw from the three-minute thesis competition could be viewed as rational, I recall the critical moment of reflexivity as a visceral embodied response. This emotional, less than conscious reaction alerted me to problems with my own positioning in relation the academic field – problems within my own developing academic habitus or, as Bourdieu (in Bourdieu and Wacquant 1992) describes, the mental and corporeal schemata of perceptions, appreciations and actions deposited in *my* body. It is likely that if I had undertaken my research outside my institution, or even with students within the institution, there would have been no embodied conflictual emotion resulting in the recognition of a "cleft habitus", nor a consequent desire to change my research approach.

My new approach has allowed me to make strategic moves, both within my own institution and the broader international field. With my developing understanding of the academic audience and my still relatively peripheral positioning within the academic field, I made the decision to present the more explicitly subversive and innovative research concepts at international forums, where they have been well received, rather than within my own institution. Spatial distance appears to offer the safety of emotional distance and lowers the risk of the concepts being viewed as a challenge to those with greater academic capital.

Methodological insights have arisen from specific critical and embodied reflexive moments, coupled with my concurrent reading of the works of Bourdieu and other scholars on the practice of insider educational research. I consider these critical reflexive moments as the points when "the exigencies of the field" either called the logic of my practice into question, such as my decision not to compete in the university's three-minute thesis competition, or freed me from the everyday exigencies of the workplace, for example, a sabbatical and attempts to sketch my thesis narrative, rather than write. These embodied moments in the development of my academic habitus have contributed to the development of a new gaze or "metanoia".

It is not possible for all doctoral candidates to change their analytical approach as late as I did. I hope that this chapter will provide insights for both doctoral candidates and their supervisors that inspire consideration of the analysis and representation of insider research early in the research process. Of course, there is no certainty that my participants and colleagues will be uncritical of my approach, but there is certainty that I am writing with the intention that my dissertation, or components of it, may be read by them, that they find it interesting, will feel positive about their participation and perhaps be inspired to develop their curriculum practices further.

REFERENCES

Bourdieu, P. (1985). The market of symbolic goods. *Poetics, 14,* 13–44.
Bourdieu, P. (1988). *Homo Academicus.* Cambridge, UK: Polity.
Bourdieu, P. (1990). *In other words: Essays towards a reflexive sociology.* Stanford, CA: Stanford University Press.

Bourdieu, P. (2007). *Sketch for a self analysis*. Cambridge, UK: Polity Press.

Bourdieu, P., & Wacquant, L. (1992). *An invitation to reflexive sociology*. New York, NY: The University of Chicago Press.

Brannick, T., & Coghlan, D. (2007). In defense of being "native": The case for insider academic research. *Organizational Research Methods, 10*(1), 59–74.

Everett, J. (2002). Organizational research and the praxeology of Pierre Bourdieu. *Organizational Research Methods, 5*(1), 56–80.

Fairclough, N. (2013). *Critical discourse analysis: The critical study of language*. Abingdon, UK: Routledge.

Grenfell, M. (2010). Being critical: The practical logic of Bourdieu's metanoia. *Critical Studies in Education, 51*(1), 85–99.

Grenfell, M., & James, D. (1998). *Bourdieu and education: Acts of practical theory*. Kindle e-book: Psychology Press.

Grenfell, M., & James, D. (2004). Change in the field—Changing the field: Bourdieu and the methodological practice of educational research. *British Journal of Sociology of Education, 25*(4), 507–523.

Haliliuc, A. (2016). Being, evoking, and reflecting from the field: A case for critical ethnography in audience-centred rhetorical criticism. In S. L. McKinnon, R. Asen, K. Chavez, & R. G. Howard (Eds.), *Text+field innovations in rhetorical method*. Kindle e-book. University Park, Pennsylvania: The Pennsylvania State University Press.

Hall, M. (2016). Playing the academic development game with control and clarity. *International Journal for Academic Development, 21*(4), 259–261.

Holmes, T., Manathunga, C., Potter, M. K., & Wuetherick, B. (2012). The impossibilities of neutrality: Other geopolitical metaphors for academic development units. *International Journal for Academic Development, 17*(3), 197–202.

Kensington-Miller, B., Renc-Roe, J., & Moron-Garcia, S. (2015). The chameleon on a tartan rug: Adaptation of three academic developers' professional identities. *International Journal for Academic Development, 20*(3), 279–290.

Labaree, R. V. (2002). The risk of 'going observationalist': Negotizating the hidden dilemmas of being an insider participant observer. *Qualitative Research, 2*(1), 97–122.

Lee, A., & Boud, D. (2009). Framing doctoral education as practice. In D. Boud & A. Lee (Eds.), *Changing practices of doctoral education*. London, UK: Routledge.

Levitas, R. (2013). *Utopia as method: The imaginary reconstitution of society*. Springer.

Mercer, J. (2007). The challenges of insider research in educational institutions: Wielding a double-edged sword and resolving delicate dilemmas. *Oxford Review of Education, 33*(1), 1–17.

Trowler, P. (2014). *Doing insider research in universities*. Paul Trowler.

Wacquant, L. J. (1989). For a socio-analysis of intellectuals: On "Homo Academicus". *Berkeley Journal of Sociology, 34*, 1–29.

CHAPTER 12

Positioning Participation in the Field of Surfing: Sex, Equity, and Illusion

lisahunter

INTRODUCTION

Surfing, a practice from ancient physical culture, is arguably a social field (Bourdieu 1977, 1990, 1998). In the modern form (re)constituted in the early to mid-1900s participants were repositioned in this field, I would argue through a patriocolonial female/male sex[1] binary. Previous findings (Booth 2001; Comer 2004; Henderson 2001; lisahunter 2006; Stedman 1997) and more recent findings concur (Franklin 2013; lisahunter and emerald 2013; Olive 2013) that in the modern field, females have either been absent as competent athletes or sexually objectified. In the contemporary post-colonial field, this dominant sex binary works strongly with performance and appearance in a way that might be hailed as feminist gains in equity. International female competitors, media, and public imagery celebrate the benefits of increasing economic, symbolic, and cultural capital for females in surfing. Yet, as I will argue, sex remains a powerful aspect of a disposition of

Freelance, Australasia.

lisahunter (✉)
Kirikiriroa, Aotearoa, New Zealand

© The Author(s) 2018   181
J. Albright et al. (eds.), *Bourdieu's Field Theory and the Social Sciences*,
https://doi.org/10.1007/978-981-10-5385-6_12

prominent female surfers to maintain their individual success within an illusion of success for women more generally. As Bourdieu (1990) notes:

> An institution, even an economy, is complete and fully viable only if it is durably objectified not only in things, that is, in the logic, transcending individual agents, of a particular field, but also in bodies, in durable dispositions to recognize and comply with the demands immanent in the field. (p. 58)

Using a Bourdieusian analytical framework (1973, 1977, 1986, 1990, 1998) to explore the logics of practice found in empirical work of an ongoing ethnography of female involvement in the surfing field, I explore the legitimisation and positioning practices within surfing to challenge the potential superficiality of such empowerment and equity celebrations. I argue that a doxa underpinned by (colonial) patriarchy is responsible for illusio, misrecognition, and symbolic violence, ultimately providing the superficial perception of participation equity for and of females. At the same time, at a deeper and ontological level, reproduction of patriarchy and its dominant/dominating practices are sustained and reworked.

PRE-COLONIAL SURFING AS FIELD (HABITUS AND PRACTICE)

> I ko Lono huipu ana me Kamalalawalu kea lii o Maui, o ka hana nui a na'lii malihini a me na'lii kamaaina, o ka heenalu, a ua oluolu ia lakou ia mea, a he mea ia e hoike mai ana I ke kanaka Akamai a me ka wahine Akamai, aole hoi oia wale. O ka hoike ana I kekahi I kanaka maikai, a ua oluolu I ka maka ka nana ana I kea no o na mea a pau, a pela na'lii a me na kanaka I lealea ai I ka heenalu. (Kamakau, Ruling Chiefs, p. 53)

> Kama'lala-walu, ruler of Maui, met him [Lono-i-ka-makahiki] and welcomed him royally, the chiefly host and guest spent much time in surfing, a sport that was enjoyed by all. It showed which man or which woman was skilled; not only that, but which man or woman was the best looking. It was a pleasing sight, and that was why chiefs and commoners enjoyed surfing. (Kamakau, Ruling Chiefs, p. 53)

> Ua lilo keia I mea waiwai nui ia wa, a pela I piha mau ain a wahi heenalu I na kane a me na wahine. – Ka Nupepa Kuokoa (May 14, 1870. p. 4)

This art [lele wa'a] was held in esteem at that time, and so the surfing places were constantly filled with men and women. – 'Ī'ī. Fragments (p. 133). (as cited in Clark (2011, p. 11)

As captured above by Clark citing early pre-colonial oral history, surfing is a *practice* with ancient roots—a physical culture in Polynesian societies, a practice that was pivotal to the social structure and ways of being. In his outlining of *ka wā kahiko* (times of old) in Hawaiian surfing, the *kama'āina* (native born Hawai'ian) Isaiah Helekunihi Walker (2011) also draws on *mo'olelo* (history, legend) such as that above, to show how human relationships, feelings, and practices identified with *he'e nalu* (wave sliding, board surfing). He notes, 'Surfing was more than competitive sport: it was a cultural practice embedded within the social, political, and religious fabric of Hawaiian society' (p. 16). *Kū mai* chants summoned waves, *ho'okupu* (offerings) were made to the surf, legends of higher beings surfing such as the goddess Hi'iaka and her brother were passed down through *mo'olelo, mele* (chants) and *kanikau* (mourning chants) referred to surfing, and great surfing feats by royalty were celebrated, such as *Halehale ke aloha*, a surfing chant honouring Queen Lili'uokalani also known as Kamaka'eha:

O Kamaka'eha ka honua nalu

A pae o Kamaka'eha I ka nalu.

Kamaka'eha on the crest

Rides the surf to shore. (Kanahele, cited in Clark 2011, p. 44)

Such recognition was, and still is, critical in Hawaiian social settings, including in the *ka po'ina nalu* (surf zone). Prior to colonisation, recognition legitimated surfing practices, and surfing as a recognisable social space, including participants' position within that space where women and men gained value or forms of capital (Bourdieu 1990) in similar ways. Valued practices of honouring others, respecting individuals, and reciprocating benevolent relations resonated in several *mo'olelo*. They also uncover specific values and rules within a Hawaiian surfing hierarchy. 'Genealogy ... social/political rank, and surfing skill were all criteria for ranking a person' (Walker 2011, p. 19), including in the *kūlana he'e nalu* (surfing lineup).[2] This positioning (rank) of one's habitus (inherited and developed bodily dispositions) as having skill is ascribed value (capital) through social relationships (social capital) made possible through surfing—a field or recognisable social space with its own language, rules, regulations, and roles.

Some possessions symbolically legitimated individuals within the social space. As an example, of the many types of boards used to wave slide, the papa olo were usually owned by chiefs. Certain breaks (wave locations or times) were reserved for royalty; if one was invited to surf these breaks, one was trading symbolic capital (being able to surf) for social capital (connecting with those who offered the invitation). Aesthetics and athleticism in the forms of 'beauty' and 'empowerment' demonstrated in the styles of women and men were also valued forms of symbolic capital. John Clark draws on a passage from *Tales and Traditions* (Kamakau 1961 p. 48) to suggest that styles, stances, and position changes on the board were thought to be 'marks of athleticism and aesthetics':

> When [Kelea] reached the place where the surf broke, she left that place to the kama'āina and paddles on out to wait for a wave to rise...when the fourth wave swelled up, she caught it and rode it to shore. As she caught the wave, she showed herself unsurpassed in skill and grace. The chiefs and people who were watching burst out in cheering. (Clark 2011, p. 32)

Kelea's physical capital, described here as 'skill' and 'grace', is celebrated by the spectators.

At this pre-colonial point in time symbolic and social capital was ascribed equally to female and male and there was a sense of equity on the waves. Surfing females were regarded to be athletic, strong, and empowered. One's sex did not differentiate access to waves or through the demonstration of aesthetics and athleticism. Instead, the surfing field provided a space for sharing the pleasures of motion on a wave, a sensuous experience on the same waves 'or even on the same board, it was stimulating for everyone and sometimes led to romantic interludes' (Clark 2011, p. 45). This is born out in Kamakau's writing:

> Elua a eha la heenalu o Kiha-a-Piilani me Koleaamoku I lilo ma ka heenalu ana, a me na hooipoipo ana no ka ike mai I keia kanaka maikai.

> Two to four days Kiha-a-Pi'ilani [male] and Kolea-moku [female] spent in surf-riding. Noticing his handsome appearance, Kolea-moku made love to him. (Ke Au Okoa. Dec 8, 1870 p. 1/Kamakau 1961 p. 25)

Drawing on Bourdieu's three-level methodological approach,[3] the field of power (first level) seemed dependent upon social relations of genetics, genealogy and marriage (second level), with classifications of 'royalty' positioning one strongly in fields such as surfing. In turn this provided access to geographical areas and waves, with surfing acting as an important cultural activity that positioned one strongly within society, in conjunction with the above mentioned positionings but also beyond them. Surfing practices seemed to rise above a sex hierarchy of female appearance and male perfomance, instead celebrating female physical prowess, positioning females and males as competent surfers.

COLONISATION AND PATRIOCOLONIAL BODIES CHANGING THE FIELD

As colonisation occurred, participation in cultural practices, including surfing, was disrupted with the colonizers' symbolic and physical violence in the form of systematic oppression and cultural marginalisation of *kamaʻāina* in nineteenth-century Hawai'i. These violence were enacted in the civil war, *Mahele* (a division of lands), dispossession of governance, missionary Christianity, and illegal annexation (Sai 2008; Walker 2011), and disrupted the very cultural framework that was embodied the field of surfing. Multiple styles of surfing disappeared and numbers declined:

> The introduction of new religions, new diseases, new economy, new forms of government, and new interests took Hawaiians in many different directions ... surfing changed into an activity practiced by individuals rather than a sport embraced by a nation. (Clark 2011, p. 33)

Also disappearing was the valuing of *wahine* (females) as strong and empowered competent surfers. *Wahine* were repositioned culturally by the colonial white patriarchal Western Christian (herein called patriocolonial) influences that positioned males as superior to females and *haoles* (Hawaiian term for people not native to Hawai'i or to denote Caucasian, European, and American ancestry) superior to *kamaʻāina* or *Kanaka Maole* (native Hawaiians). The positioning and practices of the sexes changed dramatically, this being reflected in the surfing field. Rather than colonial women being inducted into surfing and valued for their aesthetics and athleticism like wahine he'e nalu, repositioning by the dominating patriocolonial influences drastically reduced *wahine* participation and valued dependency of *haole* females on males. *Wahine* were positioned as female-below-male in a hierarchically dichotomised Western paradigm; as passive, as an object of patriocolonial gaze, as property, as servant, and as 'hula girl' (see Buck 1993; Trask 1993; Walker 2011).

At the same time, *haole* women became surfing participants as tandem riders only in relation to 'Beachboys'—*kama'āina* who were lifeguards, surf instructors, tour guides, and entertainers for tourists. As so little, to date, has been written about this relationship, it warrants greater attention to ascertain how power worked and where both were subservient within the power structures of patriocolonisation. Also needing further investigation is the assumed inactivity of *kama'āina wahine* in relation to surfing.

Haole authors, historians, and academics of the past and contemporary times, many embodying patriocolonial onto-epistemological frameworks, continue the popular narrative that *haole* (male and sometimes including male *kama'āina*) were responsible for surfing being 'pulled back from the brink of extinction and oblivion' (Kampion and Brown 2003, p. 24) for the 'revival and expansion' (Warshaw 2004, p. xii) of surfing and for the development of surfing as a modern sport, lifestyle, and leisure activity (see, e.g. Blake 1935; Finney 1966; Warshaw 2004). These accounts, prime in the construction of surfing's post-cultural-annihilation history and doxa, are pivotal to the field-habitus of the past one-hundred years. At the time of writing this chapter (2015), centennial celebrations, to which I will return, cement a convenient/particular history that denies narratives of cultural annihilation and deep forms of sexism and racism in surfing that remain today. Marginalised voices within the last hundred years have come and gone and the surfing field experienced diaspora particularly to California and Australia. The economies of exchange in surfing shifted in relation to new fields and cultural frameworks characterised by capitalism, geopolitical conditions, consumption, and technology. Counter-narratives of surfing such as the wahine/female surfing history and marginalised *kama'āina he'e nalu* history have struggled to be recognised and/or valued over time. However, as the changing field of communication diffuses hegemonic media and repositions previously marginalized authors with greater agency, these counter-narratives are proliferating. New insights or challenges to the patriocolonial histories are forming as *kama'āina* voices excavate knowledge from native Hawaiian texts and employ decolonialised epistemologies (demonstrated, for example by Clark 2011 and Walker 2011).

The surfing doxa was largely characterised by a field of power reflecting patriocolonial hegemony for over 100 years. This is established and/or illustrated in a multitude of academic and popular texts (e.g. Ford and Brown 2006; Kampion and Brown 2003; McGloin 2005; Moser 2008; Stedman 1997; Warshaw 2004. See also the burgeoning online websites for 'surfing history') the field of surfing changed dramatically from its pre-colonial roots. In summary, the 'resurgence' of surfing, as 'modern surfing', was framed through the patriocolonial pre-existing conditions. Legitimating authority was taken by *Haole* over *Kama'āina* and males over females in the surfing field, with dispositions that forefronted hegemonic masculinity and male *Haole* rights to waves and surfing history. Clearly, other factors such as race played an important part in the constitution of the field and the bodies constituting and constituted by the field. Such a claim has already been established (Walker 2011), but little work has captured the legitimating conditions of the patriocolonial sex binary, except in the more recent resurgence of female surfing in the 1970s, 1990s, and now. As I have argued elsewhere (lisahunter 2016, in press), the visibility and the repositioning of females to males off and on the waves, of *Haole* females to *Kama'āina* males, and of *Kama'āina wahine* to all meant the social and economic conditions prevailed to present a 'new' history of surfing and a differential access to resources such as waves and a physical culture associated with wave riding. Sex, and relatedly gender and heterosexuality, was pivotal in enforcing inequity, establishing a new dispositional order captured in modern surfing stereotypes of Euro-white, athletic and, strong male dominance, in relation to a relatively passive colonial femininity and sprinkled with other bodies from various geopolitical areas as surfing's diaspora spread into contemporary, perhaps post-colonial, times.

CONTEMPORARY (POST-COLONIAL) SURFING FIELD/S, HABITUS, AND CAPITAL

Surfing was 'modernised' after cultural rape and appropriation in Hawai'i. Prior to this modernisation, females and males surfed. In the modern form, (re)constituted in the early to mid-1900s, participants were repositioned in this field via sex. *Haole* males were increasingly dominant in numbers and as recipients, arbiters, and recorders of capital legitimation. *Kama'āina* males (*kane*) played a significant, if not relatively marginalised, part in developments, *haole* females played a particular role within a heterosexualized patriocolonial frame, and *kama'āina wahine he'e nalu* were almost completely erased from the field. Within the modern field, females have either been absent(ed) as competent athletes or gained symbolic capital through the (hetero) sexualized male gaze (see Booth 2001; Comer 2004; Henderson 2001; lisahunter 2006; Stedman 1997 and more recent findings that concur: Franklin 2013; Knijnik et al. 2010; lisahunter and emerald 2013; Olive 2013).

In the contemporary surfing field, as part of habitus, differentiation according to biologised sex works strongly as a marker of performance and appearance in a way that some have hailed as a feminist gain (Comer 2010). Much like that of early Hawaiian times, images of female dispositions characterised as competent surfers, athletic, strong, and empowered are beginning to be more present and celebrated. But this is only recent and, I would argue, also alongside paradoxical practices that undermine participation. The hidden, unwritten, and marginalised positioning of women in surfing is illustrated clearly in the lack of history about female surfing (lisahunter 2016) and the many barriers noted by those who did manage to surf and have these experiences recorded. The few biographies, memoirs, narratives, images, and general history captured in media about surfing females. For examples see *Gidget* (Kohner 1957); Layne Beachley's *Beneath the waves* (Gordon and Beachley 2008); Fiona Capp's (2003) *That oceanic feeling*; *Pam Burridge* (Stell 1992); as well as histories of surfing within the last one-hundred years such as Kampion and Brown (2003) and Warshaw (2004), which are witness to sexism, misogyny and the dominant sex/gender/sexuality order, undervaluing and diminishing access to economic, symbolic, and social capital for women.

Krista Comer's (2010) notion of 'critical localism' pays attention to the presence of female participation in surfing in the last century and their resistance to the alignment of surfing with masculinity and men. She accounts for females who continued to present themselves to and in the field, through physically surfing despite being the only female in the lineup. Local presence was also as competitors, often in competitions implicitly or even explicitly created for males as there were no female competitions. Some females started their own surf shops, surf lessons for females, surf magazines focusing on female surfers, and surf trips for females. Some started functional surfwear for females and some created organisations (e.g. Surfing Mums https://www.facebook.com/SurfingMumsAustralia) to encourage and support females surfing.

Layne Beachley, the recipient of much sexism and misogyny, traded her symbolic capital (seven-time ASP world surfing champion) and social capital (international and local surfing and business networks) to establish and maintain the highest prize winning purse competition—the Beachley Classic—for the World Championship Tour over seven years. Her aim was to lift the profile of female surfers and promote greater acknowledgement of their value within the field. To some extent, she resisted the sexualisation of women in the surfing field by insisting their athleticism was rewarded, with less focus on looks. While these successes have resulted in females being more strongly situated within the field and surfing being more culturally accessible for more females now as compared to twenty years ago, it is worth noting the ongoing practices of symbolic capital being tied to sexualisation and appearance for females, ongoing legitimation of surfing as masculine, and the attachment of non-athletic fashion consumption to female surfing.

The announcement of the 2015 World Surfing League schedule and prize money is telling in its economic capital afforded to surfers, dependent upon sex. Eligible females can access nine competitions as part of the Championship Tour (CT) with total prize money of US$262,500 for each competition, while eligible males can access eleven competitions each worth US$525,000. In the 'qualifying' competition (QS) schedule, where previous years' points determine who gains eligibility into the CT in the following year, 14 events are held for females, with the annual prize pool being US$462,000 and 34 events totalling US$3million are held for men (http://www.worldsurfleague.com/assets/2015_WSL_Schedule-11-29-14.pdf).

Without even going into issues of equity and equality, my point is that the economic capital available for translation into symbolic and social capital is dependent upon sex. Thirty-four male athletes have access to the CT and 332 to the QS while 17 females get CT experience and 105 are eligible for the QS. Other recent work gives detail to the way inaccessibility to economic capital afforded to male surfers' blocks female surfers' ability to develop and demonstrate their physical skill and therefore accrue various forms of capital and be positioned equally (see, e.g. Brennan 2016; Franklin 2013).

Other subtler forms of symbolic violence are practised within the field—ones those spectators are often unaware of. One such example is in the scheduling of events when female and male surfers are at the same venue. Many of my interviews with female surfers have stated they get the poorer tide and waves. This means that they cannot perform to the standard they are capable of, the men getting the most ideal conditions to show their stuff. A recent QS event, the Hurley Australian Open was won first by Laura Enever in the Women's competition and second by Kolohe Andino in the Men's competition. The recognition of this in the reporting of the event that focuses on Andino and not Enever in the website banners (http://www.worldsurfleague.com/events/2015/mqs/1199/hurley-australian-open accessed 09 February 2015) reflects the positioning of the first world champion, Phyllis O'Donnell (and no doubt many other female surfers) as absent or at best 'second' to the default champion named as the male champion.

Competitions are framed as 'Men's and Women's', females being mentioned second, 'Surfest 2015 in Newcastle, Australia, features the Burton Automotive Pro (Men's ASP 6-Star) and the Burton Automotive Women's Classic (Women's ASP 1-Star), along with supporting events' (http://www.surfest.com/live/ accessed 19 February 2015). At the same time, sexism is getting noticed and communicated in new forms of media such as blogs and social media (e.g. see http://jezebel.com/13-year-old-girl-perfectly-blasts-surf-mag-for-how-they-1554990275?utm_campaign=socialfow_jezebel_twitter&utm_source=jezebel_twitter&utm_medium=socialflow and http://www.theinertia.com/surf/13-year-old-girl-points-out-surfings-latest-problem-with-sexism-but-its-more-complicated-than-that/) where a letter from a 13-year-old to the well-known surfing magazine *Tracks* expresses her disappointment with the lack of articles and images about female surfers, a sexualised image being all that was on offer. What could be captioned as symbolic violence, when announced as such it is often met with claims of being 'too sensitive' or 'the men are better'. While both claims might be unpacked in a whole chapter each, and therefore not appropriate for this one chapter, the point is that both statements along with the original practice of male domination or female erasure reinforce the naturalised sex division with the dominant positioning of male within the field of surfing. This is in stark contrast to the state of the field described at the beginning of this chapter.

Leslie Heywood and Shari Dworkin (2003) captured the notion 'babe factor' as 'the institutionalisation in consumer culture of a new ideal of female athletic strength folded into and set atop that most classic figure of sexist discipline: female beauty' and 'the phenomenon of women posing for men's magazines in ways that call attention to their sexuality, specifically their heterosexuality' (p. 76). Such a habitus is often recognised as the embodiment of surfing, until recently only as passive female sexualised other. With the industry-led development of surfing in the late twentieth century to now, the female consumer has become a major target: 'The new Generation Y surfer girl represents big bucks. Her visualisation and emotional profile is currently exported as one highly desirable figure of normative young American femininity—a significant new player in a global marketplace selling liberated gender identities and ideals' (Comer 2010, p. 114). Comer notes that this acts to govern those who do not fit the profile being marketed. Female surfers who are claiming beauty and strength, with this practicec being considered as the stealth feminism of the Third Wave (Heywood and Dworkin 2003; Heywood 2008) are arguably alienating their non-babe sisters as the symbolic 'beauty' is still contained within a patriocolonial doxa (lisahunter, in press). I am wondering whether this acts as a form of misrecognition by those who buy into this doxa, still claiming sex as symbolic capital for personal gain—relegitimising a capital that does not really affect one's ability to surf but perhaps one's chances of being allowed more space within the surfing field, off and on the wave.

As other positions within the field are taken up by females it is interesting to note what forms of capital have brought them there and what legitimising of female surfing they are in a position to enact. For example, Rosy Hodge, a former WCT competitor, joined the commentary team for that competition in 2014 (http://surf.transworld.net/1000167081/news/asp-announces-commentary-team-2014-season/ accessed 19 February 2014). Commentary, like many of the positions within the media, has largely been staffed by men. It had not gone unnoticed by the many blogs commenting on the team that Rosy had the social capital of a recent world tour competitor but first and foremost the symbolic capital of a 'babe' or sexy blonde (for reactions see, e.g. http://stabmag.com/rating-the-2014-asp-commentary-team-so-far/). The question remains, could a 'non-babe' have been positioned as a commentator, or for that matter any other public media position in the surfing field?

A recent email prompt from WSL suggests, I celebrate '25 years of champions' with a focus on Stephanie Gilmore. The inclusion of physical capital in terms of celebrating Gilmore's 'strength' is a recent addition to women's surfing and as a marketable aspect of a habitus for females. Her 'powerful but fluid style' ... 'without fear' ... [and with] 'strength and determination' was often attributed to questionable female dispositions outside normalised patriocolonial femininity. Now, international female competitors, media, and public imagery celebrate the benefits of increasing economic, symbolic, and cultural capital for females in surfing. As a result of feminist work of earlier female surfers remaining in the field of surfing and some repositioning of females more centrally or in greater numbers in the field, one might surmise that the female athletic habitus is now highly valued and encouraged.

Females now have access to boards relative to their body and performance style, to other economic resources to travel and buy related goods, to an athletic habitus valued as athletic, to female role model biographies and histories of competence in the surf, and are beginning to enter mainstream media. However, the emphasis on female legitimation within the surfing field through practices associated with appearance still seems tied to the patriocolonial doxa supporting sexism and misogyny. The 'babe' factor acts as symbolic violence, misrecognised for capital that may be traded for resources that enhance performance, for example in the form of sponsorship as economic capital. The juxtaposition of Stephanie Gilmore as athletic and aesthetic is captured in a recent website reporting the surfer's nude photo shoot (http://indo-surflife.com/2011/10/stephanie-gilmore-poses-nude-for-espn-magazine/ accessed 19 February 2015) and 'falling ou' of surfwear clearly not designed for surfing performance (http://www.dailymail.co.uk/tvshowbiz/article-2539595/Stephanie-Gilmore-exposes-surf-skills-Vogue-beach-shoot.html). This is in stark contrast to the many surfwear advertisements using high-performance male surfers in performance boardshorts and demonstrating high levels of skill (for instance, Mick Fanning with Rip Curl http://www.ripcurl.co.nz/mens/collections/mirage-boardshorts.html or John John Florence with Hurley). I have argued elsewhere that 'Under the guise of athletic performance, a patriarchal thread continues to tie up a particular sex, gender and sexuality order that is neither new nor productive for full female participation' (lisahunter, in press).

SEX, ILLUSIO, AND SYMBOLIC VIOLENCE—PATRIOCOLONIAL LOGICS OF PRACTICE

The symbolic violence of sexism in surfing has had a long history, yet some suggest sexism is dead or that females are working with it in ways that reclaim power (e.g. Olive 2013; Rinehart 2005; Waitt 2008). In 2014 Ellie-Jean Coffey, a twice Australian national surfing champion and a World Junior runner-up, spoke on the Australian morning TV show Sunrise, introduced with 'She's putting sex into surfing, and it's making waves' (for more details see http://www.theinertia.com/businessmedia/surfing-and-sex-appeal-if-youve-got-it-flaunt-it/#ixzz3SAxvkK3f) while other (female) surfers showcase underwear or flesh or sexual poses, not surfing (see, e.g. stories on Alana Blanchard 'Sexy surfer' https://www.youtube.com/watch?v=HWZZ_Q3TbmY; Anastasia Ashley's 'Sexy surfer' https://www.youtube.com/watch?v=Txi2EQYE6-w, or Stephanie Gilmore in https://www.youtube.com/watch?v=GCji6TiJjbE). Other (male) surfers have also positioned female surfers as being 'less' (see, e.g. http://www.theinertia.com/surf/laird-on-cnn-maya-gabeira-doesnt-have-enough-skill-burle-didnt-set-world-record/#modal-close) or with explanations for competence only if 'surfing like a man' (see for instance http://www.redbull.com/en/surfing/stories/1331676061470/carissa-moore-surfs-like-a-man accessed 25 September 2014).

At the same time, others are speaking back with calls of 'hipster sexism', renaming an old problem,

Welcome to the world of hipster sexism: the brother of surfer sexism; cousin of liberal sexism; and son of retro sexism. Under the umbrella of "self-aware sexism", this is the use of mockery, irony or satire to say, "Look, we're in the post-feminist era, so it's safe to pretend we're back in the 1950s." (Sea Kin https://seakin.wordpress.com/2016/03/25/hipster-sexism-brother-of-surfer-sexism/ retrieved March 25, 2016)

And yet others are trying to (re)establish female surfers as not better but 'different' to males. Within a framework of athletic competence, Lauren Bickley notes 'And herein lies the most basic of principles. Men and women aren't the same. We are different. We are shaped differently, we are created differently, and, most importantly, we surf differently' (http://www.theinertia.com/surf/i-surf-like-a-girl-and-im-proud-of-it/ retrieved 17 February 2015). While essentialism and identity politics may indeed expose some of the complexities behind how females are positioned within the doxa of surfing, and their agency in (re)positioning themselves as an essentialised identity there remains structural inequality in access to economic resources such as sponsorship but also to acceptable dispositions outside normative versions of 'beauty' and sexiness.

Agency as Solution and Trap: Desexing Surfing

In an interview with contemporary Hawaiian surfer and cultural teacher, Tom Pohaku Stone, he talked about surfing being an embodiment of Hawaiian history, one that he works to model, relegitimate, revive, and relive albeit in a changed cultural context (Stone 2014). He spoke of women like Rell Kapolioka'ehukai Sunn, 'the queen of Makaha' and an iconic surfer in Hawai'i embodying competence in the water, like contemporary 'champions' such as Carissa Moore. As women (re)gain cultural value for their surfing habitus rather than appearance, there are certainly empowering practices in the field and dispositions. These include positive commentary by males, females taking legitimising roles and legitimating female competence, female competence becoming more visible and celebrated, and both sexes speaking against the objectification, sexism, misogyny, and sexualisation of female surfers. Yet at the same time female habitus and agency, as is the case for many of the female surfers embracing their sex for promotion, seems trapped within internalised sexism that re-establishes the attachment of capital to appearance.

In exploring the logics of practice in the surfing field, albeit mostly from the highly public and professional slice of the larger surfing field for the purpose of this chapter, I have used ethnographic methods from multiple perspectives, including historical, grassroots introductions to surfing, researching surfing, personal recreational experience, and from the position of spectator (e.g. lisahunter 2013, 2015). Unlike third wave feminism claiming empowerment, after taking up Bourdieu's methodology of field analysis to make sense of surfing, I suggest there is a reification of logics of sexism (lisahunter 2017, in press). In some instances, a form of backlash to put female surfing (back) in its place has meant the reification of sexism, where previously it had been reduced or countered (lisahunter 2014) indicating the fluid boundaries of the field and the struggle for capital. Using Bourdieu's tools to guide understanding surfing as a field with overlapping and counter-fields, where to explore surfing practices, identification of participants, capitals and their exchange and where things might not be as they seem on the surface I am convinced the continuing 'modern surfing' doxa underpinned by a patriocolonial system of values means the process of 'illusio' maintains sexism, new forms such as 'hipster sexism' reproducing hegemonic male positions and access to capitals.

Desexing surfing still seems a queer project (lisahunter 2017). Celebration of empowerment and equity for females surfing seems superficial and pre-emptive so practices continue to be scrutinised for their effect. So too does Bourdieu's field theory stimulate where to attempt to make differences and use my own research as an agency in attempting to produce more equitable and less oppressive spaces for females to surf. The ongoing project began with my experiences of surfing, an experience of distinction and 'fish out of water'. With empirical evidence from multiple sources and layers of the field, then identifying 'surfing participation' as the research object, Bourdieu's methodological guidance through the three-level field analysis provided a way to navigate and reveal the complexity of the social field. The third principle of his methodology, participant objectivation, has also been an important part of the journey. Bourdieu's notion of reflexivity (2004, 2007), not unproblematic in itself, nevertheless framed my investigation of my own position in the social space of surfing and surfing research (see, e.g. lisahunter 2013, 2014, 2015; Olive 2016) as well as guiding my sociopolitically committed practices within the field to encourage surfing to be a more positive social space (see, for instance, the instigation of http://www.waikato.ac.nz/wmier/news-events/surfing-social and collaboration in http://www.waikato.ac.nz/events/public-lectures/blue-spaces.shtml). Such practices seem to be part of a growing critical mass also attempting to impact the social field of surfing. One's presence/practice is an ongoing project of practice, for me challenged but not determined by understanding through Bourdieu, a presence aiming to reclaim positions of access to surfing resources and historical visibility in the imagination of who can be participating in surfing.

NOTES

1. The language 'sex' is used rather than 'gender' to denote the female/male binary biological classifications and set of relations that are inherently at play, significant categories used to distinguish people and mark their relations; taken for granted categories with related assumptions; and present in all historical and cultural spaces to which this chapter refers. The cultural classification system of 'gender' with femininity and masculinity as its markers is interrelated but only comes as a result of 'sex' classifications.

2. Kūlana heʻe nalu or the lineup is the social and physical order in the surf that controls who can catch the next wave. This order is played out by where the surfer sits to catch the wave at the crest, or where it first breaks. In contemporary surfing if one breaks from this order they are said to have 'dropped in' and the practice is regarded as very disrespectful.

3. Grenfell summarises these as:
  - Analyse the position of the field *vis-à-vis* the field of power.
  - Map out the objective structure of relations between the positions occupied by agents who compete for the legitimate forms of specific authority of which the field is a site.
  - Analyse the habitus of agents; the systems of dispositions they have acquired by internalising a deterministic type of social and economic condition. (2008, p. 211).

Acknowledgements I would like to thank elke emerald who provided support to complete this chapter, as well as critique and feedback on my ideas and writing. Also, to the editors Jacquie and Deb for their patience, valuable comments and copyediting.

REFERENCES

Blake, T. (1935). *Hawaiian surfriders*. Redondo Beach, CA: Mountain & Sea Publishers.

Booth, D. (2001). From bikinis to boardshorts: Wahines and the paradoxes of surfing culture. *Journal of Sport History, 28*(1), 3–22.

Bourdieu, P. (1973). Cultural reproduction and social reproduction. In R. K. Brown (Ed.), *Knowledge, education, and cultural change: Papers in the sociology of education* (Vols. 71–112). London: Tavistock.

Bourdieu, P. (1977). *Outline of a theory of practice*. Cambridge: Cambridge University Press.

Bourdieu, P. (1986). The forms of capital. In J. G. Richardson (Ed.), *Handbook of theory and research for the sociology of education* (pp. 241–258). New York: Greenwood Press.

Bourdieu, P. (1990). *The logic of practice*. Cambridge: Polity Press.

Bourdieu, P. (1998). *Practical reason. On the theory of action*. Cambridge: Polity Press.

Bourdieu, P. (2004). *Science of science and reflexivity* (Richard Nice, Trans.). Chicago: University of Chicago Press.

Bourdieu, P. (2007). *Sketch for a self-analysis*. Cambridge: Polity Press.

Brennan, D. (2016). Surfing like a girl: A critique of feminine embodied movement in surfing. *Hypatia, 31*(4), 907–922.

Buck, E. (1993). *Remaking paradise*. Philadelphia: Temple University Press.

Capp, F. (2003). *That oceanic feeling: The story of one woman's return to the water*. Sydney: Allen & Unwin.

Clark, J. (2011). *Hawaiian surfing: Traditions from the past*. Honolulu: University of Hawai'i Press.

Comer, K. (2004). Wanting to be Lisa: Generational rifts, girl power and the globalization of surf culture. In N. Campbell (Ed.), *American Youth Cultures* (pp. 237–265). Edinburgh: Edinburgh University Press.

Comer, K. (2010). *Surfer girls in the new world order*. London: Duke University Press.

Finney, B., & Houston, J. (1966). *Surfing: The sport of Hawaiian Kings (reprinted as Surfing: A history of the Ancient Hawaiian sport. San Francisco: Pomegranate Artbooks, 1996)*. Rutland, VT: Charles Tuttle.

Ford, N., & Brown, D. (2006). *Surfing and social theory: Experience, embodiment, and narrative of the dream glide*. London: Routledge.

Franklin, R. (2013). *Making waves—Contesting the lifestyle marketing and sponsorship of female surfers*. (PhD). Gold Coast: Griffith University.

Gordon, M., & Beachley, L. (2008). *Layne Beachley: Beneath the waves*. Melbourne: Random House Publishers.

Henderson, M. (2001). A shifting line up: Men, women, and *Tracks* surfing magazine. *Continuum, 15*(3), 319–332.

Heywood, L. (2008). Third-wave feminism, the global economy, and women's surfing: Sport as stealth feminism in girls' surf culture. In A. Harris (Ed.), *Next wave cultures: Feminism, subcultures, activism* (pp. 63–82). New York: Routledge.

Heywood, L., & Dworkin, S. (2003). *Built to win: The female athlete as cultural icon*. Minneapolis: University of Minnesota Press.

Kamakau, S. M. (1961). *Ruling Chiefs of Hawai'i*. Hawai'i: Kamehameha Schools Press.

Kampion, D., & Brown, B. (2003). *A history of surf culture*. Koln: Taschen.

Knijnik, J., Horton, P., & Cruz, L. (2010). Rhizomatic bodies, gendered waves: Transitional femininities in Brazilian Surf. *Sport in Society: Cultures, Commerce, Media, Politics, 13*(7), 1170–1185.

Kohner, F. ([1957] 2001). *Gidget: The little girl with big ideas*. New York: Penguin Publishing Group.

lisahunter. (2006). *Fueled by desire: Token hotties, celebrities, girls who kick arse and hardcore candy as possible representations in board cultures*. Paper presented at the Thirteenth Commonwealth International Sport Conference, Melbourne.

lisahunter. (2006, September). *'Girls Get Out There Day' and 'Surf Jam': Reinscribing gender and consumer discourses or new spaces for participation?* Paper presented as Invited speaker for the Active'06: Making a Difference Conference, Western Australian Department of Sport and Recreation, Perth.

lisahunter, (2013). What did I do-see-learn at the beach? Surfing festival as a cultural pedagogical sight/site. In L. Azzarito & D. Kirk (Eds.), *Physical culture, pedagogies and visual methods* (pp. 144–161). New York: Routledge.

lisahunter., (2014). *Shifting tides: The NZ Surf Festival 2014* (pp. 1–22). Kirikiriroa: The University of Waikato.

lisahunter, (2015). 'Stop': 'No'. Exploring social suffering in practices of surfing as opportunities for change. In W. S. Lisahunter & E. Emerald (Eds.), *Pierre Bourdieu and physical capital* (pp. 47–56). Abingdon: Routledge.

lisahunter, (2016). Becoming visible. Visual narratives of 'female' as a political position: The history, perpetuation, and disruption of patriocolonial pedagogies? In H. Thorpe & R. Olive (Eds.), *Women in action sport cultures: Identity, politics, experience and pedagogy* (pp. 319–347). Basingstoke: Palgrave Macmillan.

lisahunter. (in press). The long and short of (performance) surfing: Tightening patriarchal threads? *Sport in Society*.

lisahunter. (2017). Desexing surfing? (Queer) pedagogies of possibility. In D. Z. Hough-Snee & A. Eastman (Eds.), *Radical politics, global culture: A critical surf studies reader*. (pp. 263-283). Durham: Duke University Press.

lisahunter, & emerald, e. (2013). *A little-big event: The NZ Surf festival 2013*. Kirikiriroa: The University of Waikato.

McGloin, C. (2005). *Surfing nation(s)-surfing country(s)*. Doctoral Thesis. Wollongong: Wollongong University.

Moser, P. (Ed.). (2008). *Pacific passages: An anthology of surf writing*. Honolulu: University of Hawai'i Press.

Olive, R. (2013). *Blurred lines: Women, subjectivities and surfing*. Doctoral Thesis, The University of Queensland, Brisbane.

Olive, R., McCuaig, L., & Phillips, M. (2015). Women's recreational surfing—a patronising experience. *Sport, Education & Society, 20*(2), 258–276.

Olive, R., Thorpe, H., Roy, G., Nemani, M., lisahunter, Wheaton, B., & Humberstone, B. (2016). Surfing together: Exploring the potential of a collaborative ethnographic moment. In H. Thorpe & R. Olive (Eds.), *Women in action sport cultures: Politics, identity, experience and pedagogies* (pp. 45–68). Basingstoke, UK: Palgrave Macmillan.

Rinehart, R. (2005). 'Babes' & boards: Opportunities in new millennium sport? *Journal of Sport and Social Issues, 29*(3), 232–255.

Sai, K. (2008). *The American occupation of the Hawaiian kingdom: Beginning the transition from occupied to restored state*. Ph.D. dissertation, University of Hawai'i: Mānoa.

Stedman, L. (1997). From Gidget to Gonad Man: Surfers, feminists and postmodernisation. *Journal of Sociology, 33*(1), 75–90.

Stell, M. (1992). *Pam Burridge*. Sydney: Angus & Robertson.

Stone, T. (2014). Interview transcription, May 17.

Trask, H. (1993). *From a native daughter*. Monroe: Common Courage Press.

Waitt, G. (2008). Killing waves: Surfing, space and gender. *Social and Cultural Geography, 9*(1), 75–94.

Walker, I. (2011). *Waves of resistance: Surfing and history in twentieth-century Hawai'i*. Honolulu: University of Hawai'i Press.

Warshaw, M. (2004). *The encyclopedia of surfing*. Camberwell: Penguin Books Australia, Vic.

PART III

Explorations utilising Bourdieu and Other Methodological Approaches

Part 3 of this book includes chapters that explore the fields utilising Bourdieu with other methodological approaches. This introduction to the section will discuss these chapters in the light of the opening and closing remarks on working with field, by Albright and Hartman in the introduction to the book and Grenfell in the conclusion to this book. Utilising the processes of Bourdieu's field analysis with other theories and methods, while challenging, is entirely possible, as Bourdieu's approach to field is methodologically plastic. Bourdieu says that method should be compatible with the object of analysis, with the questions that researchers are attempting to answer. He intentionally developed field analysis as a practice to investigate specific objects of analysis and was himself willing to engage in other methods.

In addition to an engagement with Bourdieu's methodological moves in field analysis, all of these chapters are, in some ways, critiques of Bourdieu. The authors are attempting to solve specific research questions to uncover what can be seen using Bourdieu that would not otherwise have been visible. In this process, they have found the need to move beyond Bourdieu to seek answers to their methodological dilemmas. They have been drawn to other major contemporary theorists who have also addressed field in their work: Fairclough, a language analyst and social theorist; Fligstein and McAdam, social movement and social change theorists; Foucault, a philosopher and sociologist; Harvey, a historian; and Bernstein, an educational sociologist.

The authors of the four chapters in this part of the book have utilised these theorists either with, beside or against Bourdieu. Hartman and Albright, in Chap.13, and Nash, in Chap. 14, extend Bourdieu by utilising other theories with Bourdieu to overcome the perceived inadequacies or to do things that Bourdieu did not attempt. Brook, in Chap. 15, describes attempts to marry Bourdieu with Foucault and the conceptual difficulties that arise, suggesting cultural researchers undertake a different analysis alongside a Bourdieusian field analysis, rather than attempting a synthesis of Bourdieu and Foucault. In Chap. 16, Maton uses Bourdieu against Bourdieu, to point out shortcomings in Bourdieu's practice. He suggests Legitimation Code Theory (LCT), a practice originating from Bernstein, can be utilised to do the kind of relational thinking Bourdieu insists is required of social theorists.

It is important to analyse what is gained and what gets lost in these attempts to critique and extend Bourdieu. Most authors in this section explore what happens when a researcher attempts to marry methods from other theorists with Bourdieusian field analysis. They have made pragmatic decisions to ignore epistemological differences and look at their object of analysis in different ways. The chapters illustrate the different effects on the analysis that become possible utilising other approaches with and beside Bourdieu.

Some theorists sit more comfortably with Bourdieu than others. Critical Discourse Analysis as developed by Norman Fairclough analysed field in a linguistic sense. Bourdieusian scholars have explored CDA and field analysis (Grenfell, 2011); Bourdieu has explored language use in fields (Bourdieu, 1991); and indeed, Bourdieu and Fairclough (Fairclough, 2000) each saw some potential benefits, as well as some dangers in marrying each other's methods and approaches to language and field.

Hartman and Albright in Chap. 13, in this section of the book, and Widin in Chap. 5, earlier in the book, describe how they utilised CDA with Bourdieu to delve deeply into the practices of the particular fields that are the object of their analyses, to illustrate how players operate within a field using text and text features strategically to augment their cultural capital and to shore up their positions within the field. While Bourdieu did not specifically attempt this kind of analysis, utilising CDA with Bourdieu in this way is quite compatible with Bourdieu's project of analysing fields. Hartman and Albright describe the ways CDA was used in conjunction with Bourdieusian field analysis and with strategic action field analysis, to further operationalise field and illustrate how texts work as strategic moves by players in both dominant and subordinate positions in fields.

It is also possible to shore up the gaps and shortcomings found in Bourdieu by utilising other methods with field analysis. In Chap. 14, Nash utilises Harvey's notions of spacio-temporality to explore the physical and relational aspects of space and time, to overcome his perceived shortcoming in Bourdieu's construct of dualism of material space and abstract relations, which Nash suggests is not fully adequate to the task of analysing the process of change.

Some authors suggest it is possible to discover different stories by utilising a different method alongside Bourdieu. Brook, in Chap. 15, rejects attempts to theoretically bridge Bourdieusian and post-Foucauldian accounts of power and cultural practice. Instead, he argues that cultural field researchers should avoid the temptation of synthesising approaches in pursuit of an even more comprehensive theoretical construct, and articulate instead the various options for coordinating discrete methodological constructs. He argues that a more subtly differentiated account of 'practice' in studying the cultural field will bring to light the differing and local meanings and uses of culture for actors, thereby resisting the tendency to reduce all examples of cultural practice to supporting examples of a broader theory (whether that of 'social reproduction' or 'the social' as governmental assemblage).

In Chapter 16, Maton argues that while Bourdieu powerfully argues for a genuinely relational analysis that is a revolutionary transformation of our vision of the social world, field theory does not itself fully embody relational thinking. Maton suggests that Bourdieu's conceptual framework represents an unfinished 'mental revolution' that needs augmenting to achieve Bourdieu's aims. He reaches 'beyond the field theory we know' to Legitimation Code Theory (LCT), a framework that, he suggests, reveals the organising principles underlying fields, capitals, habitus and practices. Maton argues that his example of a study of Chinese students in an Australian university illustrates how LCT concepts embody Bourdieu's mental revolution and so can help others to achieve his relational gaze.

In the introduction to this book, Albright and Hartman emphasise the risks involved in taking a reflexive stance on research and suggest that Bourdieu's mature conceptual and analytical moves in certain empirical research projects offer some very useful examples and tools for analysing fields. The first three chapters in this final section of the book illustrate ways that Bourdieusian scholars are attempting to operational-ise these tools and build vertically upon them. Chap. 16, by Maton, is an attempt to realise Bourdieu's vision of relational thinking by drawing upon Bernstein's code theory.

While these attempts to extend upon Bourdieu are to be commended, it is also worth sounding a note of caution to Bourdieusian schol-ars attempting to extend upon Bourdieu. In the concluding afterword to the book, Grenfell returns to discussions of reflexivity and method, emphasising that Bourdieu's theory of practice is a single epistemological vision that he unpacks across time throughout his whole life. He reit-erates that the relationship between theory and practice in field work raises issues about our own relation to the work as researchers and with-out reflexivity researchers simply reproduce their own dispositional views and relations to the research object. Grenfell also cautions that while there is not a fixed method, nor an orthodoxy within Bourdieusian field analysis, scholars utilising Bourdieu need to be rigorous in their analy-sis of the field and in a reflexivity of their own positionality in the field. Both Grenfell and Albright and Hartman describe the range and types of moves necessary in a field analysis to ensure this rigour and reflexivity.

The chapters in this section of the book are attempting to build on Bourdieu's field theory while simultaneously attempting a reflexive stance to the object of analysis and to the methods employed. Their efforts and the degrees of success they have reached in building upon Bourdieu to continue the revolutionary work of his oeuvre are to be celebrated.

REFERENCES

Bourdieu, P. (1991). *Language and symbolic power* (G. Raymond & M. Adamson, Trans.). Cambridge: Polity Press in association with Basil Blackwell.

Fairclough, N. (2000). Discourse, social theory and social research: the discourse of welfare reform. *Journal of Sociolingusitics*, 4(2), 163–195.

Grenfell, M. (Ed.). (2011). *Bourdieu, Language and Linguistics*. London: Continuum.

CHAPTER 13

Conceptualising Strategies Open to Players Within the Field of Australian Boys' Education

Deborah Hartman and James Albright

INTRODUCTION

This chapter describes how Bourdieu's concept of field was operation-alised in a study of Australian boys' education from 1996 to 2006. Building vertically upon Bourdieu's conceptualisations of field (Bourdieu 1990, 2005), the methods of strategic field analysis (Fligstein and McAdam 2012) and Critical Discourse Analysis (CDA) (Fairclough 2003; Wallace 1992) were utilised in conjunction with Bourdieusian field analysis in the study. The methodological moves in the study enabled a forensic examination of the strategic ways newer and established play-ers attempted to work within the hierarchically structured layers of the field to enhance their cultural and economic capital, from either domi-nant or subordinate positions. Such a multi-layered analysis allowed the

D. Hartman (✉) · J. Albright
University of Newcastle,
Callaghan, Australia

© The Author(s) 2018
J. Albright et al. (eds.), *Bourdieu's Field Theory and the Social Sciences*,
https://doi.org/10.1007/978-981-10-5385-6_13

complexities and intersections of differences and identities among players and their texts to be laid bare for examination as components of possible moves open to players within the structures of the field.

THE CASE STUDY: MOVES IN THE FIELD OF BOYS' EDUCATION

The case study briefly described here was completed in 2014 as a Ph.D study by one author of the chapter (Hartman 2014) supported by the other as her primary Ph.D supervisor. During the study period, Deborah worked as a boys' education consultant to schools and an academic attached to the Family Action Centre (FAC) at the University of Newcastle. The FAC has an established reputation for strengths-based, practitioner-focused research and teaching. It played a professional development and policy advocacy role, advocating for a public health approach to the well-being of men and boys in families and communities. Academics in the FAC entered boys' education debates and activities in schools from this perspective. The Ph.D study moved beyond this perspective to an analysis of the field of boys' education. Utilising the methodological and conceptual tools of field analysis required and enabled the researcher to move beyond the sub-field she knew, working and writing exclusively as a practitioner/advocate for specific approaches to the needs of boys in education, to examine the positionality of practice and practitioners in the field of education and the sub-field of boys' education. It led towards a rigorous and reflexive analysis of her own and other positions in the field.

CONCEPTUALISING THE FIELD OF AUSTRALIAN BOYS' EDUCATION

Bourdieu's theories and practice of field analysis were particularly useful in conceptualising Australian boys' education. The field is a meta-theoretical, open concept that defines the structure of the social setting in which agents operate (Bourdieu and Wacquant 1992).

This study of the Australian field of boys' education study began with a detailed listing of events, including the production of texts, occurring in Australian boys' education from 1996 to 2006, a period of change and contestation. Following on from this initial list, field theory was utilised to examine the positionality of players instrumental in these events. The aim was to move on from the initial phase delimiting the field based on the events in the period, to a categorisation of these events and their significance in the field. The study examined positions in the field and identified how the previously unthinkable question, "What about the boys?" was read by the different players in the field. Why was it unthinkable? Who was called to arms by this question?

The overarching power of the state in a dominated field such as education was evident by examples of state intervention, such as the 1996 federal policy change from a girls' education strategy document to a gender equity in schools policy, as well as the establishment of two well-funded federal programmes, Boys' Education Lighthouse Schools Programme and Success for Boys programme (Department of Education Employment and Workplace Relations 2007). There were numerous interventions by the political field such as the parliamentary inquiry into the education of boys that received over 230 written submissions and heard 235 witnesses across all states and territories (Commonwealth of Australia 2002). Several research reports were commissioned by the government and produced by academics with established reputations (Alloway et al. 2002; Lingard et al. 2002). Newer players, such as Richard Fletcher (1997, 1999), from the FAC convened significant conferences that were well attended by practitioners and supported by state sponsorship and began to produce publications aimed at practitioners.

Examining these empirical events as actions within a field enabled the researcher to interrogate the volume and nature of events in the social field of Australian boys' education from 1996 to 2006, compared to the periods immediately prior to and after this period. Imagining these events as actions in a field brought into relief a conceptual model of the hierarchical layers of the field of boys' education and its relation to the proximal fields of politics and journalism.

The relationship between Bourdieu's notions of dominant and subordinate positions within social fields (Bourdieu and Passeron 1990) and the concept of knowing strategic actions of players (Fligstein and McAdam 2012) was applied to this analysis in ways that enabled the various and complex intersections between positions within the field to be foregrounded. This was achieved by moving in and out of the finer-grained analysis of each corpus of texts produced within each of the hierarchical layers of the field of boys' education and those produced in the proximal field of journalism, towards an overall conceptualisation of fields.

Utilising field theory in this study allowed for an interrogation of: how the field of boys' education has changed over time; which players have influenced the field; which ideas, ideologies and concepts have been transferred from one set of discourses to another and how the discourses within different genres have influenced each other; and importantly, how particular discourses can influence the actions of people in the field (Bourdieu 1993). It allowed for an interrogation of several significant aspects of strong fields suggested by Fligstein and McAdam (2012): agreements about what is at stake; who the players are and what positions they occupy; a consensus regarding the rules by which the field works; and a shared interpretive frame that allows those in the field to make sense of what other actors are doing in the field in a particular situation.

Notions of positions within the field and relations to other fields as conceived by Bourdieu and others with him (Benson and Neveu 2005; Swartz and Zolberg 2004) are the conceptual tools that were applied in the study of the intellectual field of boys' education by analysing the events that occurred from 1996 to 2006.

Fligstein and McAdam (2012) suggest that the boundaries of fields are not easy to define because boundaries are fluid and shift depending on the issues at stake and the situation at hand. They place a great deal of emphasis on the interdependence of fields, arguing that fields are often embedded within other fields in a vertical system, like a set of Russian dolls. While this is a useful metaphor for the hierarchical nature of fields, the complexity within and between fields needs to be carefully mapped in order to illustrate the multiple field relations that are possible.

Hierarchical Layers Within the Field of Boys' Education

Utilising this concept of a structured configuration of positions, the study analysed some significant interrelationships in the field. The metaphor of series of interlocking Russian dolls was operationalised to build a model of hierarchical fields within fields. This model provided a large-picture view of the location of boys' education in a series of sub-fields and proximal fields.

One set of relationships the model served to conceptualise was the interrelationships between the politics, policy, academic and practice as sub-fields of education. The heuristic of this hierarchy evokes and highlights distinctions between: the practice of education by practitioners such as teachers and principals of schools; the research conducted by academics through projects specifically commissioned or funded by the state; the policy developed by the state, in the form of the national government department overseeing all of these activities; and the products of specific political interventions into the field. It highlights the particular relationship between commissioned research and the political and policy purposes this research serves. This set of dolls evokes some significant social distinctions occurring in all fields, particularly the distinction between the practical or manual and the intellectual. The overarching power of the state dominating policy makers, academics and practitioners in the field is also highlighted here.

The hierarchical layers of the Russian dolls metaphor were also used to build a heuristic to illustrate that relationships within the equity discourses and practice in the field of education are also constructed hierarchically, with equity being only one discourse in education, and equity discourses containing gender equity in education, and discourses about girls' and boys' education as further sub-fields. This period represented a significant change from an equity focus on the education of girls, where feminist discourses were dominant, towards an equity focus on socio-economic groups and a particular focus on Aboriginal students' outcomes in education. Discourses about boys' education were framed by many players in terms of gender equity in education and by some in terms of universal and targeted education approaches relevant to boys and girls and particular groups of girls and boys. While there were some clear divisions between some feminist and some men's movement discourses, there were many complex intersections in players' positions and discourses in this highly contested period of change in education policy and practice.

In this approach to field analysis, the cultural distinctions made in each layer of fields can be highlighted and foregrounded. In singling out particular relationships, the representations are necessarily a simplification of the complexities of the whole set of possible field and inter-field relations (Bourdieu and Wacquant 1992). It needs to be acknowledged that any analysis of social reality cannot fully describe this reality. Particular distinctions were drawn to highlight what seemed significant in the analysis of boys' education from 1996 to 2006.

Taking these multiple perspectives enables the complexities and interwoven nature of fields to be shown explicitly. An important aspect of this kind of analysis is that each conceptualisation of one set of interrelationships enables a view of what could be lost in the trajectory from inner to outer layers of the field in that set of relationships. The specific cultural capital and cultural concerns of each sub-field or layer are at stake in these trajectories.

In any intellectual or social field, there are struggles for legitimisation—the right to exercise the "symbolic violence" of the domination of one set of ideas over others. This legitimisation produces an orthodoxy, or doxa in a field (Bourdieu 1990). Fligstein and McAdam (2012) theorise change and contestation as continuous in all fields, with skilled social players always jockeying for improvement in their positions or defending their privileges, depending on their positions as incumbents or challengers. A focus on these sets of field relationships allowed cultural contestations within the field to become foregrounded in ways that helped make sense of some of the major cultural struggles within the practices, academic policy and political discourses in the field at the time. Struggles over what constitutes legitimate topics for study in gender in education, which groups might legitimately be the subjects of equity studies, and what aspects of education are relevant to gender in education are highlighted. The emergence of arguments about "competing victims" and "which boys/which girls" can be made sense of in the light of the shock waves that echoed through each layer of the sets of dolls in the decade after a federal government policy change in 1996, which signalled the significant turn towards boys' education. These debates are examples of field struggles over what was at stake in the field. The rise of boys' education in this decade caused ripples and some ruptures throughout all layers of the sets of dolls. The shock waves moved through the layers of the dolls in both directions, creating instability in the field and fierce contestation over the limited capital available.

Possible Moves and Positions in the Field

Recent Bourdieusian theorists of education emphasise that the concept of the field should not lead to an objectification of social situations and social problems. They warn that merely identifying the positions, values and discourses in a field does not mean that everything is known about a social problem in that field. Indeed, they re-emphasise Bourdieu's original concept of field as metaphor for a social site, existing only relationally, as a set of possibilities or a series of moves that could be made by people or institutions engaged in a particular activity (Grenfell and James 2004; Nash 1999).

The heuristic shown in Fig. 13.1 represents possible moves and flows between positions in the field during this period of change and contestation. Following Albright (2006), this Bourdieusian heuristic allows us to make clear the relationships between the moves players in the field make in cultural struggles for the legitimisation of ideas and the strategic moves they made for the relatively small amounts of economic capital in

THE FIELD OF BOYS' EDUCATION

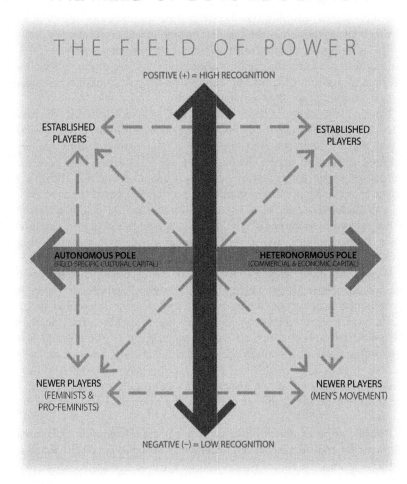

Fig. 13.1 The field of boys' education

the form of research grants, contracts and funding available to the players in the field at the time.

This heuristic represents the field of boys' education as a whole, dominated by the overarching field of power. The strategic game within any field is to achieve and maintain recognition within the field. The vertical axis represents possible positions (not people) in the field, along the continuum between high recognition in the field and low recognition. Bourdieu (1993) distinguishes between field-specific cultural capital and commercial or economic capital. The horizontal axis represents possible positions along the continuum between the autonomous pole in a field, where there is a large degree of autonomy over the cultural or ideological direction of the field, and the heteronomous pole, where commercialism or economic capital dominates the culture of the field.

Newer players entering the field are not well recognised in the field. They commence at the lower end of the recognition axis. Some established players have achieved recognition, so these positions are represented at the top of the diagram. The vertical dashed lines represent the possible trajectories towards and away from recognition. No player strives to move away from recognition, but this is a possible trajectory in field struggles if a cultural or ideological position in a field is overtaken or discredited by different ideas. This means established players can move down the recognition axis towards a similar position on this continuum with newer players who have not yet achieved recognition in the field.

Within any field, players have certain moves open to them within the agreed consensus by which the field works. Established players, or incumbents, usually operate to protect and further their field-specific capital and their established position in the field. One strategic move open to established players, to ensure domination of the cultural field, is to support newer players in their tradition, causing flows of capital to increase for both the established player and the newer player. Another is to ignore or discredit other newer players, who might be challengers to the illusio of the field and therefore to the positions of the established players.

Bourdieu argues that influxes of new players or agents in a field can be forces for transformation or conservation, depending on the situation in the field and the forces within and external to the field. Newer players can mount a challenge to the doxa of the field, challenging both the field-specific capital of established players and their positions within the field. Or they can build on the field-specific capital of established players, producing new versions of it, supported by the established players. The different actions of the players can cause flows of capital to go towards or away from established players or newer players in these different ways. A further strategy for newer players is to challenge the doxa of the field by joining together to create a new cultural tradition in the field. Depending on the stability of the field and the situation in the field, particularly in relation to the power of the state, all of these moves can cause flows either towards the autonomous pole or the commercial or heterodoxic pole in the field.

Prior to 1996, feminist and pro-feminist cultural positions dominated the field of gender equity and represented the autonomous pole of cultural capital in the field. In this period, cultural struggles in the field were between the various theoretical positions within feminism and pro-feminism and between feminist theorising and mainstream educational concerns for equity and measuring equity. The shift in focus towards boys' education after 1996 opened up different possibilities and positions for established and newer feminist and pro-feminist players. At the same time, newer men's movement players who had been instrumental in this shift entered the field, and the struggles for autonomy over doxa intensified.

The complexities of these interrelationships were examined in a number of ways, with each bringing into focus different aspects of the operations of the field. Moving between a bigger picture of the field and the various finer-grained analyses of the actions and texts in these sub-fields helped the researcher make sense of each corpus of texts produced by players in these sub-fields.

Epistemic Individuals and CDA

Bourdieu (1988) distinguishes between empirical individuals and epistemic individuals. Certain players in the field take on or represent epistemic positions in both the discourses of the field and in the social field where they operate. In order to define and identify existing potential conflicts, epistemic individuals were constructed in this study through an analysis of their position and involvement in the field of boys' education. They were identified through reference to the particular characteristics important in the analysis, such as their position as an established incumbent or newer challenger, or because of their stance on a cultural position, such as a pro-feminist male academic. These characteristics are different from those used in the ordinary description of an individual or in other scientific analyses of individuals, such as psychoanalysis.

While all players in a field seek to influence the field by the texts they produce, the texts of epistemic players are highly significant in that they show how the field as a whole is constructed by the various moves players make through texts. These moves always serve more than one purpose of the players. A critical discourse analysis of the ways texts are structured offers glimpses of the positions and claims to which the authors are prepared to commit and for which they attempt to convince others in knowing strategic ways.

Examining the texts of epistemic players enabled an analysis of texts produced for policy, practice and research in the field in relation to public and journalistic discourses about the field, seeing how agents and agencies are situated in a dynamic field of provisional balances, always subject to influence from the field of power and to change from within and without. It enabled an analysis of the field as a whole, examining how players take up positions and how discourses construct distinctions.

The study built on Wallace's (1992) use of CDA and Albright's (2008) heuristic for combining field and discourse analysis: conceptualising boys' education as a field; analysing the discourses in the field and the struggles over a normative doxa within those discourses; identifying certain epistemic individuals in the field who are illustrative of certain positions in the field; and analysing some texts produced by them as examples of the multi-layered work of text in the cultural, political and strategic struggles in the field.

Propositional, Cultural and Strategic Work of Texts

Bourdieu (1991) and Fairclough (2001) agree that in writing any text, a writer in a field has multiple purposes. The Albright model (2006) shows the interrelationships between social space, discourse practices within the field and ways texts are produced, consumed and interpreted in the field. Texts of any genre always do propositional, cultural or ideological, as well as strategic work for the author (Wallace 1992). Through the language features, authors make choices that present certain propositions or knowledge claims, they make certain assumptions about what can be taken for granted and need not even be mentioned, and they position the author within the discourses in the field in certain ways.

The framework shown in Table 13.1 was developed in the course of this study, based on Wallace's (1992) textual analysis, to illustrate how certain features of texts enable the propositional, cultural and strategic work to be done in any text in relation to the discourses in the field at the time and in relation to the strategic positions of players in the field.

An interpretation of these three aspects of the text can illustrate the different purposes of the writers. A close reading of the texts in relation

Table 13.1 The work of texts

Propositional—within the text	Cultural/Ideological—in relation to discourses	Strategic/political within the social/specialist field
Does the author assert the primacy of his or her own conceptual patterns? How do the language features enable this?	**Intertextuality** What is assumed about what the reader knows, agrees to, has heard or read elsewhere? Who is the idealised reader? Who is quoted or referenced? Who/what is not quoted or referenced? Who is named or implied as on their side/with them?	Why was this text written when it was? How does the author position him/herself in the field? Authoritative Deferential (who/what to) How do they invite the reader to interpret their text—do they invite the dominance of the author or allow other views and questioning?
	Evaluation What truth claims and actions is the author willing to commit to? What genres or discourses are named or implied as colonised or marginalised or colonising or marginalising? What ideas are regarded as obvious and unexceptional?	Who/what do they position as their ideal reader? How do they position others who are not their ideal reader? What/who do they emphasise? Why are they raising certain issues and not others, quoting certain people and not others, referring to certain themes and not others?

to activities in the field at the time can show the multiple intentions of the authors as they make propositional claims in ways that also enhance their own cultural and social capital in the field.

A forensic analysis, simultaneously examining the propositional, cultural and strategic moves by players in the field, can be seen by the textual choices within the field, tenor and mode in the texts selected. This deep analysis of individual texts provides an empirical basis for a Bourdieusian field analysis by illustrating how the authors of these texts sought to influence the cultural struggles in the field and increase their own cultural and social capital in the social space. This kind of critical reading, interpretation and processing of texts enables readers to make a deeper social analysis of the field. It allows an understanding of the operations or moves of power within the field and a mapping of the trajectory of cultural and economic capital through the intellectual, political and social fields.

Homologies Between Fields

Bourdieu (2005) writes that all fields are structured largely in the same ways and there are even more significant homologies between the political field, the journalistic field and the field of social science, where a great deal of research in boys' education sits. These homologies offer a strong explanatory lens for understanding the cultural struggles within and across these fields during the period of the research. This conceptualisation of similar aims across the three fields, and the different doxas of each field, offers a useful tool for an analysis of academic, practitioner and journalistic discourses on boys' education and the relational moves of players in these fields. The struggles to impose a particular vision and way of categorising gender in education issues, and portray this vision as legitimate, are deeply rooted in and cut across the political, journalistic and social science fields. They are embedded in the texts produced by players in the fields, with policy makers, academics and journalists taking similar cultural stances developing strong strategic alliances to enhance their positions within the constraints of their various field structures. The fields of social science (in this case especially gender studies, sociology of education and educational psychology), the political field and the field of journalism are proximal fields all vying for the right to describe and inscribe their vision of the world onto social reality.

CONCLUSION

The methods in this study enabled an analysis of the strategic ways players attempted to work within the hierarchically structured layers of the field to enhance their cultural and economic capital, from either dominant or subordinate cultural positions. The CDA of texts produced by certain epistemic players from different cultural positions in the field revealed their knowing strategic actions in enhancing their own individual positions in the field and that of their cultural positions in the field struggles over doxa. Such a multi-layered analysis allowed the complexities and intersections of differences and identities among players and their texts to be laid bare for examination.

Bourdieu and Wacquant (Bourdieu and Wacquant 1992) argue that a field is autonomous only to the extent to which it has the power to set its own agenda and to validate its own cultural capital. They suggested that education as a field has relative autonomy from economic and political power (Bourdieu and Passeron 1990). The study concluded that boys' education was not a strongly autonomous field. It was and remains a thin and dominated field. Only certain actions were open to players operating in this thin and dominated field, shaped by discourses about equity in education. Divisions were constructed by interventions of the state. Players operated both unconsciously and in knowing strategic ways to enhance their cultural capital and strategic positions within the field and to exercise the symbolic violence of their cultural positions on the field of boys' education and on the public's views of boys' education. These struggles were conducted within the hierarchical field structures of education, intersecting with the proximal fields of social sciences and journalism.

Working with concepts of the field in conjunction with CDA allowed the researcher to reach conclusions about struggles in the field that would not have been revealed by an examination of boys' education from within the positionality of strengths-based practitioner advocate within the field. It brought an awareness of the complexities of field structures and field struggles. It brought a different awareness of the forces for reproduction and change and the constraints imposed by the structures of any field. Field analyses of this type can reinvigorate and revitalise fields based on a more reflexive, strategic and knowing actions of players. Making these distinctions clear may assist in reinvigorating and reimagining the field in productive ways.

References

Albright, J. (2006). Literacy education after Bourdieu. *The American Journal of Semiotics, 22*(1–4), 107–127.

Albright, J. (2008). Problematics and generative possibilities. In J. Albright & A. Luke (Eds.), *Pierre Bourdieu and literacy Education* (pp. 11–32). New York: Routledge.

Alloway, N., Freebody, P., Gilbert, P., & Muspratt, S. (2002). *Boys, literacy and schooling: Expanding the repertoires of practice.* Canberra: Department of Education, Science and Training.

Benson, R., & Neveu, E. (Eds.). (2005). *Bourdieu and the journalistic field.* Cambridge: Polity Press.

Bourdieu, P. (1988). *Homo academicus* (P. Collier, Trans.). Cambridge: Polity Press in association with Basil Blackwell.

Bourdieu, P. (1990). *In other words: Essays towards a reflexive sociology* (M. Adamson, Trans.). Cambridge: Polity Press.

Bourdieu, P. (1991). *Language and symbolic power* (G. Raymond & M. Adamson, Trans.). Cambridge: Polity Press.

Bourdieu, P. (1993). *Sociology in question* (R. Nice, Trans.). London: Sage.

Bourdieu, P. (2005). The political field, the social science field and the journalistic field. In R. Benson & E. Neveu (Eds.), *Bourdieu and the journalistic field*. Cambridge: Polity.

Bourdieu, P., & Passeron, J. (1990). *Reproduction in education, society, and culture* (R. Rice, Trans.). London: Sage.

Bourdieu, P., & Wacquant, L. (1992). *An invitation to reflexive sociology*. Chicago: University of Chicago Press.

Commonwealth of Australia. (2002). *Boys: Getting it right. The report on the Inquiry into the Education of Boys*. Canberra: Australian Government Publisher.

Department of Education Employment and Workplace Relations. (2007). Boys' Education Lighthouse Schools. Retrieved February 12, 2007, from http://www.dest.gov.au/sectors/school_education/policy_initiatives_reviews/key_issues/boys_education/bels.htm.

Fairclough, N. (2001). *Language and power* (2nd ed.). Harlow: Longman.

Fairclough, N. (2003). *Analysing discourse: Textual analysis for social research*. London: Routledge.

Fletcher, R. (1997). *Improving boys' education: A manual for schools*. Newcastle, NSW: Men and Boys Project, Family Action Centre, University of Newcastle.

Fletcher, R. (1999). Leadership on the ground. In R. Fletcher, D. Hartman, & R. Browne (Eds.), *Leadership in boys' education*. Newcastle: Boys in Schools Program, University of Newcastle.

Fligstein, N., & McAdam, D. (2012). *A theory of fields*. Oxford: Oxford University Press.

Grenfell, M., & James, D. (2004). Change *in* the field—chang*ing* the field: Bourdieu and the methodological practice of educational research. *British Journal of Sociology of Education, 25*(4), 507–523.

Hartman, D. (2014). *Educating boys: What's your problem? A field and discourse analysis of boys' education in Australia from 1996 to 2006*. Ph.D, University of Newcastle, Newcastle Australia. Retrieved from http://hdl.handle.net/1959.13/1054694.

Lingard, B., Martino, W., Mills, M., & Bahr, M. (2002). *Research report addressing the educational needs of boys*. Canberra: Department of Education, Science and Training.

Nash, R. (1999). Realism in the sociology of education: 'Explaining' social differences in attainment. *British Journal of Sociology of Education, 20*(1), 107–125.

Swartz, D., & Zolberg, V. (Eds.). (2004). *After Bourdieu: Influence, critique, elaboration*. Dordrecht: Klewer Academic Publishers.

Wallace, C. (1992). Critical literacy awareness in the EFL classroom. In N. Fairclough (Ed.), *Critical language awareness*. Longman UK: Essex.

CHAPTER 14

Field Theory, Space and Time

Chris Nash

A scientific community is a site where people struggle for truth. Pierre
Bourdieu (Bourdieu and Chartier, 2010, p. 47) was committed to the
validity of truth as a concept and truth seeking as a practice, particularly
with respect to the social sciences (which for him included humanities
disciplines such as history). While the objective of his sociology was to
explore the social conditions of production for all practice producing
truth claims, he was in no way a relativist. Indeed, he argued that it was
the social conditions of production, in the form of a field of social relations providing the context for any specified intellectual practice, which
tested and guaranteed the calibre of truth claims. He even extended the
scope of this principle to truths that might claim trans-historical status—
social truths produced in one historical context that may hold true in
some or all other historical contexts.

The distinguished Bourdieu scholar David Swartz has argued that
scholars should resist the temptation "to talk about field, capital and
habitus as theoretical constructs" and recommends "that we think of
them more as forms of sociological practices that have a practical dispositional orientation for understanding the social world" (Swartz 2013,
p. 20). This view is certainly consistent with Bourdieu's emphasis on

C. Nash (✉)
Monash University, Melbourne, Australia

© The Author(s) 2018
J. Albright et al. (eds.), *Bourdieu's Field Theory and the Social Sciences*,
https://doi.org/10.1007/978-981-10-5385-6_14

217

scientific habitus, and also accords with Henri Lefebvre's argument that "abstract space [author's comment: such as relational space] cannot be conceived of in the abstract. It does have a "content", but this content is such that abstraction can "grasp" it only by means of a practice that *deals with it*" (Lefebvre 1991, p. 306. Emphasis in original). However, taking a Bourdieusian or practice-based approach to intellectual enquiry does not obviate the need for rigour and clarity in the conceptualisation and execution of practice. In what follows, I am following in the footsteps of those who have "used Bourdieu against Bourdieu" (Lovell 2000; Verter 2003), with the aim of augmenting and enhancing his approach.

For Bourdieu, it is the field of scientific enquiry rather than the actions of individual scientists that produces truth, and this argument gives fields a central and necessary role in the production of knowledge. The role of the scientific field is to detect error and suggest amendments in search of truth through mutual engagement among participants. That makes error the necessary counterpart of truth. The purpose of this chapter is to explore the adequacy of Bourdieu's usage of the term "field", in particular with respect to how it envisages testing of field analyses for error in real time and space, and to suggest some ways in which the work of other thinkers might augment and buttress his theory. A related and further argument is that because field theory operates at the level of meta-theory, it needs to be applied in conjunction with theory at the disciplinary level in order to account for processes of change from specific analytical perspectives. I take the term "disciplinary" to encompass both inter- and intra- disciplinary concerns. It is at the disciplinary level, within meta-theoretical frameworks, that arguments can be tested, and error is likely to be detected.

The importance with which Bourdieu regarded the concept and status of truth is readily apparent. For his valedictory set of lectures, the question he posed was

> can social science not help to resolve … the problem posed by the historical genesis of supposedly trans-historical truths? How is it possible for a historical activity, such as scientific activity, to produce trans-historical truths, independent of history, detached from all bonds with both place and time and therefore eternally and universally valid? (Bourdieu 2004, p. 1)

There is an ambiguity in this formulation and a clause that spotlights the fault line running through it: "detached from all bonds with place and time". Everything about which we claim to have knowledge exists in this universe that we inhabit, and is constituted in spatio-temporality. "Eternally and universally" does not mean "independent of history, detached from all bonds within both place and time", but inside never-ending time and unrestricted space. "Eternally and universally" are terms that express spatio-temporality, and depend on it for their meaning. To say that something is eternal is to say that it exists in time and will never cease to do so from its inception, and that something is universal that it exists in all possible places and spaces within the universe we inhabit. Trans-historical (across history) is not synonymous with ahistorical (outside history). The theoretical and empirical testing of Bourdieu's field theory therefore depends on the theorisation of spatio-temporality, and conversely, it requires theories of spatio-temporality compatible with Bourdieu's relational approach. But before turning to that issue, we need to examine his usage of the term field in relation to truth.

Bourdieu's approach to the conceptual status of truth was to triangulate among debates in history, sociology and philosophy. His concept of field was central to the argument.

> We know – and Pascal pointed this out long ago – that it is the dogmatic idea or ideal of absolute knowledge that leads to scepticism: relativistic arguments have their full force only against a dogmatic and individualistic epistemology, that is to say knowledge produced by an individual scientist who confronts nature alone with his [sic] instruments (as opposed to the dialogic and argumentative knowledge of a scientific field). (Bourdieu 2004, p. 3)

What empowers dialogue and argument in a field, and the relentless elimination of mistakes, blind alleys and falsehoods, is the search for error. The possibility of error is fundamental to the concept of field. Errors can range from mere mechanical mistakes in observation through mistakes in interpretation to paradigmatic flaws in conceptualisation, which last can precipitate a rupture or revolution in scientific thinking (Bourdieu 2004, p. 14ff). Bourdieu references Bachelard approvingly on this point:

> Opposing the idealisation of scientific practice, Gaston Bachelard pointed out many years ago that epistemology had thought too much about the truths of established science and not enough about the errors of science in progress, scientific activity as it actually is. (Bourdieu 2004, p. 3)

The recognition of error is fundamental to Bourdieu's theory of practice, because without error, there can be no reflexive argument to establish truth, particularly multidimensional and dialectical truths that entail ambiguity, ambivalence and change. Reflexivity depends on methodologies that can detect inconsistency and error, analyse them and either discard or transcend them.

The same argument extends to the other key concepts in Bourdieu's framework: capital and habitus. Capital in Bourdieu's usage is accumulated through learning processes where the capacity to detect and avoid errors in understanding and practice is acquired, which capacity then manifests itself as disposition or habitus in engaging with new social situations as they arise. The ongoing refinement of habitus as it adjusts to new contexts is a product of the recognition of inappropriateness or error in alternative responses: "error in progress" is essential to practice. So the status of error and how it might be produced in a process, and understood by participants and observers, are issues that field theory has to engage with.

The enormous attraction of field theory, particularly to disciplines and professions requiring real-time responses in dynamic environments such as education, journalism, legal and medical practice, is that it addresses "activity as it actually is", that is to say, practice. Practice offers a way of understanding and analysing agency—social, individual, physical, emotional and intellectual—as activity not frozen in a snapshot of time for *post mortem* examination but available for real-time apprehension and self-conscious response through further activity. It is practice that makes reflexivity possible, and it is reflexivity, socially enabled by dialogue and argumentation, that empowers the field as "a site where people struggle for truth" (Bourdieu and Chartier 2010, p. 47).

Notably, given the importance of the concept of field to Bourdieu's framework, it was absent from his originating work *Outline of a theory of practice* (1977). In that book, the concept of field is not elaborated, and indeed, the term does not appear in the index. Nor is it present in the magisterial *Distinction* published two years later (1986 [1979]). It was in *Le sens pratique* (1980), published in English as *The logic of practice* ten years later, that Bourdieu "can be seen to gradually substitute the word field (associated with what he called 'institutions' such as the church or the economy) for structure" (Reed-Danahay 2005, p. 133). The French words that Bourdieu used for field and place were *champ* and *lieu* respectively. In a detailed discussion of his developing usage of these terms,

Deborah Reed-Danahay suggests that "[i]n using this metaphor of *champ* as field, Bourdieu drew on the physics concept of force field in order to characterise a realm of social interaction, which did not necessarily imply being physically in the same place" (Reed-Danahay 2005, p. 133). In other words, it is a set of relations structured by force or power. Bourdieu himself spelt out this relational definition of the term in *Practical reason*:

> That is what I mean when I describe the global social space as a field, that is, as both a field of forces, whose necessity is imposed on agents who are engaged in it, and as a field of struggles within which agents confront each other, with differentiated means and ends according to their position in the structure of the field of forces, thus contributing to conserving or transforming its structure. (Bourdieu 1998, p. 32. Italics in original)

In both aspects of this definition, as "forces" and "struggles", or "positions" and "stances" (Bourdieu and Waquant 1992, p. 105), a field is an abstract analytical concept created by relations among participants defined both subjectively and objectively. "To think in terms of fields is to *think relationally*" and "*the real is the relational*" (Bourdieu and Waquant 1992, pp. 96, 97. Italics in original). It is the activity or practice of the participants that produces relationships and transcends the bipolarity of subjectivity/objectivity (or agency/structure), because the objective positions are produced by the past practice of participants, and the contemporary subjective practice of participants reproduces or transforms those objective positions. Bourdieu describes fields as "structured structures" and "structuring structures"—using the same word in its (past and present) verb and noun forms—in a perhaps slightly mannered way in order to capture the unifying role of activity or practice in both subjectivity and objectivity. Another consequence of the relational character of fields is that they have parameters, which themselves are contingent upon the reach of the relations that constitute the field and are always themselves open to contestation (Bourdieu and Wacquant 1992, p. 100). Moving the goalposts or the sidelines is a tried and true strategy for winning a contest.

So the term *champ* or field is both an analytical concept and a spatial metaphor, but it is constituted in its both subjective and objective dimensions by relational activity or practice that occurs in real time and space. Relations are abstract, and therefore not empirically observable, but activity is material, and therefore empirically observable. Although both relations and activity are produced in real space, only the latter is directly observable and the former has to be imputed or induced by participants in or observers of the activity. Habitus is largely comprised of this imputation or induction. Clearly, if practice is to be observed in real space and time and critically evaluated, then the conceptualisation of space has to move beyond metaphor, as David Harvey has noted (Harvey 2006). A metaphor cannot be tested for exactitude or accuracy, but its pertinence only accepted or rejected by the reader/listener.

Bourdieu himself recognised dual physical and relational aspects of space in his usage of *lieu* for what in English translation has been termed place, site or location.

> The site (le lieu) can be defined absolutely as the point in physical space where an agent or thing is situated, "takes place", exists: that is to say, either as a *localization*, or from a relational viewpoint, as a position, a rank in an order. (Bourdieu 1999, p. 123. Italics in original)

In this usage, place is both a definable stable location in material space and the abstract intersection of contending relations of force that are immaterial but "concrete abstractions", as Marx put it. By that he meant that values and relations that are abstract and invisible in themselves nonetheless can produce material effects that are empirically observable; they do this through the exertion of force, which involves process. Bourdieu's own account of process commonly used another metaphor or analogy, that of the game (Bourdieu and Wacquant 1992, p. 98). Although this metaphor is powerful in its generic depiction of the operations of a field, it is nonetheless a metaphor. As such, it is not very useful in testing for error in any particular analysis of a given field's operations. The limitations of metaphor become clear when considering the contestability of empirical analyses done by Bourdieu and his team of associates.

For example, in *The weight of the world: Social suffering in contemporary society* (Bourdieu et al. 1999), Bourdieu and his team of sociologists conducted detailed interviews with French workers and socially disadvantaged people in a wide range of socio-economic contexts, and for each set of interviews offered a field analysis. The analyses typically consist of a description of their physical and social context, and an account of the socio-economic conditions and relations that are producing their difficulties. The analyses reflect the dualism of material space and abstract social relations in Bourdieu's field theory, and also the limitations of meta-theory in dealing with specific empirical situations, in that no relevant disciplinary theoretical framework is elaborated. In so far as the analyses offer an account of the *process* by which the social relations have produced the material circumstances of the interviewees' context, that account tends to be a didactic narrative that is prescriptive of how the social forces played out, rather than testing of a particular argument for its adequacy against alternative accounts. If one is generally sympathetic to the broad political sympathies that Bourdieu and his colleagues manifest, then their accounts are attractive, but even so if one has a detailed empirical or professional knowledge of the situations being described, then one might well want to criticise the theoretical and/or empirical adequacy of the account being offered. For example, in my own area of disciplinary expertise, journalism studies, Patrick Champagne in *The view from the media* (Champagne 1999, pp. 46–59) offers an analysis of how journalists operate in relation to their sources in conducting investigations and producing discourses about instances of social *malaise*. But the theory of journalist-source relations is a richly contested topic in journalism studies, as is the role of journalistic discourse with respect to socially disadvantaged classes, ethnicities, genders, etc. It is perfectly feasible for a critic to endorse field theory as a productive meta-theoretical approach to social analysis and yet query the particular theoretical analysis of process being presented in a specific case study of a given field.

The underlying problem here is that a dualism that comprises material space and abstract relations is not adequate to the task of analysing process, whereby relational forces play out their contests to achieve material change in the world, as well as change in the configuration of abstract relations. What is required is a theorisation of spatiality that adds the dimension of change or temporality, in other words spatio-temporality. An account of process or change in a specific discipline depends not only on a meta-theoretical account of spatio-temporality, but also on discipline-specific theory within which the account can be tested for its conceptual adequacy.

In contrast to Bourdieu's dualism, David Harvey in 1973 theorised space in three dialectically inter-connected modes, two of which are empirically observable—absolute space and relative space—and one of which is abstract—relational space (Harvey 1973/2009, p. 13). Like Bourdieu, Harvey is a relational thinker and concerned with meta-theory and has referenced Bourdieu favourably in his writings, particularly with respect to the concept of habitus. Bourdieu has not referenced Harvey's work that I know of. Harvey has also referenced Henri Lefebvre (another meta-theoretical relational thinker) extensively throughout his work from the early days. In 2006, Harvey put together into "a general matrix of spatialities" (Harvey 2006, p. 135) his tripartite theory of spatio-temporality—absolute, relative and relational space—with Lefebvre's tripartite theorisation of spatial practice—experienced, conceptualised and lived space (Fig. 14.1).

It was the last (to date) of a series of matrices that Harvey has produced over the years to reconcile his own conceptual framework with that of Lefebvre, and to my mind, the most fertile. Harvey cautions that this matrix provides a checklist for what has to be included in any fulsome analysis of spatiality, and emphasises that it is in the dialectical relations *among* elements of the matrix as much as *within* them that meaning can productively be sought: "with a bit of imagination it is possible to think dialectically across the elements within the matrix so that each moment is imagined as an internal relation of all the others" (Harvey 2006, p. 134).

I suggest that the Harvey-Lefebvre matrix provides a very productive vehicle for moving beyond Bourdieu's metaphorical or analogical usage of spatiality to a theorisation that is empirically verifiable and methodologically contestable. In return, Bourdieu's field theory offers Harvey and Lefebvre a way of "clarifying", as Harvey puts it, the ways in which social agency links a flexible subjectivity with the structural objectivity of relations constituted in fields (Harvey 1989, p. 263). Harvey's spatiality is produced by practice, and Lefebvre's spatial practice engages with socially produced spatiality. Together, they resonate strongly with the formulation that Bourdieu gives to the concept of field: "structuring structures" and "structured structures". This is not to suggest that we should substitute the matrix for field theory. The matrix is not a theory as such, but is bringing two cognate and complementary theories into a relationship with each other. As Harvey, referencing Marx, put it in another context, he is seeking to

> rub different conceptual blocks together to make an intellectual fire ... In a friction of this kind, one should never altogether give up one's starting point – ideas will only catch fire if the original elements are not completely absorbed in the new ones. (Harvey 2000/2011, p. 237)

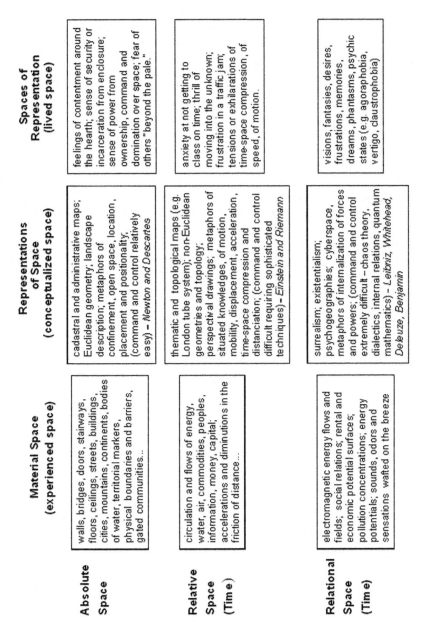

Fig. 14.1 Harvey (2006, p. 135): A general matrix of spatialities

What I am proposing here is that we should add Bourdieu's field theory to Harvey's and Lefebvre's sets of "conceptual blocks", without giving up the starting points in each of the three. Harvey himself had earlier rubbed Lefebvre's theory of spatial practice up against Bourdieu's concept of habitus and found they complemented each other productively (Harvey 1989, pp. 261–263). In the rest of this chapter, I want to introduce the Harvey-Lefebvre matrix in more detail, and then conclude with some comments on its efficacy in the application of field theory to empirical situations.

Harvey (2006, 1973/2009) argues that space can be conceptualised in three modes: absolute, relative and relational space. These are conceptual categories, and any given spatial phenomenon will manifest all three of them; their relative salience will depend on the analytical need. Absolute space "is a "thing in itself" with an existence independent of matter. It then becomes a structure which we can use to pigeonhole or individuate phenomena" (Harvey 1973/2009, p. 13). Absolute space contains the material world of physically manifest objects (mass and/or energy). It is the world as we perceive it. The characteristics and dimensions of its content can be ascertained empirically, named and verified: for example, the appearance, dimensions and construction materials of a building; the contents of a speech by a politician; the attendees at a meeting or social gathering; or the information in a financial statement or company report. In other words, it encompasses the full range of facts that can be located for verification purposes with reference to specific points in time and space. It includes the stable physical elements of a Bourdieusian field. The empirical characteristics of objects in absolute space appear to be stable and unchanging for the given point or period of time. Put another way, absolute space does not include (absolute) time within itself, but time can be used as an external marker to identify when the attributes of the objects existed in space, just as absolute space can be used as an external marker to identify where the attributes of the objects existed in time. Absolute space and absolute time are the space and time of Newtonian physics, Cartesian philosophy and Euclidean geometry (Harvey 2006, p. 121).

Relative space refers to "a relationship *between* objects which exists only because objects exist and relate to each other" (Harvey 1973/2009, p. 13. Emphasis in original). It includes distance and direction so that objects that exist in space can be located relative to each other, and therefore it involves duration or time for movement across that distance;

in other words, objects and events in relative space, whether they comprise mass or energy, are subject to the impact of movement or process. Relative space necessarily incorporates time into the equation, and can therefore be spoken of as spatio-temporality. Spatio-temporality is the space and time of Einsteinian relativity, in which all objects in the universe are moving with respect to each other; it involves the mathematics of calculus and the spherical geometry of Gauss (Harvey 2006, p. 122). At slow rates of movement, the stability of space and time of Newtonian physics seems to apply, but at velocities approaching the speed of light, space and time "curve" and are no longer stable. A comparable phenomenon exists for spatio-temporal relativities in the social world where individuals and collectivities are undergoing processes of varying velocities with respect to each other and to the object world.

Harvey's examples in the matrix refer to "circulation and flows" of energy and objects such as water, air, commodities, people, money and capital. Harvey uses Marx's phrase of "the annihilation of space through time" (Marx 1973, p. 539) for the phenomenon of increases in the speed of transport and communication both extending the spatial range of processes (what he terms the "geographical fix" and what Bourdieu calls changing the parameters of a field) and lessening the time required to travel though space and therefore diminishing (and effectively wiping out in the case of electronic communication) the experience of space between points of departure and arrival of objects or messages. Process is produced by relationships of force or influence and is what Bourdieu analogises as "the game" played by subjective agents in a field constituted by objective relationships. Processes produce objects or events in absolute space which then impact back on the processes; for example, the purchase of goods or services at a specified price in a market will impact on other prices being paid elsewhere in that market, or the fact of an electoral victory by a certain politician may have far-reaching effects on other processes in that field of politics.

Harvey's examples of "circulation and flow" in relative space are drawn from the worlds of the natural and social sciences. They demonstrate the requirement and role of disciplinary theory in understanding the nature of processes, for example, finance market theory, political theory, hydrology and climate science. Disciplinarity is necessarily unstable because as a way to organise thought and analysis, it is always responding to new or different conceptual and empirical challenges. Theory is always contestable; it always engages with process and necessarily resides in spatio-temporality. Harvey's relative space is a necessary extension of Bourdieu's dualism of absolute and relational space.

Relational space is "regarded, in the fashion of Leibniz, as being contained in objects in the sense that an object can be said to exist only insofar as it contains and represents within itself relationships to other objects" (Harvey 1973/2009, p. 13). It is the conceptualisation of physical and social space according to the relations that drive processes which produce objects or events and occur with respect to those objects or events. While profoundly meaningful, Harvey argues it is impossible to verify relations directly, but only through an examination of the processual and objective effects of their power (Harvey 2006, p. 141). For example, the physical layout (absolute space) of a Christian church includes a pulpit and maybe an altar at the front and a series of seats arrayed in front of and facing the pulpit. The space contains or is configured to the advantage of a certain set of social relations—one person generally speaks from the pulpit, and those in the seats generally listen. The power relations implicit in this physical layout are familiar to someone who has experienced the process of a Christian religious service, but at first encounter, might appear incomprehensible to someone who hasn't. Likewise, the material attributes of a shopping centre will convey powerful signals of social relations that encompass class, gender, ethnicity, age and therefore identity to someone who has experienced the social relations produced within it.

The important point from the perspective of field theory is that verification and understanding of necessarily abstract relations requires consideration of the processes driven by those relations as well as the objects and events produced by those processes, which in turn impact back on the abstract relations and resultant processes. To reiterate, Bourdieu's dualism of absolute and relational space requires the third partner of relative or processual spatio-temporality.

Harvey argues that relative space encompasses absolute space, but not vice versa, and that relational space encompasses relative and absolute space but not vice versa. If one thinks of Newtonian space being a subset of Einsteinian spatio-temporality, and process in spatio-temporality being produced by relations of force, then the three states might appear to be a set of Russian dolls, the one secreted inside another. Nonetheless, Harvey explicitly desists from identifying a hierarchy of conceptual categories of space, and prefers "to keep the three categories in dialectical tension" (Harvey 2006, p. 131). Because there is no part of our spatial universe that is not subject to temporality, from the opposite extremes of quantum physics to geological time, I would argue that absolute, relative and relational space are always applicable everywhere. The spatio-temporal dialectic is universal, constant and eternal. Facts and events in material space (e.g. a landslide or an argument) can impact on relations between natural and social forces, and processes (such as military conflict) can modify the relations between social forces that produced the processes in the first place. It is in the understanding of this unceasing dialectical activity that the concept of field makes a valuable, even necessary contribution to Harvey's model.

It does this in two main ways: firstly, by highlighting the role of parameters or limits to any set of relations, and therefore whether forces might be autonomous or heteronomous to a field of activity and specific processes. In astronomy, for example, the identification of gravitational forces heteronomous to known masses has led to the search for and discovery of planetary bodies. Similarly, it is a basic principle of forensic investigations to identify anomalous evidence and to hypothesise potential causes for the events and processes being examined. Secondly, the concept of habitus in field theory spotlights the capacity of agents in social situations to respond to processes and their outcomes through learning, and so to develop a set of dispositions that is efficacious for achieving their objectives in such situations. It is this constantly developing set of dispositions that enables the continuation of social relations as processes, and their outcomes impact on situations and modify the structural context of social relations. However, habitus as a concept needs to be analysed for its component dimensions, and this is where Lefebvre's theory of practice offers some insight.

Lefebvre (1991) identified three modes of socio-spatial practice whereby people act in material space to produce empirically observable outcomes (objects, facts and events), but also ways of understanding space and the objects in it, and also ways of living socially, culturally, emotionally, imaginatively and so on within that space and with those objects and practices. He labelled these three modes the space of experience, the representation of space and spaces of representation, or more simply as experienced space, conceptualised space and lived space respectively. The first is the space that we experience and apprehend through the physical senses of touch, sight, etc. and wherein we can produce physical objects and events; the second is space as we conceptualise it and produce intellectual frameworks such as the laws of physics, political

systems, the rules of sports games, etc. but also psycho-cultural conceptualisations such as surrealism, cyberspace, virtual space, etc.; the third
is space as we live and represent it psychologically, emotionally, culturally and imaginatively to ourselves and each other. Again, they are not
hierarchically related but to be held in dialectical tension (Harvey 2006,
p. 131).

Bourdieu's concepts of capital and habitus range across the three
modalities of spatial practice proposed by Lefebvre, and not just the third
category of lived space. The capacity to produce a particular experienced
event in a sports game such as a goal involves both an understanding of
the rules and the lived experience of the game. As with the vertical axis
of Harvey's matrix, the three elements are dialectically necessary to each
other and separable only for analytical purposes. It is particularly in the
middle category of conceptual practice that theories can be tested for the
adequacy and correctness of their formulation, and errors produced in
experienced space identified as such.

To conclude, there are several things to say about the Harvey-
Lefebvre matrix in relation to Bourdieu's field theory. Firstly, the matrix
is not a "theory of space" as such. Rather, it represents the product of
the "conceptual rubbing together" of the theories that Harvey and
Lefebvre have developed in their own attempts to understand spatiality—Harvey in theorising the ways in which spatio-temporality exists in
our universe as a result of natural and social production, and Lefebvre in
theorising the ways in which human practice engages with the world as
it finds it. This chapter has proposed that Bourdieu's field theory could
be added to the conceptual mix in ways that are mutually beneficial.
Like field theory, the matrix is a meta-theoretical checklist that identifies what sorts of dimensions need to be considered when dealing with
any given phenomena in the world. Underneath meta-theory will sit the
theory specific to the specified phenomena, e.g. climate theory and practice for climate change, military theory and practice for war, and medical theory and practice for health. The matrix is a useful tool because it
gives a structure to reflexivity that encompasses contestability and also
points to the (inter) disciplinarity that is a core dimension of any empirical investigation.

Secondly, while absolute and relative space are amenable to precise
observation, measurement and calibration, and therefore direct verification, relational space is not measureable, though it can be understood and
qualitatively appreciated from its effects in relative and absolute space.

Harvey derives this conclusion from the abstract nature of social relations: "[A] social relation … is impossible to measure except by way of its effects (try measuring any social relation directly and you always fail)." And again: "Social relations can only ever be measured by their effects" because social relations are an abstraction—"immaterial but objective" to quote Marx (Harvey 2006, p. 142). Therefore, in order to establish the way in which social relations produce results that are observable objects or events in the world, it is necessary to understand the processes by which the relations produce the objective results. Without understanding process, all conceptualisation is speculative, and therefore Bourdieu's field theory of practice requires a theorisation of process, or spatio-temporality as Harvey puts it, in order to achieve the contestability that makes the field the guarantor of truth status. Bourdieu's dualism of objects and relations is missing the crucial component of process that connects the two into the totality of practice.

Thirdly, process is empirically observable, and therefore open to rigorous procedures of verification for analytical purposes to identify error. As Harvey's examples in the matrix make clear, that requires theorisation specific to the empirical phenomena being analysed, or in other words, a level of disciplinary theory below the meta-theories of field and spatio-temporality. It is this level that is always present, because it is fundamental to the role of habitus in adjusting to new situations, but is often not contestably addressed in much Bourdieusian analysis.

Fourthly, each slot or intersection within the Harvey-Lefebvre matrix is a fractal dimension of a spatio-temporal whole and, because each dimension is socially produced in its meaning, each can be understood and contested as a field by its participants, as Harvey suggested. This will bring us to Bourdieu's theory of contestation within the field, but in a way that displaces the spatial metaphor of the field into the specifically defined spatio-temporal characteristics of the matrix. This generates a framework of enormous complexity and subtlety that is amenable to empirical and conceptual interrogation and testing. It should again be emphasised that Harvey did not propose that each slot be interrogated in isolation, but in dialectical relation to other slots (Harvey 2006, p. 134).

Fifthly and finally, it is all very well to criticise conceptual adequacy and suggest an alternative as I have done above, but how would it work in practice? "Using Bourdieu and against Bourdieu" requires bringing the theoretical and empirical into mutual engagement through practice. In exploring the validity of my own field of intellectual practice—journalism—as a valid disciplinary (and therefore scholarly) research practice (Nash 2013, 2014), I have applied the Bourdieu-Harvey-Lefebvre framework to a detailed examination of journalism practice in climate change reporting (Nash 2015), to the nexus between art and journalism and the reporting of contemporary and historical conflicts (Nash 2016). Readers will make their own judgements, but I have found this approach to be enormously invigorating and revelatory in moving the critical analysis of journalism beyond tired nostrums of fairness and balance. But in the true spirit of contestability and the search for error, the value of this framework will be determined in the fields of disciplinary scholarship where people struggle for truth.

References

Bourdieu, Pierre. (1979/1986). *Distinction: A social critique of the judgement of taste*. London: Routledge.

Bourdieu, Pierre. (1980/1990). *The logic of practice*. Stanford, CA: Stanford University Press.

Bourdieu, Pierre. (1993/1999). Site effect. In Pierre Bourdieu et al. (Eds.), *The weight of the world: Social suffering in contemporary society* (P.P. Ferguson, Trans.). Cambridge: Polity Press.

Bourdieu, Pierre. (1998). *Practical reason: On the theory of action*. Cambridge: Polity Press.

Bourdieu, Pierre. (2001/2004). *Science of science and reflexivity*. Cambridge: Polity Press.

Bourdieu, Pierre et al. (Eds.). (1993/1999). *The weight of the world: Social suffering in contemporary society* (P.P. Ferguson, Trans.). Cambridge: Polity Press.

Bourdieu, Pierre, & Chartier, Roger. (2010/2015). *The sociologist and the historian*. Cambridge: Polity Press.

Bourdieu, Pierre, & Waquant, Loïc J. D. (1992). *An invitation to reflexive sociology*. Cambridge: Polity Press.

Champagne, Patrick. (1999). The view from the media. In Pierre Bourdieu et al. (Eds.), *The weight of the world: Social suffering in contemporary society* (P.P. Ferguson, Trans.). Cambridge: Polity Press.

Harvey, David. (1973/2009). *Social justice and the city*. Athens, GA: University of Georgia Press.

Harvey, David. (1989). *The urban experience*. Baltimore: Johns Hopkins University Press.

Harvey, David. (2000/2011). Reinventing geography. In Francis Mulhern (Ed.), *Lives on the left: A group portrait*. London: Verso.

Harvey, David. (2006). *Spaces of global capitalism*. London: Verso.

Lefebvre, Henri. (1974/1991). *The production of space*. Oxford: Blackwell.

Lovell, Terry. (2000). Thinking feminism with and against Bourdieu. *Feminist Theory*, *1*(1), 11–32.

Marx, Karl. (1973). Grundrisse. London: Penguin.

Nash, Chris. (2013). Journalism as a research practice. *Pacific Journalism Review*, *19*(2), 123–135.

Nash, Chris. (2014). Research degrees in journalism: What is an exegesis? *Pacific Journalism Review*, *20*(1), 76–98.

Nash, Chris. (2015). Atolls in the ocean—Canaries in the mine? Australian journalism contesting climate change impacts in the Pacific. *Pacific Journalism Review*, *21*(2), 79–97.

Nash, Chris. (2016). *What is journalism? The art and politics of a rupture*. London: Palgrave Macmillan.

Reed-Danahay, Deborah. (2005). *Locating Bourdieu*. Bloomington: Indiana University Press.

Swartz, David. (2013). Metaprinciples for sociological research in a Bourdieusian perspective. In Philip Gorski (Ed.), *Bourdieu and historical analysis*. Durham: Duke University Press.

Verter, Bradford. (2003). Spiritual capital: Theorizing religion with Bourdieu against Bourdieu. *Sociological Theory*, *21*(2), 150–174.

CHAPTER 15

Governing Cultural Fields

Scott Brook

Introduction

It is now common for studies on cultural practices to engage Bourdieu's field theory alongside a focus on governmentality. Indeed, the theoretical bridging of Bourdieusian and post-Foucauldian accounts of power and cultural practice has been a major theme of methodological discussion (Brook 2010; Bennett 2010), and it is easy to appreciate the attraction of this. Both approaches have generated sophisticated general theories of aesthetic culture that are capable of applied research, and both would appear complementary in highlighting different elements of cultural phenomena. We might say that where cultural field theory brings to light the embedded forms of "practical economy" that reproduce a relational space of social positions and trajectories, post-Foucauldian governmentality studies enable attention to the rationales and techniques by which cultural practices are harnessed by governmental apparatuses that "act on" the social, whether at the level of individuals or populations.

From the perspective of cultural field research, such a turn would be one way of addressing some of the widely acknowledged shortcomings of

S. Brook (✉)
Centre for Creative and Cultural Research, University of Canberra, Canberra, Australia

© The Author(s) 2018
J. Albright et al. (eds.), *Bourdieu's Field Theory and the Social Sciences*,
https://doi.org/10.1007/978-981-10-5385-6_15

235

cultural field theory. In general, these concern the overemphasis on the role of culture as a positional good achieved through relations of competitive striving, and a lack of attention to the local and distinct uses of culture whose meanings are not reducible to Bourdieu's broader account of social reproduction (Warde 2004. See also Martin 2003). Drawing on a major empirical study of the French authors, Bernard Lahire has questioned the extent to which the dynamics of the literary field are sufficient as an explanation of literary works (rather than literary positions), as well as the extent to which the literary field is in fact primary in orienting the involvements and career moves of authors (Lahire 2010, 2015). In a review of Bourdieu's turn to cultural field theory from the late 1970s, Alan Warde has argued that although the notion of field enabled a robust and empirically productive methodology for investigating particular domains of social interaction, it became overstretched as it neglected the routine forms of conduct that are purposeful and planned, yet neither strategic (unconsciously or otherwise) nor orientated by competitive circumstances. (See also Noble and Watkins (2003) on the problem of this model for understanding professional sports training). Although Warde is motivated by the need to revise Bourdieu's key concepts in the light of observed social practices rather than forge a link with governmentality studies, his discussion nonetheless proposes a more circumscribed account of the relation between cultural fields and practices, one that is (as I argue below) amendable to the post-Foucauldian account of culture as "governmental".

However, despite these good reasons for a "turn to Foucault", researchers have yet to outline the terms on which it is possible to coordinate such different approaches, or the limits of doing so. Noting Bernard Lahire's call for a more Wittgensteinian approach to the thinking the relation between empirical inquiry and Bourdieu's methods (Lahire 2011), this chapter argues cultural field researchers should avoid the temptation of synthesising approaches in pursuit of an even more comprehensive theory and, instead, articulate the various options for coordinating discrete methodological constructs. This is a move that sets aside the idea that a single methodology might be adequate for a total explanation of cultural phenomena and returns attention to the limits of particular methods. In support of this more modest goal, this chapter follows Warde in reconsidering a basic unit of analysis in Bourdieu's lexicon, namely "practice". While the notion of practice was a philosophical cornerstone in Bourdieu's work, arguably becoming subsumed within Bourdieu's turn to field theory from the late 1970s (as Warde suggests), it is germane in the current context practice was also an assumed if under-acknowledged concept in the post-Foucauldian governmentalities literature. While references to "governmental practices" and the "practice of government" are routine, scant attention has been paid to which theory of practice is in play. The premise of this chapter is that a more subtly differentiated account of "practice" in studying the cultural field will bring to light the differing and local meanings and uses of culture for actors, thereby resisting the tendency to reduce all examples of cultural practice to supporting examples of a broader theory (whether that of "social reproduction" or "the social" as governmental assemblage). Ultimately, this is to situate both Bourdieusian and Foucauldian approaches to culture in the broader history of post-war practice theory (Reckwitz 2002).

Governing Cultural Fields

Before turning to Bourdieu, it is worth considering two well-known and influential studies from the social sciences that demonstrate this theoretical convergence as well as some of the strategies for negotiating it. In *Flexible Citizenship: the cultural logics of transnationality*, Aihwa Ong (1999) seeks to describe transformations in citizenship under conditions of transnational mobility. To do this, Ong looks to Bourdieu to interpret the activities of diasporic agents in terms of strategies for the accumulation and conversion of different forms of capital within an emergent transnational field of the Chinese diaspora. Ong highlights the strategies by which Chinese business professionals convert economic capital gained in one national context (Hong Kong) into the cultural, symbolic and social capital necessary for further capital accumulation in another (California). "Flexible citizenship" is hence understood as an embodied and intergenerationally transmitted strategy (Bourdieu's term would be "practical sense") of elite diasporic agents within a transnational field. However, when Ong comes to describe the policies of government that enable this field, she looks to Foucault's notion of "biopower" in order to describe a set of modern rationalities and techniques of government which are coordinated by a focus on population. Accordingly, Ong notes the newly flexible labour policies in China that have sought to capture transnational capital flows, as well as the forms of migration policy in Britain and the USA that seek to enable diasporic business networks in the interests of national economy. Here, "flexible citizenship" refers not to a practical economy of a transnational field of social elites, but rather the contingent outcome of intersecting programmes and policies for governing populations.

My second example is a well-known study that drew on governmentality studies within the context of a major empirical engagement with Bourdieu. In *Accounting for tastes: Australian everyday cultures*, Tony Bennett, Michael Emmison and John Frow sought to road-test the plausibility of Bourdieu's distinction thesis in mid-1990s Australia via a national survey that enabled an analysis of the variable relations between cultural practices and occupational class (Bennett et al. 1999). Despite this clear objective, a number of forms of analysis and description associated with governmentality studies were drawn upon *en route*, such as Foucault's account of the governmentalisation of the State (p. 227), Nikolas Rose's notion of advanced liberalism as a post-war mentality of rule (p. 228) and the concept of "technologies of the self", as when the authors discuss the practices of dieting and exercise as means to shape both the physical and moral self, and whose origins, in the case of exercise, lie "in the disciplines of the body that Foucault describes in *Discipline and punish*" (p. 124). Such references are relatively uncontentious in cultural studies research, reflecting more a relaxed pluralism rather than any strong methodological commitment. Nevertheless, we might legitimately ask how it is possible to explore Bourdieu's account of the relation of class reproduction to cultural practices, such as dieting, if those same practices can also be understood as "technologies of the self" that are distributed by governmental programmes for the reform of populations. Noting Bourdieu's caution not to mistake "the things of logic" for "the logic of things", we might ask: How do we know when the social logic of a cultural practice answers to the logic of governmentality as opposed to class reproduction? How do we know that the governmental discourses on cultural practices aren't evidence of a process of "officialisation" that *misrecognises* the logic of practice? (Bourdieu 1990, 107–110).

Fortunately, neither of these studies propose a grand synthesis of Bourdieu and Foucault, nor play off one methodology against the other in order to deduce a theory with greater explanatory power. We might say the different approaches are accommodated through being applied to different objects. In *Flexible citizenship*, for instance, the study of field-specific capitals is limited to the practices of individual agents who are the targets of various forms of governmentality. There is no corresponding attempt to scale up the analysis of capitals to consider the development of government policies within those fields Bourdieu would cite as central to the State, such as the fields of departmental bureaucracies, party politics and the media (Bourdieu 2005).

To note that Bourdieu developed a distinct sociology of fields of government brings us to key problem: while a focus on government as a distribution of "resources with which the name 'State' is associated" (Bourdieu 2014, p. 38) might address a number of internal critiques of governmentality studies as normative (e.g. Malpas and Wickham 1995), such a project sits uneasily with the reformist agenda of many applications of Bourdieu. This at least is one way of understanding the normative case for the utility of Bourdieusian analysis that is made by the authors of *Accounting for tastes*. Despite the eclectic references to Foucault cited above, arguably it was the articulation of a Bourdieusian focus on the politics of distribution to the post-Foucauldian concern with government at the level of *address* that provides a model for how the two approaches might be coordinated in practice. Although the study sought to test the distinction thesis as a matter of intellectual clarification, it also sought to steer the attention of cultural policy research towards the normative objectives and requirements (e.g. statistics) of government interventions in culture. In a passage on the different ways in which the research is addressed to the practical requirements of governmental reform, the authors are explicit about these differing rationales:

> The first, taking its cue from Foucault, stresses the importance of bending the inherited apparatuses of public culture to new purposes in the aid of "governing differences": that is, managing the relationships between the increasingly diverse ways of life that make up civil society. The second, derived from Bourdieu, concerns the role of the nexus between public culture and public education in enhancing and equalising the cultural life-chances of citizens, while, at the same time, reducing its ability to organise, symbolise and thereby legitimate class differences. (p. 247)

So, the reason for annexing Bourdieu to a focus on governmentality is normative and instrumental; it is about operationalising Bourdieusian critique *within* established apparatuses of government. And as with Ong's study, the Bourdieusian gaze is directed at populations who "consume" culture, but not the populations that manage its distribution.

Such an analytic separation reflects a pragmatic choice on the part of the researcher. As relatively flexible mid-level theories, the models of cultural field and governmentality are not restricted to a particular level of analysis. As with the case of dieting mentioned above, the notion of government can work at the micro-scale of practices of the self, while, as Bourdieu demonstrated in his study of the neoliberal reform of French housing policy in the 1970s, government policy can be analysed as the outcome of the process of competitive striving within the bureaucratic fields of the "State" (Bourdieu 2005; See also Bourdieu 2014). However, the need for this separation should alert us to the fact that the two approaches are strikingly incompatible in terms of their understanding of the relation of culture to "social structure" (for Bourdieu) and "the social" (for post-Foucauldian scholarship). Just how incompatible they are becomes clear whether we consider their respective analyses of literary education. For instance, in the seminal study on Parisan students, *The inheritors: French students and their relation to culture* (Bourdieu and Passeron 1964/1979), it is claimed the function of aesthetic disciplines is to enable the intergenerational transmission of the capitals of the dominant classes, a process in which the class-based inheritance of cultural capital is disguised as the logical result of a meritocratic process. Indeed, Bourdieu (1986) would later claim the concept of "cultural capital" was developed as shorthand for this process. Such a distribution is fundamental to understanding the structure of the field of cultural production with its own ideology of "the gifted artist" and provided the conceptual foundation for Bourdieu's argument in *Distinction*, where the social function of cultural capital in the school is generalised to all fields of cultural consumption. Here, it is the social field that stands in for the role of the school in a process of misrecognised social selection.

Of course, we could not be further from the post-Foucauldian account of aesthetic culture. If we turn to a founding exhibit in governmentality studies—i.e. Ian Hunter's *Culture and government: The emergence of literary education* (1988)—we encounter a detailed history of English literary education that explicitly rejects the idea that literary studies represented the success of the bourgeoisie in deploying their own cultural patrimony in the reproduction of class domination. Applying Foucault's late work on ethics, government and discipline, Hunter contended that during this period the caste-specific practices of Romantic aesthetic culture had been incorporated into the popular school and university departments in order to develop the ethical capacities of a national population in an ongoing project of liberal settlement. Hunter argued that the teaching practices specific to English represented a functionally coordinated (if institutionally dispersed) system of ethical training: such a system faced both outwards towards the general population as a new modality of "pastoral power" via the school, and inwards towards a specialised caste of teachers whose *persona* was the vehicle for such power. The emergence of modern literary studies hence did not reflect a process whereby education systems were bent towards the interests of either class domination (due to the specific patrimony of middle-class professions) *or* cultural democracy (due to the "universal corporatism" of those located in the autonomous pole of the cultural field); rather, it represented the annexing and redeployment of literary culture by a governmental apparatus whose purpose was the management, care and training of populations.

At stake here are not only differences in research sites (elite universities/the popular school) or methodologies (sociology of education/historical philology) but differences in the concepts of "culture" which the choice of research site is designed to support. For Bourdieu, culture in the final analysis is to be understood as a form of patrimony. Although culture is to be quantified in terms of specific instruments and techniques—that is, cultural capital in its various States (Bourdieu 1986)—the hypothesis that culture is a *capital* is intended to recall the basic structuralist position that its primary social value is a function of its distribution (through strategies of inheritance, monopoly and exchange); and this over and above any technical functions it may have as an instrument of knowledge, of person formation, of training, of civic development and so on. Indeed, for Bourdieu, to prioritise these technical aspects of cultural capital over their positional value within shared social space would be to misrecognise (i.e. collude in disguising) its objective function as an instrument of class reproduction.

Cultural Field, Practical Economy

At the centre of Bourdieu's account of the field of cultural production is the notion of an "economy of practice" in which symbolic capital is a central stake. The practical economy of symbolic capital (i.e. the peer-recognised capacity to represent the field through embodying its values) is peculiar in the cultural field, as it supports a conspicuous rejection of economic capital. Indeed, it is with the appearance of this capacity to reject the market in the name of field-specific (i.e. aesthetic) values that Bourdieu claims the field came into existence in the second half of the nineteenth century (Bourdieu 1996). Much like the description of the Parisian literary field in Honore de Balzac's novel *Lost illusions*, Bourdieu highlighted the economic interests that are euphemised in aesthetic discourses and which disguise the interpolated processes of social selection and economic exchange. The model also drew on his earlier anthropologies of gift economy in order to explain the key role of temporal delay in mediating this economy. It was through the temporal delay between "gift" and "counter gift" as mediated by all sorts of field-specific forms of service (e.g. introductions) and forms of recognition (titles, awards) that interested exchanges might be experienced as gratuitous and hence publically celebrated as evidence of a higher commitment to culture.

The great virtue of this model is its compelling account of the practical economy of social actions and discourses that otherwise defy classical economic explanation. As such, it moves the explanation of the economic sociology of artists' careers well beyond the notion of a "psychic income" (such as feelings of professional autonomy, community, self-actualisation, prestige and creative freedom) in order to explain why some individuals might be oriented towards these forms of psychic income in the first instance when others are not. It offers a coherent theory for exploring why some artists may persist in economically impoverished positions as a "calling" beyond economic calculation (e.g. bohemia), while others successfully seize opportunities to improve their economic position in the field via strategies of capital conversion and multiple position-holding (gravitating towards bourgeois art or commercial entertainments) and others again (for economic reasons that become apparent over time) "cut their losses" by exiting the field altogether.

However, it does assume that such as model is sufficient for explaining the logic of cultural practices. As such, it overlooks a range of social phenomena that can be encountered in the field, such as "non-strategic action, purposeful behaviour in non-competitive circumstances, internal goods arising from participation in practice, and discrepancies between competence and social position" (Warde 2004. p. 2). This last point picks up on one of the consequences of Bourdieu's account of the relation of the habitus to the field; namely that the capacities of social actors are assumed to be calibrated with their positions, as the habitus seeks out "the relatively constant universe of situations tending to reinforce its dispositions by offering the market most favourable to its products" (Bourdieu 1980/1990, p. 61)

In order to clear a space for explanation of cultural phenomena that do not confirm the deep logic of the field, Warde proposes a disaggregated approach to the concept of "practice". His first move is to note Bourdieu used the term practice in several senses, as in *Distinction*, where it used in three distinct senses: to denote the observed *performance* or carrying-out of an activity (manifest behaviour), practices (plural) as socially recognised sets of activities (such as writing or photography) and practice (singular), in the sense of a "logic of practice" that stands in opposition to theoretical or scholastic knowledge. This last sense of practice refers to activities orientated by an embodied "sense" that differs from scientific reason, what Bourdieu often glosses as a "feel for the game". This third definition was clearly theoretically dominant for Bourdieu; it is elaborated in the book-length study the *Logic of practice*, which was written around the same time as *Distinction*, and was the definition that underpins his enduring references to a concern with the "economy of practices" which are to be explained by reference to the field, rather than the ways in which actors try to rationalise their practice according to "nativist" discourses. The logic of this form of practical awareness is economic, insofar as "practical conduct neither requires nor exhibits the level of conscious reflexive thought characteristic of theoretical reason" (Warde 2004, p. 6).

However, it is the second notion of practice listed above that interests Warde (2004). Practice in the plural ("cultural practices") is used to identify "some kind of more or less coherent entity formed around a particular activity" (p. 6). Such practices might be highly dispersed units of everyday life, such as explaining or walking, or they might be more complex, coordinated and institutionally supported ensembles of activity with a recognised history, such as art practices, games and sporting codes. Although *Distinction* recognises this second notion of practice, it was eclipsed by the critical project of analysing the logic of practice.

Warde then draws on Andreas Reckwitz to clarify these two *distinct* theories of practice in terms of a distinction between *Praxis* and *Praktik*:

"Practice" (Praxis) in the singular represents merely an emphatic term to describe the whole of human action (in contrast to "theory" and mere thinking) [...] A "practice" (Praktik) is a routinized type of behavior which consists of several elements, interconnected to one other: forms of bodily activities, forms of mental activities, "things" and their use, a background knowledge in the form of understanding, know-how, states of emotion and motivational knowledge. (Reckwitz 2002, p. 249)

For Warde, it is the notion of *Praktik* that answers the need to describe cultural practices in terms of structured forms of conduct whose logic is specific to the formal and rational properties of the activity, rather the social contexts in which it is performed. Drawing on his study of culinary practices in Britain, Warde disputes the idea that all social action takes place within fields and that even when it does, the field is sufficient for an explanation of observed practices. Warde (2004) suggests social *Praktik* can be absorbed into fields and hence become subject to the dynamics of the field, but this does not necessarily eliminate their other features as an instituted practice, nor does it fully explain them;

Formalisation and rationalisation of a domain of activity is prerequisite for it becoming ripe for absorption into a field or fields. But institutionalisation does not, per se, create a field. Nor does incorporation into a field eliminate its other features as a practice. (p. 25)

The real virtue of Warde's account, however, is that it does not eliminate the other major definition of practice; it simply notes they posit different objects of description. For instance, we might ask how routine social *Praktik* are "made practical" at the level of performance (*Praxis*), according to the different social trajectories and positions of individuals within the field, their capacities (capitals) and their embodied sense of social space. Warde's discussion hence proposes a more modest account of both the scope and intensity of fields in social life.

Culture as Governmental *Praktik*

Such a plural approach enables some important questions about the relationship between fields and governmentality. But firstly, let me present one statement by Foucault on "practice" made in the context of a round-table discussion:

In this piece of research on the prisons [Discipline and punish: The birth of the prison], as in my other earlier work, the target of analysis wasn't "institutions", "theories" or "ideology", but practices – with the aim of grasping the conditions which make these acceptable at a given moment; the hypothesis being that these types of practice are not just governed by institutions, prescribed by ideologies, guided by pragmatic circumstances – whatever role these elements may actually play – but possess up to a point their own specific regularities, logic, strategy, self-evidence and "reason" [...] To analyse "regimes of practices" means to analyse programmes of conduct which have both prescriptive effects regarding what is to be done [...] and codifying effects regarding what is to be known. (Foucault 1977/1991, p. 75. Original emphasis).

Note the norms-saturated language: rules, regularities, regimes, prescriptions and codes. Although Foucault's account of governmentality as consisting of practices for the "conduct of conduct" is highly distinctive in its emphasis on the rational and reflective nature of practices, let me submit that the general category of practice at work answers to the second sense cited above, practice as assemblage-based routine. While this model of practice is hence unexceptional, Foucault's application was distinctive for the way it historicised a range of intellectually prestigious objects (government, sexuality, knowledge, ethics) that had evolved distinct domains of authoritative discourse (political theory, psychology, philosophy, classical philology), across which Foucault's analysis cut a tangent, connecting major academic disciplines to relatively minor areas of inquiry, such as government administration, urban planning, penal discipline, medicine and education. In so doing, he explicitly refused the distinction between social action and thought/theory that was so central to Bourdieu's critique of knowledge (i.e. it refuses the premise of Reckwitz's first sense of practice (*Praxis*)). For Foucault, practices thus understood were rare, as they were "systems of action *in so far as* they are inhabited by thought" (Foucault 2000 [1984], pp. 200–201. Original emphasis). Furthermore, and in a reciprocal argument worthy of Bourdieu's own grammatical constructions, the criterion for "thought" was that it too was a practice, insofar as it exhibited a level of formal reasoning, techniques and technical supports for mental conduct.

If it is accepted that the general model of practice that subtends the object of governmentality studies is indeed this model of *Praktik*, then this approach enables two reciprocal lines of inquiry concerning the relation of cultural fields to cultural practices. On the one hand, we might investigate how established cultural practices for the government of conduct (of individuals or populations) are made "practical" at the level of performance. That is, how are "regimes of practice" performed by individuals and groups whose socially embedded trajectories and positionings inflect the application of the received practice? Furthermore, how might the explanation and justification of such practices (*Praktik*) made by such individuals reflect the logic of this performance, as examples of "misrecognition" as Bourdieu suggests? To what extent do cultural practices (*Praktik*) in fact "govern" the practical economy of their application, including the discourses that articulate their application?

On the other hand, what role might the practical economy of a discrete cultural field play in the historical constitution of practices (*Praktik*)? How do practices evolved within distinct fields of cultural production—such as poetry writing—articulate with institutional assemblages for the government of conduct (such as the popular school) that ensures their survival outside the field? How might such governmental rationales for cultural practices constrain the dynamics of the field?

To analyse the same phenomena in the light of both accounts of practice is to acknowledge two distinct objects of description, neither of which is assumed to eliminate the other. Whether we attribute greater explanatory power to one concept of practice over the other can only be settled in the light of available evidence and critical purpose. In terms of cultural field research, what we have is a methodology for investigating cultural fields which registers the contours of an entirely different model of the logic of cultural practice, one that can support the general modern account of culture as "governmental". Such an approach not only permits a more nuanced appreciation of the scope and intensity of cultural fields in everyday life through positing objects that answer to a different logic, but more importantly an account of how institutionalised cultural practices (*Praktik*) designed to act on the social are differently purposed as they come under the sway of particular fields in which technical competencies and their tools are transvalued into positional goods.

I've argued there are good reasons for a turn to governmentality studies within Bourdieusian cultural sociology and that recent attempts to revise Bourdieu's notions of field and practice are amenable to this project, in particular the attempt to reduce the explanatory reach of the notion of field in favour of a more rigorous and differentiated account of practice. To ask these questions is, I think, to bring field theory into a dynamic relation to a set of post-structuralist accounts of culture: such as a more materialist account of culture as assemblage and the historical contingencies that impact on social structures. It is certainly to bring a more historically reflexive account of "the social" to bear on our conception of the preconditions for the emergence of the cultural field.

Acknowledgements The research behind this chapter was supported by the Australia Research Council Discovery Project "Working the Field: Creative Graduates in Australia and China" (DP#150101477). I would like to thank John Frow and Jen Webb for their useful feedback on an earlier draft of this discussion.

REFERENCES

Bennett, T. (2010). Culture, power, knowledge: Between Foucault and Bourdieu. In E. Silva & A. Warde (Eds.), *Cultural analysis and Bourdieu's legacy: Settling accounts and developing alternatives* (pp. 102–116). London: Routledge.

Bennett, T., Emmison, M., & Frow, J. (1999). *Accounting for tastes: Australian everyday cultures.* Cambridge: Cambridge University Press.

Bourdieu, P. (1980/1990). *The logic of practice* (R. Nice, Trans.). Stanford, CA: Stanford University Press.

Bourdieu, P. (1986). The forms of capital. In G. J. Richardson (Ed.), *Handbook of theory and research for the sociology of education* (pp. 241–258). New York: Greenwood Press.

Bourdieu, P. (1996). *The rules of art: Genesis and structure of the literary field* (S. Emanuel, Trans.). Stanford, CA: Stanford University Press.

Bourdieu, P. (2005). *The social structures of the economy* (C. Turner, Trans.). Cambridge: Polity.

Bourdieu, P. (2014). *On the state: Lectures at the Collège de France 1989–1992.* Cambridge: Polity.

Bourdieu, P., & Passeron, J.-C. (1964/1979). *The inheritors: French students and their relation to culture* (R. Nice, Trans.). Chicago: University of Chicago Press.

Brook, S. (2010). *Governing cultural fields: Creative writing as liberal discipline and cultural practice.* Ph.D. thesis, University of Melbourne, Melbourne.

Foucault, M. (1977/1991). Questions of method. In G. Burchell, C. Gordon, & P. Miller (Eds.). *The Foucault effect: Studies in governmentality* (pp. 73–86). Chicago: University of Chicago Press.

Foucault, M. (2000). *Ethics: Subjectivity and truth: The essential works of Michael Foucault, 1954–1984* (Vol. 1). P. Rabinow (Ed.). London: Penguin.

Hunter, I. (1988). *Culture and government: The emergence of literary education.* London: Macmillan.

Lahire, B. (2010). The double life of writers. *New Literary History, 41*(2), 443–465.

Lahire, B. (2011). *The plural actor.* Cambridge: Polity.

Lahire, B. (2015). Literature is not just a battlefield. *New Literary History, 46*(3), 387–407.

Malpas, J., & Wickham, G. (1995). Governance and failure: On the limits of sociology. *Australian and New Zealand Journal of Sociology, 31*(3), 37–50.

Martin, J.L. (2003). What is field theory? *American Journal of Sociology, 109*(1), 1–49.

Noble, G., & Watkins, M. (2003). So, how did Bourdieu learn to play tennis? Habitus, consciousness and habituation. *Cultural Studies, 17*(3–4), 520–538.

Ong, A. (1999). *Flexible citizenship: The cultural logics of transnationality.* Durham: Duke University Press.

Reckwitz, A. (2002). Toward a theory of social practices: A development in culturalist theorizing. *European Journal of Social Theory, 5*(2), 243–263.

Warde, A. (2004). *Practice and field: Revising Bourdieusian concepts* (CRIC Discussion Papers, no. 65). Manchester: Centre for Research on Innovation and Competition, the University of Manchester.

CHAPTER 16

Thinking like Bourdieu: Completing the Mental Revolution with Legitimation Code Theory

Karl Maton

Introduction

How can we think like Bourdieu? This is a crucial question for understanding and enacting field theory. Bourdieu argued that the essential task of social science is to produce a "new gaze" that moves beyond everyday sensual experience to grasp the relational principles underlying the empirical world (Bourdieu and Wacquant 1992, p. 251). However, achieving such a relational gaze is not easy. Bourdieusian commentators often criticise applications of his ideas as offering a veneer of concepts over empirical description rather than a genuinely relational analysis. Bourdieu himself acknowledged that achieving this new gaze "cannot be done without a genuine conversion, a *metanoia*, a mental revolution, a transformation of one's whole vision of the social world" (p. 251). In this chapter I argue that while Bourdieu powerfully argues for this transformation, field theory does not itself fully embody relational thinking. The conceptual framework represents an unfinished

K. Maton (✉)
LCT Centre for Knowledge-Building, University of Sydney, Sydney, Australia

© The Author(s) 2018
J. Albright et al. (eds.), *Bourdieu's Field Theory and the Social Sciences*,
https://doi.org/10.1007/978-981-10-5385-6_16

249

"mental revolution" that needs augmenting to achieve Bourdieu's aims. To do so I reach "beyond the field theory we know" to Legitimation Code Theory (LCT), a framework that reveals the organising principles underlying fields, capitals, habituses and practices. I illustrate how LCT can help realise Bourdieu's vision by briefly discussing a major study of Chinese students at an Australian university. I show how LCT reveals the principles characterising their habituses, pedagogic environments, experiences and learning practices. This analysis identifies a "code clash" between students' habituses and the attributes valorised by their teachers that explains both their negative experiences and a "hysteresis of habitus" effect whereby they continued strategies that mismatched the "rules of the game". Crucially, this analysis offers a relational account by showing the organising principles underlying these dispositions, positions and practices. It thus illustrates how LCT concepts embody Bourdieu's mental revolution and so can help others to achieve his relational gaze.

BOURDIEU'S GAZE

As Wacquant argued,

> the enduring significance of Bourdieu's enterprise does not reside in the individual concepts, substantive theories, methodological prescriptions, or empirical observations he offers so much as in the manner in which he produces, uses and relates them ... it is the *modus operandi* of Bourdieu's sociology... that most fully defines its originality. (in Bourdieu and Wacquant 1992, p. ix)

For Bourdieu, this *modus operandi*—"the craft of sociology"—is embodied in a way of seeing and thinking. He emphasised that to "master in a practical state everything that is contained in the fundamental concepts: habitus, field, and so on" (Bourdieu et al. 1991, p. 253), one must acquire a "gaze' or "sociological eye" (Bourdieu and Wacquant 1992, p. 251). However, Bourdieu repeatedly emphasised that achieving this gaze was not easy because it involves a "break" or "rupture" with understandings of the social world that focus on sensual experience. The difficulty arises from such understandings being easily taken for granted as self-evident, an illusion of immediacy and transparency that naturalises the social world. For Bourdieu (1984), one must especially break with thinking in terms of separate and visible empirical entities, a "substantialist" form of thinking that lends itself to essentialism by treating properties as located *within* specific entities (p. 22). In contrast, Bourdieu emphasised a *relational mode of thinking* that conceives phenomena as realisations of generative principles that are relationally defined. For Bourdieu, "*the real is the relational*" (Bourdieu and Wacquant 1992, p. 97).

In Bourdieu's approach, "the relational" has horizontal and vertical dimensions. First, Bourdieu (1990, pp. 52–65) viewed practice as arising from relations between "two histories" or evolving logics: agents' dispositions ("habitus") and the positions they occupy (by virtue of their "capital") within an evolving system ("field"). As illustrated by the formula "[(habitus)(capital)] + field = practice" (Bourdieu 1984, p. 101), this *horizontally* relates concepts, offering a corrective to accounts that explore only either the attributes of agents or their social contexts. Second, each of these logics is itself relationally conceived: an agent's dispositions (habitus) are understood as one structure among a range of possible structures; and positions are explored in terms of an agent's status and resources (capital) in relation to those of other agents within a structured social universe (field) that is itself defined in relation to other social universes. This is to take field, capital, habitus and practice separately and *vertically* relate the specific structure of each to other possible structures. In other words, Bourdieu emphasises the need to analyse the organising principles *underlying* empirical realisations of each concept, where the specific setting of those principles (its "structure") derives its characteristics from relations with other possible settings. Grasping both these horizontal and vertical dimensions of relational thinking is crucial to achieving Bourdieu's "mental revolution" and acquiring his "new gaze".

However, the difficulties of thinking relationally are demonstrated by applications of Bourdieu's ideas. A series of Bourdieusian commentators have described many studies using his concepts as shallow, reductive and partial (e.g. Reay 2004; Grenfell 2010; Atkinson 2011; James 2015). Often criticisms effectively highlight a lack of one or both dimensions of relationality. Horizontally, analyses of practice are often solely in terms of *either* agents' dispositions (using "habitus") *or* positions (using "capital" or, less frequently, "field"). Vertically, concepts are often used to re-label empirical characteristics rather than to examine the organising principles underlying dispositions, positions and practices. Such analyses veneer description with theory; for example, social background becomes "habitus", valued attributes become "capital", and context becomes "field". This reintroduces substantialism into field theory, rendering the approach anything but 'Bourdieusian'. As commentators argue, without deep relationality the concepts are reduced "to a meaningless descriptive vocabulary" (Atkinson 2012, p. 169).

In short, Bourdieu's concepts have been more widely adopted than his way of thinking: ideas from field theory are often applied without a relational gaze. However, it would be unrelational to lambast scholars but ignore the framework they are using. In this case the framework plays a role because Bourdieu's concepts do not fully embody the relational thinking he called for. This is not easy to see. It is hard to point to what is hidden by a blind spot, though it can become evident through seeing what new concepts reveal, as I show below. Moreover, Bourdieu intended the concepts to be relational, called them relational and repeatedly cautioned against non-relational thinking. Nonetheless, as highlighted by Boudon's (1971) distinction between "intentional" and "operative" definitions, there is a difference between intending to construct an object of study relationally and implementing that intention, which may not be possible "because the necessary mental tools are not available" (p. 51). In this case, the tools cannot fully implement a relational gaze: they are "intentional" rather than "operative".

X Marks the Blind Spot

Consider Bourdieu's notion that practice results from the meeting of "two histories", dispositions and positions, each with its own logic or structure. This raises questions of the nature of those logics, or the organising principles underlying dispositions, positions and practices. These principles are pointed to by Bourdieu's concepts but not relationally conceptualised. For example, Bourdieu (1994) defines "habitus" as a "structured and structuring structure" (p. 170) but does not provide the means to conceptualise that structure as, say, X among a range of possible structures W, X, Y, Z. Accordingly, the effects of habitus are typically shown by scholars describing the practices to which it gives rise, rather than habitus itself being analysed in terms of its underlying principles and the system of possible settings of those principles that give a particular setting its meaning (cf. Bourdieu 1990, p. 4). Without exploring those principles, one can argue that agents feel like "fish out of water" because their habituses do not match the field (to take an oft-used example), but one cannot show the *basis* of that mismatch: one cannot reveal the X structure of the habitus and the Y structure dominating the field.

Moreover, without conceptualising these structures, one cannot systematically show similarity and difference or change over time. What is, for example, the structure of a "working-class habitus" and how does it differ from that of a "middle-class habitus"? (I mention social class but these points hold for other categories, including gender and ethnicity.) How can one show when an agent's habitus has changed or remained the same between different situations or over time? The same questions can be asked of similarity, difference and change in the structures of "capital", "position", "field" and "practice". To avoid using these concepts as a veneer requires a "break" or "rupture" with empirical description into a conceptual language that reveals these structures without merely recounting agents' practices. The aim is to reveal the organising principles (the X) underlying a specific set of empirical instances and show how they may be varied (e.g. to W, Y, Z) to generate different empirical instances. As Bourdieu (in Bourdieu and Wacquant 1992) insisted:

> The challenge is systematically to interrogate the particular case by constituting it as a 'particular instance of the possible,' as Bachelard (1949) put it, in order to extract general or invariant properties that can be uncovered only by such interrogation. (p. 233)

In his major studies Bourdieu began to reveal these properties, typically through binary categories. For example, in his study of French cultural taste (Bourdieu 1984), the distinctive lifestyles and consumer preferences of working-class and bourgeois subcultures were characterised by "virtue of necessity" and "freedom from necessity", respectively. Similarly, in his study of the academic field, Bourdieu (1988) characterised agents striving for "intellectual capital" (such as scholarly renown) as oriented inwards towards the field's specific activities and agents striving for "academic capital" (institutional power as oriented outwards to economic and political forms of success). However, while these dichotomous types highlight what needs to be conceptualised as relational principles, those principles remained just out of reach; in these examples, there are no concepts for analysing degrees of distance from necessity or strengths of external boundaries.[1] Without those concepts, the analysis does not extract "general or invariant properties" that could be used in studies of other fields—the binary categories are locked into their objects of study. This matters because, lacking such concepts, many scholars using Bourdieu's approach rely instead on the pre-constructed notions he warned against, such as citing social classes to proclaim, for example, a disjuncture between the "working-class habitus" of a student and a "middle-class" educational institution. By using such pre-constructed categories, such descriptions present as self-evident the very things that need to be analysed: the structure of the habitus and the structure of the capital valorised by that position in the field. The concepts then add little to empirical description beyond a veneer of theoretical sophistication. Bourdieu often emphasised the need for "vigilance" to avoid these problems but conceded that the "mere fact of being on the alert is important but hardly suffices" (Bourdieu and Wacquant 1992, p. 238). One also needs relational concepts.

In sum, to understand practice relationally one must conceptualise "vertically" by revealing the relational X of, say, a habitus in order to analyse "horizontally" by relating that X to the X, W, Y or Z of capital, position, practice, etc. This entails a break from description in terms of pre-constructed categories into a conceptual language capable of revealing and relating these relational structures. Relational analysis thus requires not only a relational gaze but also relational concepts. However, while Bourdieu made clear what a relational gaze entails, his concepts do not fully embody that gaze. This is not to dismiss Bourdieu's ideas—they are extremely powerful. Rather, it is to recognise the limits of the concepts as they currently stand and to highlight why they need augmenting if we are to implement Bourdieu's intentions. Specifically, we require a means of conceptualising the organising principles (the X) underlying dispositions, positions and practices. Without those concepts, the framework will continue to lend itself to veneering of empirical description by scholars lacking a relational gaze. Moreover, it will remain extremely difficult for anyone to acquire that gaze, as even prolonged and sustained use of Bourdieu's concepts cannot shape, enact or sustain a relational gaze—they lack the X factor. The need, then, is for relational concepts that convert Bourdieu's gaze into tools capable of helping others acquire that gaze. For this, I turn to Legitimation Code Theory.

LCT: An Invitation to Relational Sociology

Legitimation Code Theory or "LCT" is a sociological framework that extends, *inter alia*, Bourdieu's field theory and Bernstein's code theory (Maton 2014). Since emerging at the turn of the century, LCT has grown rapidly as the basis of research by an international and multidisciplinary community into a widening range of issues in education, politics, law and other social fields (Maton et al. 2016).[2] The framework of LCT comprises a multidimensional conceptual toolkit. Each dimension includes concepts for analysing a particular set of organising principles as a species of *legitimation code* (Maton 2014). These dimensions are "simultaneous": they explore not different objects of study but rather different organising principles that may underlie the same object. Thus, empirical studies often adopt more than one dimension in analysis. Any of the dimensions of LCT could be used here to reveal relational principles underlying dispositions, positions and practices. For brevity, I focus on one, Specialisation, which is centred on *specialization codes*.

The dimension of Specialisation begins from the simple premise that practices are about or oriented towards something and by someone. One can thus analytically distinguish: *epistemic relations* (ER) between practices and their object or focus; and *social relations* (SR) between practices and their subject, author or agent. When applied to knowledge practices, these highlight questions of *what* can be legitimately described as knowledge (epistemic relations), and *who* can claim to be a legitimate knower (social relations).

Each relation may be more strongly (+) or weakly (−) emphasised as the basis of legitimacy. These two strengths may be varied independently to generate *specialization codes* (ER+/−, SR+/−). As shown in Fig. 16.1, the two continua of strengths can be visualised as axes of the *specialization plane*, a topological space with four principal codes:

- *knowledge codes* (ER+, SR−), where possession of specialised knowledge, principles or procedures of specific objects of study is emphasised on the basis of achievement, and attributes of agents are downplayed;
- *knower codes* (ER−, SR+), where specialised knowledge and objects are downplayed and attributes of agents are emphasised as measures of achievement, whether viewed as born (e.g. "natural talent"), cultivated (e.g. "taste") or social (e.g. standpoint theory);
- *élite codes* (ER+, SR+), where legitimacy is based on both possessing specialist knowledge and being the right kind of knower; and
- *relativist codes* (ER−, SR−), where legitimacy is determined by neither specialist knowledge nor knower attributes—"anything goes".

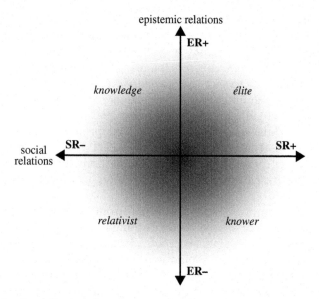

Fig. 16.1   Specialisation plane (Maton 2014, p. 30)

To understand these concepts in terms of field theory consider Bourdieu's (1991) description of a "social topology":

> the social world can be represented in the form of a (multi-dimensional) space constructed on the basis of principles of differentiation or distribution constituted by the set of properties active in the social universe under consideration, that is, able to confer force or power on their possessor in that universe. Agents and groups of agents are thus defined by their *relative positions* in this space. (pp. 229–230; original emphasis)

Specialisation visualises one dimension of this space as the *specialization plane* (Fig. 16.1), in which agents occupy relational positions. Specialisation codes are one set of the "principles of differentiation" constructing the social universe. The specialisation plane outlines the full range of possible positions that could be occupied. The particular specialisation codes that are "active in the social universe" are determined by empirical research. Bourdieu describes such social universes as "fields of forces", where these forces within which agents are positioned are (contrary to substantialism) irreducible to interactions among them.

Specialisation codes conceptualise one dimension of those forces that constitute fields. They are able to "confer force or power on their possessor": a dominant code is both privileged (having priority) and privileging (conferring power upon possessors). Accordingly, agents attempt to maximise their positions by ensuring their own codes are dominant in the social universe.

Specialisation codes conceptualise one set of the organising principles underlying dispositions, positions and practices. Put simply, the basis of legitimacy for each code is: what you know (knowledge codes), the kind of knower you are (knower codes), both (élite codes), or neither (relativist codes). A specific specialisation code may dominate as the basis of achievement, but may not be transparent, universal or uncontested. Not everyone may recognise and/or be able to realise what is required, there may be more than one code present, and there are likely to be struggles among agents over which code is dominant. One can thus describe degrees of *code match* and *code clash*, such as between learners' dispositions and pedagogic practices (see below), education policies and disciplinary conventions, different approaches within an intellectual field, etc. For example, studies of a large-scale educational initiative in Australian schools (Howard and Maton 2011) show the policy successfully integrated technology into subject areas matching its knower-code intentions but was less successful in subjects with other specialisation codes, where code clashes were evident. The dominant code may also change, such as between subject areas, classrooms and stages of a curriculum in education or, for dispositions, over the lifecourse. These *code shifts* can change the "rules of the game". For example, research into music in English schooling (Lamont and Maton 2010) revealed the curriculum shifted from a knower code at primary school to a knowledge code in the early years of secondary school, and then towards an élite code for formal school qualifications in senior secondary school. Such code shifts can have profound implications, such as causing previously successful agents to struggle or, in the case of music, reducing the take-up rate of qualifications.

Relational Concepts

Specialisation codes are but one species of legitimation code—there are more organising principles conceptualised by LCT (Maton 2014). Moreover, these concepts are better understood within the wider context of the sociological approach of LCT, one which builds on Bourdieu's field theory of practice. Space precludes summarising here his accounts of how society comprises a series of relatively autonomous social fields of practice, how agents struggle to maximise their positions within the hierarchies of those fields, how they differentially acquire a "feel for the game", how their past experiences are embodied in habituses that shape practices in relation to the evolving structures of the fields, and so forth. Space also precludes demonstrating the centrality of this understanding to LCT, though it will be recognised by anyone familiar with Bourdieu's approach. More pertinent here are three characteristics of legitimation codes (including specialisation codes) that explain how the concepts embody a relational gaze.

First, legitimation codes explore organising principles—they reveal the X, enabling vertical relationality. Rather than using pre-constructed categories, offering ideal types or veneering descriptions, legitimation codes conceptualise the principles or structures *underlying* empirical realisations of dispositions, positions and practices.

Second, legitimation codes are "operative" relational concepts—the Xs they reveal are relationally constructed. For example, when determining the specialisation codes characterising a set of practices, the strength of their epistemic relations is relative to strengths of epistemic relations of other possible practices, and the strength of their social relations is relative to strengths of social relations of other possible practices. These relative strengths locate the practices on the y-axis and x-axis of the plane (Fig. 16.1), giving their specialisation code. Thus, each instance is constructed as a "particular instance of the possible" by showing both its position on the plane (and code) and the full range of possible positions (and codes) not occupied. The topology of the plane allows for an infinite number of relational positions. Legitimation codes are thus neither binary categories nor simply a typology. One can chart every instance of, say, interaction in a classroom or publications in a discipline as a scattergraph reaching across the plane, revealing both the dominant code and the diversity of codes at play. Similarly, one can chart change over time by tracing positions across the plane, such as movement from a knowledge code to a knower code.

Third, legitimation codes are not limited to a specific phenomenon, enabling horizontal relationality. They can be used to conceptualise the principles underlying habituses, configurations of capital, structures of a field, sets of practices, and numerous other phenomena, such as affordances of technology or attributes of institutions. Each can be coded using the same concepts, so each X can be related to other Xs. Thus, as mentioned above, one can show degrees of *code match* or *code clash*, such as between the knower code of an agent's habitus and the knowledge code dominating a field. Moreover, by showing changes over time *within* the organising principles of phenomena (field, capital, habitus, etc.), the concepts enable analysis of changes in relations *among* them. For example, one can reveal where an agent's experiences engender "code shifting" of their habitus from knower code to knowledge code to match the dominant code of a field. By revealing Xs underlying all the phenomena highlighted by Bourdieu, the possibilities for deepening Bourdieusian explanations are manifold.

It should be clear that LCT concepts are complementary to, rather than in competition with, Bourdieu's tools. They offer a conceptual language that "breaks" with substantialist description and embodies relational thinking, as Bourdieu argued. Indeed, by revealing the organising principles of field, habitus, capital and practice, they boost the explanatory potential of his concepts. LCT thereby enables field theory to achieve a deep relational analysis and so generate greater explanatory power. In short, Bourdieu highlighted what needs to be analysed and how; LCT provides additional tools for putting those intentions into practice. To illustrate how, I shall briefly discuss a major study by Rainbow Chen (2010) that used the concepts of specialisation codes to explore the experiences of Chinese students at an Australian university.

A Case from the X-Files

Most research into Chinese students who are overseas exhibits substantialism. Typically, studies focus on the ostensible attributes of students and neglect the educational environments they experience, leading to an essentialist and deficit model of students. In contrast, Chen's relational study analysed: (1) the dispositions to education brought by Chinese students; (2) the educational environments they encountered in Australia; and (3) their experiences and practices. In short, the study viewed agents' practice as resulting from the meeting of dispositions with positions and analysed each of their organising principles. Data comprised: (1) focus groups with Chinese students across the university; (2) interviews with teaching staff and analysis of teaching materials; and (3) in-depth, recurrent interviews with seven Chinese students in a single faculty (41 hours total) through the course of their postgraduate learning. I can give only the briefest précis of this research, see Maton and Chen (2017) for a summary and Chen (2010) for the full study. Here I simply highlight how the concepts of specialisation codes revealed the principles underlying student habituses, the environments they encountered, their experiences and resulting practices, and then brought these diverse phenomena together to generate explanatory power.

Student Dispositions

When describing the experiences and expectations about education they brought from China, participants emphasised learning strongly bounded "academic" knowledge; for example: "the information in the textbook, decided by the teacher, was what the study unit was all about".[3] Teachers were described as experts in this content knowledge and teaching as explicit and clear procedures with strong control over selection, sequencing and pacing of knowledge. What was required of students in assessment was similarly explicit, unambiguous and concerned this knowledge. In short, the students described achievement as emphasising specialised knowledge and procedures: *relatively strong epistemic relations* (ER+). In contrast, students rarely considered their personal experiences as relevant to learning. They also emphasised the need to adopt self-effacing roles, such as asking questions only when sure they contribute to learning for the whole class. One described a cardinal rule of classroom behaviour as: "Don't disturb the class. Even if your question is brilliant". Similarly, academic achievement was said to require withholding one's own views. Students stated that assessment should require textbook-based answers affording limited latitude and avoiding personal opinions; for example: "if I had written my answers on exams according to what I thought, not the book, they wouldn't have been standard, right answers". In short, education was described as downplaying personal experiences and views: *relatively weak social relations* (SR–).

As Fig. 16.2 highlights, the dispositions to education brought by the Chinese students embodied stronger epistemic relations and weaker social relations or a *knowledge code* (ER+, SR–). In other words, they valorised capital based on specialised knowledge, procedures and skills and devalorised capital based on personal attributes of knowers. This knowledge-code habitus was empirically realised in education contexts as valorisation of: curriculum emphasising academic knowledge and

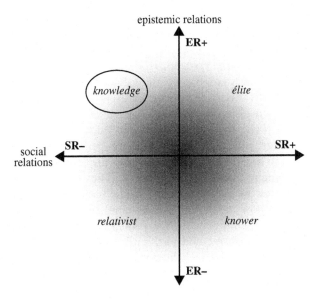

Fig. 16.2 Knowledge-code dispositions

downplaying personal experience; pedagogy involving procedural delivery of teachers' expert knowledge of subject content and downplaying personal dimensions of learning; and assessment comprising explicit and impersonal criteria for evaluating learners' understanding (Chen 2010, pp. 90–118).

Learning Environments

The Chinese students were studying at an Australian university's Faculty of Education but were taught primarily online. In these learning environments teaching blurred all boundaries around "academic" knowledge. There was little core content to the units, and teachers encouraged students to treat reading materials as optional. They also denigrated as "instructivist" any teaching where teachers select, sequence or pace knowledge. Instead, they advocated "constructivist" pedagogy, described themselves as "facilitators" or "co-learners" and stressed they did not claim expert knowledge. Assessments similarly downplayed guidelines, comprising "authentic" assessments that "situate the assignment in the context in which these people work and live" and eschew explicit evaluative criteria, ostensibly legitimating all forms of knowledge. The educational environment thus downplayed specialised knowledge, skills or procedures: *relatively weak epistemic relations* (ER−).

In contrast, teachers emphasised the value of personal experience and viewed students as already legitimate knowers. Students were expected to make their own decisions with minimal guidance about the relevance of readings to their own practices beyond education. They were also expected (though not compelled) to share personal experiences with other students in online discussions. Similarly, the "authentic" assessments focused on students' personal experiences. Thus, each student formed the basis of her or his own legitimacy; as one teacher described: "What I want to know is how much you, the student, can make the connections between your beliefs and your theory, your beliefs and your practices and can you share that with me and justify it". However, this was not "anything goes"—teachers valued a willingness to self-organise, participate and share their experiences in online discussions. The ideal student by which they measured work was thus independent, self-directed, confident and reflective. In sum, the educational environment based legitimacy on specific dispositions of knowers: *relatively strong social relations* (SR+).

As Fig. 16.3 shows, the learning environments embodied weaker epistemic relations and stronger social relations or a *knower code* (ER−, SR+). Thus, this position in the academic field devalorised capital based on specialised knowledge, skills and procedures and valorised capital based on attributes of knowers. This knower-code position was empirically realised as: curriculum downplaying content knowledge and valorising personal experience; pedagogy downplaying teacher involvement in favour of self-regulating learners creating their own understandings; and assessment where knowers evaluate themselves based on personal rather than shared criteria (Chen 2010, pp. 119–158).

Student Experience and Strategies

Students with knowledge-code dispositions occupying a knower-code position creates the potential for a code clash. However, this is not to say the students viewed the learning environment as a knower code. As Bourdieu (2000) emphasised, one must avoid the "scholastic fallacy" of confusing the outcome of conceptual analysis with the viewpoint of participants. The experience of agents is mediated by the codes of their

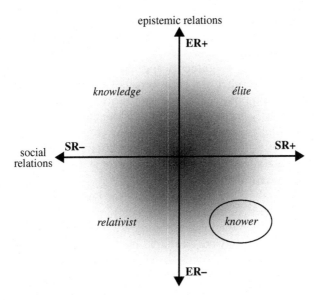

Fig. 16.3   Knower-code position

habituses. In this case, the Chinese students viewed the environment not as a *knower code* but as a *relativist code* (ER–, SR–), one lacking any basis for legitimacy.

On the one hand, students' characterisations of the learning environment embodied weaker epistemic relations but viewed negatively. They experienced latitude concerning curriculum knowledge as a lack of structure and viewed constructivist pedagogy as an absence of structured guidance with teachers acting as like "tour guides" or "passive assistants". Almost all students expressed sentiments akin to the following:

> I feel that teachers do not teach in online classes. They raise a lot of questions for us to discuss. What do they teach us? They teach us nothing. They ask us to think, but what if I can't think of anything? I can sit there thinking all day, not sleeping at all, but I still can't think of anything. So I don't think they are teaching me.

Similarly, students described assessment criteria as lacking clarity and voiced frustration at being unable to obtain explicit instructions from teachers they approached for help.

On the other hand, students did not recognise the legitimacy of practices based on stronger social relations, such as sharing personal experience and peer discussion. They did not view their own experiences and beliefs as relevant to assignments and dismissed online discussions as "pointless" because other students were not experts in content knowledge. This was compounded by the hands-off approach of teachers; for example: "Even if I got a reply from my classmate, it's unlikely that the teacher would post a message afterwards to confirm whether what my classmate said was correct or not". Accordingly, none felt part of an online learning community, repeatedly expressing isolation and doubting whether they were learning at all.

As discussed above, students with knowledge-code habituses (ER+, SR−) were seeking stronger epistemic relations and predisposed to downplay social relations. When encountering knower-code learning environments (ER−, SR+), they were frustrated by the weaker epistemic relations and unable to see the stronger social relations, viewing self-disclosure and peer discussion as not legitimate. As depicted in Fig. 16.4, the Chinese students perceived the environment as embodying *both* weaker

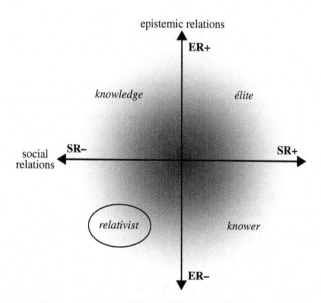

Fig. 16.4 Relativist-code experiences

epistemic relations *and* weaker social relations: a *relativist code* (ER–, SR–). This code was experienced as a vacuum and related by students to feeling inferior, insecure, anxious, frustrated, helpless, guilty and depressed (Chen 2010, pp. 159–209). In short, the students were like "fish out of water" because their habitus code not only clashed with the environment code but also rendered its rules of the game invisible, leaving them floundering.

The students were unable to simply repeat their previous learning strategies from China, for their assignments were fundamentally different. However, they continued following their knowledge-code habituses through strategies such as treating previously learned academic knowledge as personal experience and synthesising personal experiences from examples found in readings. In other words, they exhibited what Bourdieu (1984) termed "hysteresis", whereby the habitus remains unchanged in new circumstances. Here, students' coping strategies reflected their existing knowledge-code dispositions. This was not without cost: they described the courses and studying overseas as a waste of time and often blamed themselves for failing to discern the learning requirements.

CONCLUSION

Bourdieu argued that "the most vital task of social science ... is to establish as a fundamental norm of scientific practice the conversion of thought, the revolution of the gaze, the rupture with the preconstructed" (Bourdieu and Wacquant 1992, pp. 251–252). This revolution involves a shift to relational thinking that horizontally relates dispositions, positions and practices through vertically revealing their organising principles. In this chapter I argued that LCT offers concepts that complement Bourdieu's tools in ways that embody this relational gaze. As the example above begins to illustrate, LCT enables analyses to reveal and relate the organising principles (the X) underlying the diverse phenomena denoted by habitus, field, capital, practice, etc. In this case, the study analysed the specialisation codes of student dispositions, teaching practices, student experiences, and student learning strategies.[4] These codes were then related together to explain student experiences. The analysis conjectured that knowledge-code students (ER+, SR–) in knower-code environments (ER–, SR+) experience the weaker epistemic relations as an absence and do not see the stronger social relations as legitimate, generating relativist-code experiences (ER–, SR–) which they negotiate by continuing knowledge-code practices, with damaging emotional and educational effects. Put another way, LCT can add codes to each element of Bourdieu's formula "[(habitus)(capital)] + field = practice". One can summarise this study's findings as: knowledge-code (habitus and capital) + knower-code position = relativist-code experiences + knowledge-code strategies.

By using specialisation codes, the study was thereby able not only to argue that students felt like "fish out of water" but also to show the *basis* of that mismatch: a code clash between knowledge-code habituses and the knower-code environment. The study was also able to systematically show similarity or difference and, moreover, change between contexts and over time; for example, despite empirical differences between their learning strategies in China and Australia, analysis showed that students' habituses exhibited hysteresis by maintaining a knowledge code.

As the study illustrates, code concepts are not locked onto habitus, field or capital but rather apply to all the phenomena highlighted by Bourdieu's tools. Similarly, the conjectures they enable are not locked into specific contexts. In this case, the explanation encompasses all knowledge-code agents in all knower-code environments, regardless of location, social background, form of practice, etc. LCT thus provides a means for exploring potentially "general or invariant properties" of social fields. Moreover, using specialisation codes allows this conjecture to avoid the terms "Chinese", "Western", "Australian", "constructivist", etc., illustrating how LCT enables the "rupture" with pre-constructed categories essential to Bourdieu's gaze.

Finally, by embodying relational thinking, LCT can propose new possibilities. The study suggests ways to avoid the code clash, such as teachers making explicit the code underlying success and modelling the knower-code practices required of students. Indeed, as a growing body of teaching practice shows, teachers can use LCT as an explicit metalanguage for making the "rules of the game" visible to students (e.g. Clarence 2016; Kirk 2017).

LCT is far more than the concepts I have illustrated here, and these concepts are more complex than I have shown. Rather than simply an "X", specialisation codes are a combination of settings of two principles, each of which can exhibit a range of strengths. There are four main specialisation codes, but each code can take many forms (Maton 2014). Moreover, there are four other species of legitimation code, each revealing different dimensions of practice, such as temporality. Legitimation codes can embrace as much complexity as required by the object of study. Nonetheless, the example highlights how LCT can help fulfil the promise of field theory. By converting a relational gaze into relational concepts, the framework can enable others to complete that "mental revolution" required to practise what Bourdieu preached. LCT can help us think like Bourdieu.

NOTES

1. Bourdieu (1993) elsewhere described "the autonomous principle" and "the heteronomous principle", but the X that underlies these dichotomous "principles" was not conceptualised. (Both this and degrees of distance from necessity have been conceptualised within LCT as "autonomy codes" and "semantic gravity", respectively; Maton 2005, 2014).
2. For LCT research, see http://www.legitimationcodetheory.com.
3. All student and teacher quotes are from Chen (2010).
4. Analysis of teachers' positions in the university field would help explain their adoption of constructivist stances, but that was not the focus of this study. The aim was to analyse the organising principles characterising their position to explain the experiences of Chinese students.

REFERENCES

Atkinson, W. (2011). From sociological fictions to social fictions: Some Bourdieusian reflections on the concepts of 'institutional habitus' and 'family habitus'. *British Journal of Sociology of Education, 32*(3), 331–347.

Atkinson, W. (2012). Where now for Bourdieu-inspired sociology. *Sociology, 46*(1), 167–173.

Boudon, R. (1971). *The uses of structuralism*. London: Heinemann.

Bourdieu, P. (1984). *Distinction: A social critique of the judgement of taste*. London: Routledge.

Bourdieu, P. (1988). *Homo academicus*. Cambridge: Polity Press.

Bourdieu, P. (1990). *The logic of practice*. Cambridge: Polity.

Bourdieu, P. (1991). *Language and symbolic power*. Cambridge: Polity.

Bourdieu, P. (1993). *The field of cultural production: Essays on art and literature*. Cambridge: Polity.

Bourdieu, P. (1994). *In other words*. Cambridge: Polity.

Bourdieu, P. (2000). *Pascalian meditations*. Cambridge: Polity.

Bourdieu, P., & Wacquant, L. J. D. (1992). *An invitation to reflexive sociology*. Cambridge: Polity.

Bourdieu, P., Chamboredon, J.-C., & Passeron, J.-C. (1991). *The craft of sociology*. Berlin: Walter de Gruyter.

Chen, R. T.-H. (2010). *Knowledge and knowers in online learning*. unpublished Ph.D. thesis, University of Wollongong, Australia.

Clarence, S. (2016). Exploring the nature of disciplinary teaching and learning using Legitimation Code Theory semantics. *Teaching in Higher Education, 21*(2), 123–137.

Grenfell, M. (2010). Working with *habitus* and *field*: The logic of Bourdieu's practice. In E. B. Silva & A. Warde (Eds.), *Cultural analysis and Bourdieu's legacy* (pp. 14–27). London: Routledge.

Howard, S. K., & Maton, K. (2011). Theorising knowledge practices: A missing piece of the educational technology puzzle. *Research in Learning Technology, 19*(3), 191–206.

James, D. (2015). How Bourdieu bites back: Recognising misrecognition in education and educational research. *Cambridge Journal of Education, 45*(1), 97–112.

Kirk, S. (2017). Waves of reflection: Seeing knowledge(s) in academic writing. In J. Kemp (Ed.), *EAP in a rapidly changing landscape*. Garnet: Reading.

Lamont, A., & Maton, K. (2010). Unpopular music: Beliefs and behaviours towards music in education. In R. Wright (Ed.), *Sociology and music education*. London: Ashgate.

Maton, K. (2005). A question of autonomy: Bourdieu's field approach and policy in higher education. *Journal of Education Policy, 20*(6), 687–704.

Maton, K. (2014). *Knowledge and knowers: Towards a realist sociology of education*. London: Routledge.

Maton, K, & Chen, R. T.-H. (2017). Specialization from Legitimation Code Theory: How the basis of achievement shapes student success. In J. R. Martin, K. Maton, Pin Wang Pin, & Wang Zhenhua (Eds.), *Understanding academic discourse*. Beijing: Higher Education Press.

Maton, K., Hood, S., & Shay, S. (Eds.). (2016). *Knowledge-building: Educational studies in Legitimation Code Theory*. London: Routledge.

Reay, D. (2004). 'It's all becoming a habitus': Beyond the habitual use of habitus in educational research. *British Journal of Sociology of Education, 25*(4), 431–444.

CHAPTER 17

Afterword: Reflecting In/On Field Theory in Practice

Michael Grenfell

In this Afterword to a book that deploys Bourdieu's approach in a number of research studies, I want to return us to issues of method; in particular the strength and integrity of the concepts offered by him and what it is to use them. I do this by considering their provenance and issues of language between theory and practice in working with them. The chapter reflects on field theory in practice and indeed what reflexivity means within it and in its terms.

I

For those of us who have worked with Bourdieu and his methods—for some decades now—one of the key aspects that this endeavour has had to face is the way that the prominence of his ideas has grown throughout that time, and with that a proliferation of adaptations and 'extensions' of them. Of course, in many ways, this is to be celebrated and attests to the value of the work. However, I want to revisit the original context of his

M. Grenfell (✉)
University of Southampton, Southampton, England, UK

© The Author(s) 2018   269
J. Albright et al. (eds.), *Bourdieu's Field Theory and the Social Sciences*,
https://doi.org/10.1007/978-981-10-5385-6_17

ideas, how they arose and the implications these have for our own work with them in terms of reflexivity and method.

Bourdieu first came to the attention of scholars in what he often referred to as an 'Anglo-Saxon', English-speaking academic world as somewhat of a 'vulgar Marxist' cultural critic and as a 'sociologist of education' (see Bredo and Feinberg 1979; DiMaggio 1979; Young 1971). For the former, his work on museums and photography formed part of a reassessment of cultural norms and practices, and the values underpinning them. For the latter, he was the 'cultural capital' man who, along with British-based sociologists such as Basil Bernstein, showed up how clashes between the cultures of school and home actively led to differences in academic achievement which, ultimately, contributed to the reproduction of social classes. In this early period at least, the two constituencies were often distinct despite sharing a concern with the nature and operations of *culture* as each defined it (and let us remember that Bourdieu's own use of the term is particular—see Bourdieu 1971). Both read Bourdieu with little reference to his voluminous work on Algeria carried out in the 1950s and early 1960s. If we had done so, we may have understood better the ways that culture for him was not just an adjunct of society but synonymous with it, and what that meant in terms of research method and practice.

Certainly, the significance of this early work in shaping the later work is now appreciated much more with a number of readers on Bourdieu and his work appearing in recent years (e.g. Grenfell 2004). It did not help at the time that so little of the earlier work was translated into English—much of it is still not—or, that when it did appear (e.g. *Outline of a Theory of Practice*, 1977/1972), it did so with significant cuts from the empirical data that were used in the original to substantiate the arguments presented. With a more comprehensive reading of these, such extended texts as *Distinction* (Bourdieu 1984/1979), *The Logic of Practice* (1990/1980), *Homo Academicus* (1988/1984) and *The State Nobility* (1996/1989) might have been less shocking, as might the range of topics Bourdieu was covering—economics, politics, philosophy, gender, art, literature, religion, fashion, media, etc. Of course, the former are each large tomes, and they took some time to digest, and in relation to each other—even once the translation arrived. The *Sociologist's Craft*—a major statement of the methodological approach Bourdieu was adopting—did not appear until 1991, even though it was first published in France in 1968.

I make these points not to be a bibliographic pedant but to raise issues about what Bourdieu himself referred to as 'the social conditions of production' of cultural artefacts and, thus, how they are received and interpreted—ultimately used. He warned about dangers of the 'international circulation of ideas' (1999) and, in interviews I did with him (Bourdieu and Grenfell 1995), quoted J.B. Thompson approvingly that English-speaking academics sometimes catch French ideas like 'French flu'—from which they most certainly need curing! Elsewhere, he pleads for a 'sociogenetic' reading of his work (1993), one which builds in contextual elements of provenance and construction.

This line of argument clearly risks discarding any application or extension of Bourdieu's ideas as 'inauthentic' if not built on both a comprehensive reading of his entire oeuvre and the intellectual French tradition from which it emerged. Clearly, such a position would be foolish and unwarranted. Nevertheless, there is something to be said about Bourdieu's own relationship to theory and practice, how one evolved from the other, and how analytical concepts emerged from this work which may help us in guiding our own, especially with respect to that most elusive of dimensions—reflexivity.

It is commonly recognised that Bourdieu underwent somewhat of an intellectual epiphany when faced with the shock of being transported into the Colonial war then playing out in Algeria in the 1950s, and from which his first publication emerged (1958). This experience clearly meant that Bourdieu, the philosopher, had to 'make sense' of a *practical* reality of what was occurring at that time and place. However, the kind of epistemological epiphany on which his entire work is based came a little while later:

When I came back from Algeria, I was an assistant at the Sorbonne and Aron said to me, 'You are a Normalien, you can teach Durkheim'. And, for me, that was terrible – to have to teach Durkheim. Nothing could be worse! I had read Durkheim as a student – *The Rules of Method*. Then, I had to read it again to teach it and it began to interest me because it could help me with my empirical work on Algeria. Mauss even more. Then, I went on to Weber. I taught Weber and I found the notion of field which I had confusingly in my mind while teaching it…It irritated me a lot and I could not see the logic. And, then, one day, I started to make a scheme on the blackboard and I said to myself, 'Well, it's obvious, it is necessary to study people 'in relations' …. I was doing structuralist studies of parenthood, the Kabyle house. So, I was reading a pre-structuralist text with a structuralist way of thinking. (1995, p. 4–5)

At another moment in the interview, Bourdieu makes the statement that he has only managed to produce the 'works of his youth' (ibid., p. 32). The point I would make is that this epistemological epiphany can be read backwards and forward: back to his own biography and intellectual training and forward to the rest of his academic career. We see that the early book on Algeria makes very little use of the sort of concepts, which were to become synonymous with Bourdieu, although it may be possible to see them in germinal form. *Habitus*, for example, is referred to as *habitat* (itself a phenomenological concept developed by Husserl). But, it was not until 1966, that the concept of *Field* was employed explicitly (1971/1966) as a principal tool of analysis and later still that the relationship between *field* and *habitus* (objectivity and subjectivity) was set out (see Bourdieu 1991a/1968, p. 68). In fact, I am not sure those of us who were using Bourdieu and his methods in the 1980s and 1990s, or indeed reading texts from him at this time, saw it necessarily as work in *Field Theory* per se; yet, his final *leçons* at the *Collège de France* were badged indeed as *Further Explorations in Field Theory*. Along the way, of course, a whole other arsenal of Bourdieusian concepts had been developed and deployed (see Grenfell 2014 for an elucidation of the most basic).

Again, I raise these issues, not as an example of intellectual archaeology but with a sense that they seem crucial to our current use of Bourdieu and his ideas in our own practice. How so? I will make three major points. Firstly, what we have with Bourdieu is a single epistemological vision that he spent the rest of his life articulating. It is one thing to see it in 'a flash', another to unpack it across time. Secondly, this relationship between theory and practice in field work raises issues about our own relation to and work with it. Thirdly, and somewhat autologically implied by the above, is the question of reflexivity: What is it? How does it feature in Bourdieu's work and what role might it have in our own?

Before turning specifically to reflexivity, I would make some points about research methodology and the analytic concepts themselves.

II

In other contexts, I have set out what I considered the essential 'phases' and 'levels' of a Bourdieusian methodology (Grenfell 2014, Grenfell and Lebaron 2014). In terms of phases, they go as follows:

1. Construction of the Research Object
2. Field Analysis
3. Participant Objectivation.

The first of these—the Construction of the Research Object—is perhaps the most critical and radical of the entire undertaking, as it is here that the object of research is 'rethought' as against the orthodoxy of the field in order to break with the historic assumptions embedded within its representations, rethought that is in Bourdieusian terms. It obviously attests to the power of the approach that it is now adopted in such a wide range of academic fields. However, there is a danger—through natural processes of *elective affinities*—that those within these fields take what they like and discard the rest; this risks undermining the potential a Bourdieusian perspective has to uncover aspects of discipline areas not yet seen. In other words, without a radical view of the construction of the research object, the researcher simply reproduces their own dispositional views and relations to it.

Subsequent 'Field analysis' then involves work at three levels:

1. The field in relation to the field of power
2. The field itself.
3. The habitus of those holding positions within the field.

There is then 'participant objectivation', about which more below.

I set these phases and levels out in this way, not to 'police' what is done in terms of Bourdieusian method but to encourage *a certain conformism* in key aspects to adopting the approach. Otherwise, it seems to me, it is so easy simply to pick and choose what suits, pass over difficult elements and reconstruct the method in one's own image in the name of celebrating diversity and development. It is not so much that any Bourdieusian orientated study must include all of these; it is just that, anyone utilising this theory and practice will hardly be doing justice to it without at least considering each of these phases and levels in some depth.

A similar point might be made about the use of the concepts themselves: they need to be understood in terms of these phases and levels as well as being used to work within them. There is frequent use in some research of the term 'seeing the world through a Bourdieusian lens'. But, what does that mean? It is all too easy to *metaphorise* data; in other words, simply employ terms such as *habitus, field* and *capital* in order to discuss research findings. Such can lead to a weak form of constructivism, where biographical incident is interpreted in terms of what is and is not valued in various contexts. Here, there is little attempt to undertake a 'field analysis' per se in terms of structure—positioning and the quantities of various forms of capital leading to hierarchies of salience within. Such research is done in a descriptive, qualitatively narrative based way. There are other common 'abuses' and 'misuses' (see Grenfell 2010). We should also be careful about 'correcting' Bourdieu, or pointing out what he 'does not do', 'avoids', 'sidesteps', 'ignores'. We do certainly need to build on what he did but, firstly, we must be clear about exactly what he claimed and, indeed, what he did and did not do—and why. Any subsequent developments then need to build on such an understanding in order to ascertain 'what it can buy us'—rather, that is, than (too easily) fall into misplaced revisionist variations of his approach. Not to do so threatens both the potential and the integrity of the analytic concepts and indeed approach more generally.

We know that Bourdieu's theory of practice was built in twin opposition to both Sartrean subjectivity and the structuralist objectivity of Levi-Strauss and Althusser (see Grenfell 2014 parts I and II). Objects of research for him can never be seen as *objects in themselves*—a view, which underpins *substantialist* science—but are understood *in relation*; that is, they are always set within their socio- historical environment. In effect, this is a science of movement and process rather than one of stasis; an ontology of relations rather than substance—'existential analytics' (see Dreyfus and Rabinow 1993). But, relations and structures in terms of what?

Bourdieu's conceptual terms—*habitus, field, capital,* etc.—were developed as part of a practical engagement with the object of research and the data collected in its terms. Such concepts arose for him as *logically necessitated* by this relationship, which also needs to be seen as personal in the first instance (e.g. based on Bourdieu's own philosophical and empirical biography) before leading to the formulation of scientific claims on its behalf. All of Bourdieu's later comments on reflexivity point in this direction.

What the emerging concepts do all share is a common *structural* epistemology: *structure* as the co-incidence between the cognitive, phenomenological and the socio-anthropological (see Grenfell and Lebaron, 20, Part I). Hence, the vivid dialectic of *structuring and structured structures* as set out in the *Outline of Theory of Practice* (op. Cit.). I might add that this phrase in English does not quite capture the dynamic of the French equivalent: '*les structures structurées qui se structurent en se structurant*'. A key point here is not only *what* is being signified but *how*—in what concepts and language?—and the role of the latter in the process of generating knowledge: relations and structures are expressed in a certain sort of language for Bourdieu which means we must understand the relationship between signifier and signified within his method.

III

It is to note that when asked what advice he would give to a young researcher, amongst Bourdieu's first statements was the warning to 'beware of words' (1989: 54). He then makes the point that sometimes the language of research can become *more real* than the object it aims to represent; this is why there is a need to focus on the language of representation in the constructing of the research object, as it is here that historical *misrecognitions* are hidden. Indeed, language can almost create what it refers to, or might refer to; that is both the form and the content of social phenomena. Bourdieu draws attention to this way that language shapes experience in terms of the phenomenology of the affective life— the topic of a Masters thesis he apparently never completed:

> There is a wisdom that is recorded over millennia, of symptoms which are translated into language (stomach knots, makes me feel sick) .... or is it that language has produced the symptoms?'. It was interesting because (in my work in Algeria) there was no language of emotions to do a comparative sociology of affective lives, which would employ language as a means of structuring perceptions and also bodily experiences. (Bourdieu: 2008, p. 352)

Here, language actually structures perception a little like the Sapir-Whorf hypothesis. This feature somewhat leads us to questions of language, the philosophy of language and ultimately post-modernist issues about the relationship between language in representing the world and/or explaining it.

The play-off between language (conceptual terms) and perceived experience—in research itself—must therefore go to the heart of our epistemological concerns. It is tantamount to saying our thoughts not only shape what we see but in fact almost produce (and indeed limit) what *we can see* and *think*—so, on what are they based? This is not just a question of linguistic relativity with respect to the signified but of actual exegesis and what is claimed in its name. In the same way that, in contemporary physics, if scientists look at electrons as discrete entities, they are discrete entities, and if they look at them as a wave, they (somewhat mysteriously) become a wave, maybe our enquiry into the empirical world requires us to understand the nature of our own conscious viewpoint itself and the language we use to express it, in order for us to appreciate the way it shapes what we (can) see.

I believe these perspectives are very close to Bourdieu's view of social space and phenomena as emergent processes. They certainly raise questions about how we conceptualise the social world and ourselves in it—empirically and as science researchers. We do, therefore, need to understand the epistemological status of the concepts we have—*habitus*, *field* and *capital*, etc.—beneath the language used to express them; what they allow us to see—and not see.

The most direct response to this ambition is set out in the *Theory of Practice* itself, and the characteristics of the knowledge outcome intended is made at the beginning of the *Outline of a Theory of Practice* where Bourdieu writes of a series of 'epistemological breaks': firstly, from *empirical knowledge*—the naïve state; secondly, *phenomenological* subjective/sense *knowledge*; and thirdly, from *structuralist* objectivist knowledge. There is then, significantly, a final break with theoretical knowledge itself—a *theory of theory*—which is the true characteristic of the *practical rationality* and thus *reflexive objectivity* to which Bourdieu aspires. It is this final element that enshrines principles of reflexivity, which were not fully articulated until later in Bourdieu's intellectual trajectory. This place, Bourdieu argues, is achieved by *constructing the generative principles* of research practice; in this case, *in their moment* of its accomplishment. This *science of practices* is predicated on creating the *conditions of possibility* of its realisation. So, what is this epistemological *generative principle?* And, what are its *conditions of possibility?* Such questions imply a need to understand the relationship between the individual, the world, knowledge arising from it and the language used to express this knowledge? Once again, the language we use—the concepts—is clearly crucial in communicating our answers such questions. For Habermas:

> ...individuals, when they act communicatively, go through the natural (empirical) language, make use of interpretations that are culturally transmitted and make reference to something in the objective world, in the social world, which they share and make, and each one makes reference to something in its own subjective world simultaneously. (Habermas 1987a, pp. 499–500)

However, for Bourdieu, such can never arise from ordinary, empirical language; only from special scientific concepts, themselves generated out of practical exegesis. As such, concepts such as *habitus, field* and *capital* can be seen as providing the foundations for a kind of Bourdieusian 'communicative competence'—a 'language of association' (linking subjects, the subject and the object, and the objects themselves) for those working from this perspective. Here, the individual is seen as being somewhat 'at one' with the collectivity. The 'social' world is 'objective'—that is, communicable—and thus pertaining to a reality beyond the empirical self, but which can be accessed through it. At such points, the self and the collectivity become one and the same thing; not just empirically, but in some more 'heightened', emancipated realm beyond everyday subjective identification. It follows that the power of such language—the way it is used and the valued outcome of its deployment—carries with it the potential to both change relations to the empirical world and how we act as a result. Epistemological principles underlying these relations are hence critical in ascertaining certain forms of scientific knowledge and their effects.

In Habermasian epistemology, three epistemological *modes* are presented—*hermeneutic, nomothetic* and *critical*—pertaining to substantive *interests* (see Grenfell 2014, pp. 151–168 for a Bourdieusian interpretation of such): law-giving, interpretive and emancipatory (Habermas 1987b). Given the above, however, such modes do not simply represent discrete, implicit epistemological interests—ways of knowing—but also need to be defined and expressed in terms of whole social relations to the world, which have practical, ultimately political, consequences. Bourdieusian science, therefore, implies a different form of relationship to the world and thus with a different interest. Such can be expressed as *praxeological knowledge*, which might be understood as a fusion of the three Habermasian modes and sharing each of their corresponding *interests*—interpretative, law-bound (structural) and emancipatory. This is why Bourdieu insists on maintaining *epistemological vigilance*. Keeping these *interests* discrete can never amount to Habermasian *communicative action* or *competence* for him, since each implies a particular scholastic rather than practical understanding of (and thus relation to) the social world. This distinction needs to be objectified in presenting scientific knowledge as part of a reflexive undertaking in its constitution. Indeed, reflexivity then becomes a principal pre-requisite condition of the possibility of Bourdieusian science. Before looking at the way reflexivity is operationalised in Bourdieu's method, it is first necessary to examine further elements of practice, the subject-object relationship and the way these play out between the researcher and the object of research.

III

It is again important to stress that Bourdieu's *theory of practice* begins in practice and ends in practice—the first empirical, the second scientific—its generative principle is therefore practice, as are its *conditions of possibility*. So, how do we achieve this reflexive *practical gaze* of practice *in* practice expressed practically? The short answer is by not simply employing these concepts in research but going beyond them and turning them on the research product and researcher as well; and not as some post hoc adjunct but as a central part of the entire research process.

As noted above, Bourdieu clearly saw empirical data through his own (developing) *habitus* to the objective conditions of their own creation: both needing to be considered as the subject and the object of science. This is partly why he argues that researchers must not feign objectivity as some sort of 'disinterested other' and would do better to rely on their own subjective experience in understanding 'the objective' (Bourdieu 2000). But not, it must be stressed, subjectivity as the empirical—non-reflexive—self, but 'scientifically', by thinking in terms of structural relations and developing a language—static—to express a dynamic process. This way of acting is more an ontology than epistemology as it acts both on the object of research and the objectifying subject. The fact that this theory of practice is embodied in the concepts—*habitus, field* and *capital*—means that these then need to be regarded as active epistemological matrices capable of affecting ontology and consequent understanding in terms of the phenomenological relationship to the social world—ultimately, both scientifically *and* empirically. Bourdieusian language (concepts) is then epistemologically charged and can provide the *possibility of understanding of* (empirical) practice *as* practice *in* practice finally to be lived in (emancipatory) practice:

> The science of this mode of knowledge finds its foundation in a theory of practice as practice, meaning an activity founded in cognitive operations, which mobilize a mode of knowing, which is not that of theory and concept... (but) a sort of ineffable practicipation in an object known (in practice). (Bourdieu 1992, p. 433 my translation and brackets)

Such a position is also consistent with Bourdieu's theory of language per se. In a very Wittgensteinian sense, Bourdieu argues that language only has meaning in terms of the *situations* within which it is immersed at any one time and place—literally, a game! For him, the schemes of perception, which individuals hold and the language, which carries them are each homologously linked to social structures, which act as both their provenance and social destiny. Just as social agents exist in *network relations*; therefore, words also exist in *networks of semantic relations* to each other—and partly acquire their meaning in terms of difference and similarity *with respect to each other* instantiated at specific times and places. Sense and meaning, then, are always determined by the interplay between individual meaning and the social context in which language is being expressed. Such contexts are set within *social spaces*—often as *fields*—that are bounded areas of activity, for example education, culture and politics. Words form a part of such *social space* and *fields* and are ultimately used to represent their *particular way of thinking*. By entering a *field* (implying a semantic network), a word thus takes on meaning *from that field* and defines meaning; which itself differs according to its position within the overall *field* and thus semantic *space*. The attribution of meaning is therefore also a kind of imposition (originating from the *field* context)—a kind of *transformation* and *transubstantiation* where meaning is changed from one context to another: 'the substance signified is the signifying form which is realized' (1991b, p. 143) in practice. In other words, what is signified and signifying is socially co-terminus for Bourdieu; the meaning necessary to a *field* context is realised in the particular lexical/semantic form. So, words can have one meaning in one context and another elsewhere. It is an imposition because any specific meaning can be projected onto a word—signifying signifier—prior to it being signified as a sign (word). This is true both empirically and scientifically, which is why Bourdieusian concepts take on the epistemological power of their provenance, which can then be further re-actualised in research practice, with the corresponding effects.

Such analytic concepts as *habitus* and *field* therefore have an epistemological status outside of their empirical norm, upon which they act in order to generate knowledge that is somewhat *snatched* from the assumptions of everyday reality and is, as such, *scientific*. It is, therefore, easy to see why they are central to Bourdieu's ambition to found such a *praxeological* science, since they mediate the relationship between subject, object and context.

Of course, Bourdieu somewhat infamously wrote that the divide between objectivity and subjectivity was the most 'ruinous' in the social sciences. But, what is it to get beyond them, to this 'a science of the dialectical relations between objective structures...and the subjective dispositions, within which these structures are actualised, and which tend to reproduce them' (1977, p. 3). The subject-object relation itself rests at the base of phenomenology, the view of structure of which Bourdieu so evidently shares. In the *Phenomenology of Perception*, for example, Merleau-Ponty writes:

> This subject-object dialogue, this drawing together, by the subject, of the meaning diffused through the object, and, by the object, of the subject's intentions – a process which is physiognomic perception – arranges round the subject a world which speaks to him of himself, and gives his own thoughts their place in the world. (Merleau-Ponty 1962, 45, p.132)

In this way, subject is always immanent in an object and vice versa. Indeed, the world as constituting sense is immanent and speaks to us *of ourselves*. But, who is this self?—our empirical or scientific selves? Whatever the answer to this question, a further one arises concerning what we understand each—empirical and scientific—to be and the relationship between them. At base, both involve an 'embodiment'—what

Bourdieu would refer to as *hexis*—not simply based on mental activity, but one where the objective also creates the subjective in the process of incorporation. The former gives meaning to the latter on the basis of what is perceived—and can be perceived. 'I understand the world and it understands' me', Bourdieu quotes approvingly from Pascal (2000c, p. 408). This is a clearly a very subtle point: Merleau-Ponty above (and with him Bourdieu) does not intend that the world is sentient, as human. It is subject consciousness that 'sees' the world; but this world still 'calls' on the subject to know what it already knows, to be conscious of what it is already conscious of (a kind of *interpolation* in Foucauldian terms). Such again leads us to a consideration of the nature of consciousness as reflexivity in the relationships between the two.

This viewpoint hence sees the subject-object dyad existing as a single '*flesh*', so to speak: they are intimately connected, and one only leaves off where another begins and vice versa. This is not to say that the visible blends into us, or we to it; rather 'the seer and the visible reciprocate one another and we no longer know which sees and which is seen' (Merleau-Ponty 1968/1964, p. 139). The *flesh* then appears as an element—such as water, air, fire and earth—rather than an actual thing: spiritual/material, mind/matter, idea of thing. Such goes to the heart of modern metaphysics and the relationship between knowledge and impressions as initiated by Kant (Kant 1956/1788, 1961/1781, 1987/1790—see Grenfell and Hardy 2007, p. 36–39 for summary).

For Kant, when sense data as an object is intuited by imagination, there is a point of intuitive resonance that lies beyond the individual judgement—of right and wrong, for example—and represents the power to form judgments itself: that is, a sense of understanding that is literally beyond knowing, an empathy or identification but of universal assent. If we take artistic aesthetics, for example, the distinction between '*sensation*' and '*the beautiful*' is useful here, where the faculty of feeling replaces structure derived from concepts (expressed in language). The beautiful—a sub-set of sense data—is presented to understanding (in time and space) by imagination, but is not converted via conceptual categorisations because non-cognitive feeling accompanies intuition: in other words, non-cognitive feelings replace concepts. Since there is no conceptual categorisation to provide form, what is experienced is *the power to form concepts itself*—which is very close to consciousness—a consciousness without anything to be conscious of. Hence, it is 'disinterested' (beyond value)—that is, contemplative rather than cognitive (conceptual/theoretical). In Kant's philosophy of art, therefore, this is *transcendental aesthetics—the disinterested pure gaze*—that lies beyond sensation. However, the key point here is that for Bourdieu, this realm cannot be one of *universal* pure aesthetics but is the reflection of a certain—bourgeois—relationship to the world (see *Distinction* 1984): superior, detached, masterful, but empty—a kind of absence because it reflects its own detached position in the social world (neither one thing nor another)—a kind of *nothingness*. 'Objective knowledge' in science can be seen as also sharing the same ambition of 'disinterestedness'—'knowledge for knowledge sake': what Bourdieu would call the aspiration of *'knowledge without a knowing subject'*—a Popperian World 3. In this case, it is less that data are presented by imagination to understanding without concepts, but that pre-existing—a priori—(theoretical) concepts (expressed in language) provide the power to form understanding within particular cognitive (theoretical) structures. Here, it is 'concepts' with a particular scientific disciplinary provenance and relation to the world and thus interest. Such would be scientific objectivity within the positivist paradigm. In effect, this knowledge—and thus relationship—might even be understood as the cognitive/intellectual effect of the aesthetic side of the bourgeois power to transcend—but, this time in the expression of objective knowledge—by asserting not so much *the truth* but a certain kind of *truth* (objectivist) which carries with it its own undisclosed *interest* (control) and thus legitimacy and consecration—this time in the name of reason. We might even say that *knowledge without a knowing subject* is akin to the pure aesthetic gaze in its claim to a *transcendent objectivity*, which, in effect, can be understood as nothing other than the transcendental sense of the bourgeois intelligentsia, and its relative structural relationship to the world; what Bourdieu once described as 'thoughtless power and powerless thought' (1991b, p. 98). Such knowledge is criticised by Bourdieu since it is un-reflexive and so does not disclose its *interest* in asserting a certain way of knowing the world, and thus misrecognises its inherent relative positing with respect to it. Reflexivity is therefore a necessary part of the endeavour in order to escape this trap—what might be more politely termed the *scholastic fantasy*.

IV

It is a moot and not uncontested issue as to the extent to which reflexivity features across Bourdieu's oeuvre; still more whether or not it is the essence of his methodological purpose. It might seem that reflexivity does not feature explicitly from the early and mid-period. Some even find the personal 'revelations'—summed up as 'le rose-bud de Pierre Bourdieu' in *Le Nouvel Observateur* at the time of his death—or his final lecture at the *Collège de France*, published later in the *Sketch for a Self-Analysis* (2007/2004) to be a somewhat post hoc formulation of how 'he would wish to be read' (Lamont 2012). They do not see the empirical studies carried out in the Béarn, or Algeria and indeed in Education, as necessarily reflexive. Even *Homo Academicus* can only be read as Bourdieu reflecting on his own professional field in retrospect. At the same time, reflexivity was clearly an inherent part of Bourdieu's initial research endeavours in the way he brought his own *habitus*—both professional and personal—to the objects of his studies. Moreover, the original French version of *Outline* had a chapter on 'the observer observed' (pp. 225–234) and, from the leçons given in Paris from the mid-1980s, we see an explicit awareness of the need for a 'sociology of sociology' as a way of breaking out of the box in which contemporary sociologists have shut themselves (Bourdieu 2016, 1116). By the last decade of his career, of course, reflexivity was clearly central to Bourdieu's concerns (see Bourdieu 1990c, 1992b and 2004). Finally, he extended the reflexive element of his work as an attempt *to objectify the social forces that acted upon him* (Bourdieu 2007/2004; Eakin 2001); offering the method as of use equally to a general and academic public (e.g. Bourdieu 2000). At base of such reflexivity is the epistemological epiphany I described at the outset. The outcome of this vision can itself be expressed as the ontological *separation* he made between his own *empirical subject* and *scientific subject*:

> The scientific habitus can be independent in relation to the habitus. Basically, there are two subjects. There is the empirical subject. Myself, when I go to a meeting, I am like everyone. I am nervous. I am angry. I say, 'this guy is an idiot, why does he say that? I agree with the other one'. Like everyone. When I analyse that, it is not the same subject. It is a subject that objectifies that, who understands why Bourdieu is angry. It is another subject which is very difficult to maintain in life. In everyday life,

one becomes an empirical subject once again...but it is possible to create a kind of torn out subject...and the more it is collective and reflexive, the more it is separate from the empirical subject...I have learnt with age and experience that the knowing subject can change the naive subject a little. There are things that one understands better and suffer from less. (1995, op. Cit. p. 38–39)

In sum, Bourdieu wants to replace *empirical* and *objective knowledge* as alluded to above with a form of *reflexive objectivity—practical rationality* and *praxeological knowledge*; and, concepts such as *habitus, field* and *capital* are the means to do this. There is also an issue here with respect to 'semantic density'; in other words, they are not just conceptual terms or descriptive metaphors but contain a kind of epistemological 'genome' through which sense data are apprehended and understood. In a sense, the ultimate source behind such concepts is not bourgeois nothingness alluded to above with respect to that certain relationship to society but emancipatory knowledge, which again represents a different relationship to society. Here, *habitus, field* and *capital* might even be seen as acting as a *kind of epistemological mordant* between subject and object (the empirical and scientific subject): an a priori epistemological understanding which conveys the principle of practice instantiated in the present— as they speak *to* us and *of* us: to see oneself as *habitus, field and capital* at the point of seeing and of what is seen. These terms hence carry the notion of contingent understanding, but not tentativeness or conjecture. Rather they lead a form of *radical doubt* on the part of the researcher; a kind of Rortyan *final vocabulary* (Rorty 1980) as a pragmatic expression of the best we can do at any one particular time. They also stabilise knowledge in a way, which shares many of the features of Popperian theory—predictability, generalisability, open to articulation, useful and simple. Such amounts to an ambition to form a theory of practice that aims to be distinct from both objectivist abstraction and the intoxicating familiarity of common sense interpretation apprehended in its everyday obviousness.

V

To sum up, phenomenologically, Bourdieusian concepts seem to define not only what we see but what we *can* see. The empirical state deploys empirical concepts to make sense of the world; the would-be researcher deploys their own conceptual frame in understanding the object of its research. As noted, this is why it is so important to objectify the *construction of the research object* since without a reflexive reconstruction it will express a pre-existing scholastic orthodoxy (for itself) rather than the thing (in itself) in praxeological terms. We know that the objectifying subject is prone to three forms of bias: the conceptual orthodoxy of their field; their own background and position within it; and the very non-empirical relation that the researcher takes up—*skholè*—*vis-à-vis* the object of investigation (Bourdieu 2000c, p. 10). There seem to be two prime ways of doing this. Firstly, there is the need to think conceptually of oneself in terms of *habitus, field* and *capital*, the very use of which would seem to purge the undertaking of any transcendent, substantialist objectivist (control) in favour of a genuine relational science (emancipatory). Secondly, the need to place oneself in the field of knowledge in terms of connections with the field of power, connections and relations to the field, and one's individual personal relationships in terms of *habitus* and its position and proximity to others.

Source of Bias

1. Position in Social Space (Habitus/Cognitive Structures)
2. Orthodoxy of the Field Site (language)
3. *Skholè*—Scholastic Fantasy (Relations to the world—Substantialist/Relational

Reflexive View

1. Fields in relation to the field of power—my connection/connecting.
2. My relationship to the doxa in the field; held in institution. What am I connected to? Doxa of the discipline—Aims. Position in field.
3. My habitus and that of other people in the site context;

Their habitus and mine; personal relationships/networks. My position and proximity.

This is what Bourdieu means by *participant objectivation* and it is something, which is logically predicated from the very instant of his epistemological vision even if it only gained prominence in the last decade of his career. It has to be, because his epistemology of practice is too comprehensive to leave the researcher on the outside of it. Indeed, not to include the researcher in it is an act of intellectual bad faith, even if it requires them to vacate the position they have acquired in undertaking the research and *disarming* themselves of the intellectual weapons they have employed to gain it. Why? Because 'the truth is that truth is at stake' (Bourdieu 1990b, p. 195). Moreover, such is not accomplished without a cost. Indeed, 'one must choose to pay a higher price for truth while accepting a lower profit of distinction' (1991, p. 34). This can be read as a warning for all of us who adopt a Bourdieusian approach simply because of the symbolic capital it can confer in terms of implied distinction within the academic field. Ultimately, his philosophy is corrosive: both professionally and personally—if taken to its logical conclusion.

Clearly, such a reflexive approach cannot ultimately be only an individual enterprise but necessitates a collective commitment; others have pointed out the necessity of a collective response (see Deer 2014), what Shirato and Webb (2003) refer to as a field 'meta-literacy'. There is a paradox because Bourdieu was so scathing about other forms of reflexivity—with their illusion of being able to 'transcend thought by the power of thought itself'. Rather, for him, it is a question of transcending both empirical and conventional scholastic thinking by the power of his theory of practice and the epistemological vision it makes available. No wonder he referred to it as a *metanoia*.

The difficulty is when the subject makes for themselves an object—*in their own image*—and thus with all the implied assumptions of view. This is inevitable to a certain extent. However, if that making is carried out in terms of Bourdieusian concepts—praxeologically validated—then, as I have argued, terms such as *habitus*, *field* and *capital*, etc. can mediate between subject and object in a way that constitutes a *different interest*: an interest with a different ethical, value-based generative principle. Basically, such offers, and indeed allows, a different—emancipatory—view of the world. Consequently, instead of a subject objectifying an object *as an object*, the subject sees itself literally in it but not as a subjective mirror of individual empirical identity but at an epistemological moment grounded in the same generative principles as their scientific practice. In this way, as Bourdieu states it in *The Weight of the World* (1993, p. 609), it is less about seeing oneself in another as being 'able to take up all possible points of view', recognising that, faced with the same conditions, one would likely *be* and *do* the same. This is not to be every man/woman, and everyone to be the same, but to see the structural

relations and principles in exegesis—immanent—which manifest themselves in *this way at this particular time and place and individual,* knowing that given the same conditions *we may well act and be the same.* One
acknowledges and sees oneself in others and others in oneself as the outcome of particular formative conditions; not as a separate object-other.
Bourdieu calls this knowledge a 'spiritual exercise' (ibid., p. 612) and a
sort of 'intellectual love' (ibid.)—a 'non-violent' method since it offers
no imposition of meaning, no *symbolic violence.* There is here no authority, and the faculty to 'think things independently'.

It is also a kind of love because it is based on mutual recognition and
regard; a high form of attention. It is the product of Being reflecting
on Being in a state of collective social identity. At this point, Bourdieu's
epistemology does indeed become an ontology. We might call this
Objective Subjectivity or Subjective Objectivity, which amount to and
are the same. To articulate this level of understanding and knowledge is
always *a posteriori.* But, mostly, it is realised at a point of instantiation.
It is also a case of the past and the future literally *being* in the present,
which is, really, the only place they can exist. This is a consciousness or
reflexive refraction through Bourdieusian theory of practice and concepts
such as *habitus, field* and *capital.* The empirical *habitus* is scientific and
the scientific *habitus* is empirical. The transcendental sense beyond the
power to form concepts then becomes less the Bourgeois sense of nothingness—the pure objective or aesthetic gaze—but *the logical essence of
practice itself,* which is nothing other than the past (a sociological history) instantiating itself in the present (a historical sociology)—a kind of
sociological *karma.* This power *to be* present—this process—is 'grasped'
at the point *of* and *in* becoming rather than in the thing itself formed.

Finally, therefore, reflexivity is less concerned with 'how *to do* it' than
'how *to be* it'. The researcher is implicated in his theorising; the gaze is
necessarily 'personal' but with the potential for praxeological science. It
might be seen as a theory that is a gaze and a gaze that is expressed in
theoretical terms, but one that also furnishes us with a theory that can
generate the gaze in practice—if understood in terms beyond the concepts to their generation—in and through practice. The gaze is then subject to the gaze which is subject to the gaze which is subject to the gaze
as a kind of internal recurrence, but is not eternally recurrent in a post-
modernist way as it is bounded by reflexive concepts of practice in practice. Basically, we always return to the same principles of practice. Time is
the deciding factor here.

At the end of Arthur Miller's biography *Time Bends* (1987/1995) he writes about looking out at the field behind his house from the writing desk on which he had created so much work. He comments that he looked at the trees, the ones he had seen through so many seasons. And, at one point, a sort of chiasmic reversal takes place as he realises that it is the trees that are looking at him. This is the gaze that lies at the heart of Bourdieu: a subjectivity that does not make of itself an object; a subject that instead sees itself in the object, and the object as an expression of the subject, but this time not empirical and un-reflexive but as a 'scientific' presence. In the same way, Bourdieu calls on all of us, to see ourselves in society but also society in ourselves; not as two separation events but as co-terminus—the individual and the collectivity—especially as researchers. God and Man—he reminds us at the end of *Pascalian Meditations* that 'society is God' (2000c, p. 245), meaning that such is not simply an academic or intellectual activity, but an expression of truth—a consciousness/attention that is a higher form of love—identification of same and difference as one and the same thing. We then see the social forces of what is potential, impossible and necessary—even what is good and bad in the world. To grasp this, if only for an instant, is certainly beyond the words we use but can guide what we do as a result.

VI

In this Afterword, I have attempted to show how Bourdieu's theory of practice was instantiated by a particular epistemological vision, which he then took the rest of life to articulate. I have discussed the way in which his conceptual map emerged and why, and the philosophy of practice behind it. As they are expressed in language, I have focused on issues of signification and signified in drawing distinction between the very thoughts and the words used in them, and what the same entails within a Bourdieusian methodological framework as a particular gaze, or *metanoia*. Getting beyond words, in a sense, or at least using them within a *praxeological attitude* leads us to the nature and use of reflexivity within this method; which in turn returns us to issues of subject-object and the conditions of possibility for reflexive objectivity. Finally, as with Bourdieu, it is worth stressing that this is an unfolding journey—both practically and philosophically. Indeed, we might even see using Bourdieu as characteristic of certain 'levels' of understanding and use:

- Level 1: Use of Key Concepts to animate Narrative;
- Level 2: Planning a Research Project from a Bourdieusian 'Lens'. Common focus on the biographical and qualitative analysis.
- Level 3: More Critical Approach to Research Object Construction—a sustained attempt to map the field and fields within fields. Greater use of Quantitative methods.
- Level 4: Consolidation of the above—more refined sense of Reflexivity.
- Level 5: Praxeological.
- Level 6.......

It goes without saying that these should not be read as linear or hierarchical but as *potentia*—and can be realised temporarily at any one instant in conducting research. I leave this Afterword, and indeed book, there in this realm of both personal and professional reflexivity with the question of where it leads us next?

REFERENCES

Bourdieu, P. (1958). *Sociologie de l'Algérie.* (New Revised and Corrected Edition, 1961). Paris: Que Sais-je.

Bourdieu, P. (1971). The thinkable and the unthinkable. *The Times Literary Supplement,* 15 October, pp. 1255–1256.

Bourdieu, P. (1971/1966). Intellectual field and creative project. In M. F. D. Young (Ed.)—'Champ intellectual et project créateur', *Les Temps Modernes,* Nov., pp. 865–906.

Bourdieu, P. (1977/1972). *Outli ne of a Theory of Practice* (R. Nice, Trans.). Cambridge: CUP (*Esquisse d'une théorie de la pratique. Précédé de trois études d'ethnologie kabyle.* Geneva: Droz).

Bourdieu, P. (1984/1979). *Distinction* (R. Nice, Trans.). Oxford: Polity (*La Distinction. Critique sociale du jugement.* Paris: Editions de Minuit).

Bourdieu, P. (1988/1984). *Homo Academicus* (P. Collier, Trans.). Oxford: Polity (*Homo Academicus.* Paris: Les Editions de Minuit).

Bourdieu, P. (with L. Wacquant) (1989). Towards a reflexive sociology: A workshop with Pierre Bourdieu. *Sociological Theory,* 7(1), 26–63.

Bourdieu, P. (1990/1980). *The logic of practice* (R. Nice, Trans.). Oxford: Polity (*Le sens pratique.* Paris: Les Editions de Minuit).

Bourdieu, P. (1990/1987). *In other words: Essays towards a reflexive sociology* (M. Adamson, Trans.). Oxford: Polity (*Choses dites.* Paris: Les Editions de Minuit).

Bourdieu, P. (with Chamboredon, J.-C. and Passeron, J.-C.). (1991a/1968). *The craft of sociology* (R. Nice, Trans.). New York: Walter de Gruyter (*Le Métier de sociologue*. Paris: Mouton-Bordas).

Bourdieu, P. (1991b/1988). *The political ontology of Martin Heidegger* (P. Collier, Trans.). Oxford: Polity Press.

Bourdieu, P. (1992a). *Les règles de l'art: gènese et structure du champ littéraire*. Paris: Seuil.

Bourdieu, P. (with Wacquant, L). (1992b). *An Invitation to Reflexive Sociology* (L. Wacquant, Trans.). Oxford: Polity Press (*Réponses. Pour une anthropologie réflexive*. Paris: Seuil).

Bourdieu, P. (1993). For a sociogenetic understanding of intellectual works. In C. Calhoun, L. Lipuma, & M. Postone (Eds.), *Bourdieu: Critical perspectives*. Oxford: Polity Press.

Bourdieu, P. (with Grenfell, M). (1995). *Entretiens*. CLE Papers 37: University of Southampton.

Bourdieu, P. (1996/1989). *The State Nobility. Elite Schools in the Field of Power* (L. C. Clough, Trans.). Oxford: Polity Press (*La noblesse d'état. Grandes écoles et esprit de corps*. Paris: Les Editions de Minuit).

Bourdieu, P. (1999). The social conditions of the international circulation of ideas. In R. Shusterman (Ed.), *Bourdieu: A critical reader*. Oxford: Blackwell.

Bourdieu, P (2000a). 'Participant Objectivation', address given in receipt of the Aldous Huxley Medal for Anthropology, University of London, 12th november, *Mimeograph*, 12 pp.

Bourdieu, P. (2000b). Move over shrinks. *Times Higher Educational Supplement*. 14th April, p. 19.

Bourdieu, P. (2000c/1997). *Pascalian Meditations* (R. Nice, Trans.). Oxford: Polity Press (*Méditations pascaliennes*. Paris: Seuil).

Bourdieu, P. (2004/2001). *Science of science and reflexivity*. Oxford: Polity Press (*Science de la science et réflexivité*. Paris: Raisons d'Agir).

Bourdieu, P. (2007/2004). *Sketch for a self-analysis*. Cambridge: CUP (*Esquisse pour une auto-analyse*. Paris: Raison d'Agir).

Bourdieu, P. (2008). *Esquisses Algériennes*. Paris: Seuil.

Bourdieu, P. (2016). *Sociologie Générale: Cours au Collège de France 1983–1986*. Paris: Raisons d'Agir.

Bredo, E., & Feinberg, W. (1979). Meaning, power, and pedagogy: Pierre Bourdieu and Jean-Claude Passeron, Reproduction in Education, Society and Culture: Essay Review. *Journal of Curriculum Studies, 11*(4), 315–332.

Deer, C. (2014). Reflexivity. In M. Grenfell (Ed.), *Pierre Bourdieu: Key Concept* (2nd ed., pp. 195–210). London: Routledge.

DiMaggio, P. (1979). Review essay on Pierre Bourdieu. *American Journal of Sociology, 84*(6), 1460–1474.

Dreyfus, H., & Rabinow, P. (1993). Can there be a science of existential structure and social meaning. *Bourdieu: Critical perspectives*, 35–44.

Eakin, E. (2001, January 6). Social status tends to seal one's fate, says France's master thinker, *New York Times*.

Grenfell, M. (2004). *Pierre Bourdieu: Agent Provocateur*. London: Continuum.

Grenfell, M. (2010). Working with Habitus and Field: The logic of Bourdieu's practice. In E. Silva & A. Warde (Eds.), *Cultural analysis and Bourdieu's legacy: Settling accounts and developing alternatives* (pp. 14–27). London: Routledge.

Grenfell, M. (Ed.). (2014). *Pierre Bourdieu: Key concepts* (2nd ed.). London: Routledge.

Grenfell, M., & Hardy, C. (2007). *Art rules: Pierre Bourdieu and the visual arts*. Oxford: Berg.

Grenfell, M., & Lebaron, F. (2014). *Bourdieu and data analysis: Methodological principles and practice*. Berne: Peter Lang.

Habermas, J. (1987a). *Theory of communicative action* (Vol. I). Oxford: Polity Press.

Habermas, J. (1987b). *Knowledge and human interests*. Oxford: Polity Press.

Kant, I. (1956/1788). *Critique of practical reason*. New York: Liberal Arts Press.

Kant, I. (1961/1781). *Critique of pure reason*. London: Macmillan.

Kant, I. (1987/1790). *Critique of pure judgement*. Cambridge: Hacket.

Lamont, M. (2012). How has Bourdieu been good to think with? The case of the United States. *Sociological Forum, 1*, 228–237.

Merleau-Ponty, M. (1962/1945). *Phenomenology of perception*. London: Routledge and Kegan Paul (*Phénoménologie de la perception*. Paris: Gallimard).

Merleau-Ponty, M. (1968/1964). *The visible and invisible*. Evanston, IL.: Northwestern University Press (*Le Visible et l'invisible, suivi de notes de travail*. Paris: Gallimard).

Miller, A. (1995/1987). *Time bends: A life*. London: Bloomsbury.

Shirato, T., & Webb, J. (2003). Bourdieu's concept of reflexivity as metaliteracy. *Cultural Studies, 17*(3–4), 539–552.

Rorty, R. (1980). *Philosophy and the mirror of nature*. Oxford: Blackwell.

Young, M. F. D. (Ed.). (1971). *Knowledge and control: New directions for the sociology of education*. London: Collier Macmillan.

INDEX

A

Aboriginal affairs reporting
  people, 134, 136–139, 141, 142
  representation, 136, 137, 143
Academic
  development, 165, 168, 169, 175
  literacy, 67, 68, 71, 72, 74–77
  literacy support services, 72, 74
Aesthetics, 184, 185, 281, 282
Agency, 2, 11, 12, 28, 30, 34, 43, 76,
    186, 193–195, 220, 221, 224
Algeria, 104, 168, 270–272, 275, 283
Audience, 56, 61, 64, 150, 151, 154,
    157, 166, 168, 170, 172, 173,
    175, 177, 178
Australia, 57, 58, 63, 70, 73, 75, 77,
    102, 120, 125, 136, 143, 149,
    159, 160, 186, 190, 205, 238,
    259, 266
Autonomy/Autonomous, 5, 7–9, 11,
    12, 23, 25–28, 35, 42, 56, 57,
    59, 60, 83, 84, 94, 150, 153,
    155, 156, 158, 159, 161, 210,
    211, 214, 229, 241, 242, 258,
    267

B

Bachelard, G., 22, 219
Boudon, R., 252

C

Candlin, C. N., 118, 121–123
Capital
  academic, 67, 69, 70, 169–172,
    174, 178, 253
  cultural, 4, 5, 7, 8, 10, 12, 60, 67,
    68, 72, 74, 75, 77, 78, 86, 88,
    93, 137, 138, 141, 144, 146,
    159, 181, 192, 207, 210, 211,
    214, 240, 241, 270
  economic, 4, 5, 7, 8, 10, 34, 35, 61,
    70, 73, 74, 77, 86, 88, 90–92,
    119, 126, 127, 137, 144, 189,
    192, 203, 208, 213, 214, 237,
    242
  linguistic, 68, 75, 121
  statist, 9
  symbolic, 10, 47, 59, 60, 63, 73,
    77, 137, 144, 145, 184, 188,
    191, 241, 286
Champ, 220, 221

© The Author(s) 2018   293
J. Albright et al. (eds.), *Bourdieu's Field Theory and the Social Sciences*,
https://doi.org/10.1007/978-981-10-5385-6

Cicourel, A.V., 121, 122
Civil service, 7, 10
Code
  clash, 250, 257, 259, 262, 265, 266
  knower, 255, 257, 258, 262–266
  knowledge, 255, 257–260,
    264–266
  legitimation, 250, 254, 255,
    257–259, 266
  match, 257, 259
  shift, 159, 211, 259, 265
  specialization, 255, 257, 258, 260,
    265, 266
Collaboration, 45, 72, 123, 133, 134,
  136, 138, 195. See also Field;
  Strategy
Commissions, 6, 10
Communicative competence, 277
Community engagement
  of consumption, 118, 124, 126–128
Community partner, 136, 139, 141,
  142
Conditions of possibility
  production, 54, 108, 217
Consecration, 56–59, 62, 64, 282
Construction of the research object,
  166, 273, 285
Critical Discourse analysis, 167, 203,
  212
Critically reflexive, 135, 136
Cultural production, 54, 56–58, 149,
  151–153, 155, 157–159, 240,
  241, 246

D
Delegitimised journalism practices and
  products, 134
Dialectical, 220, 224, 228, 230, 231,
  280
Disciplinary, 145, 218, 223, 227, 231,
  232, 255, 257, 282

Discourse analysis, 118, 120, 128,
  167, 203, 212
Disinterested, 107, 278, 281
Dispositions, 2, 6, 9, 10, 12, 23, 40,
  41, 43, 45–50, 62, 76, 106,
  109, 119, 136, 182, 184, 187,
  188, 191, 193, 194, 229, 243,
  250–252, 254, 255, 257–260,
  262, 265, 280
Doctoral education, 165, 166, 169,
  175
Domination
  cultural, 137, 210
  dominant position, 5, 9, 35, 70, 71,
    73, 75
Double object, 134
Doxa, 5, 8, 56, 60, 75, 167, 169, 182,
  186, 191–194, 208, 210–212,
  214, 285
Durkheim, E., 83, 106, 271

E
Elective affinities, 273
Élite code, 257. See also Specialization
  code
Empirical subject, 2, 283, 284
English for Academic Purposes, 72
Epiphany, 166, 271, 272, 283
Epistemic, 100, 106, 110, 260,
  262. See also Specialization;
  Specialization code
  players, 14, 211, 214
  relations, 255, 258, 260, 262–265
Epistemological breaks, 107, 109,
  122, 276
Epistemology, 219, 275, 277, 278,
  285, 287
Established players, 161, 203, 210
Existential analytics, 274

F

Fairclough, N., 167, 203, 212
Female, 104, 181, 182, 184–194
Field
  analysis, 1, 2, 4, 5, 10, 14, 20, 22,
    24, 35, 54, 68, 69, 72, 77, 81,
    95, 134, 145, 159, 166, 168,
    194, 195, 203, 204, 207, 213,
    222, 273, 274
  bureaucratic, 6, 7, 25, 240
  cooperation, 145
  economic, 5, 6, 9–11, 14, 36, 119,
    120, 126, 127, 242
  higher education, 165, 168, 169,
    171
  intellectual, 2, 7–9, 69, 174, 206,
    207, 213, 257
  journalistic, 9, 12, 134–140, 145,
    214
  juridical, 7, 27
  of learning, 40, 41, 46
  meta-field, 6–8, 14
  political, 7, 9, 12, 21, 57, 70, 205,
    213, 214
  position, 3–5, 7–9, 13, 36, 45, 47,
    55, 60, 73, 74, 135, 139, 144,
    145, 204, 208, 210, 214, 215,
    242
  of power, 4–7, 9, 11, 14, 23, 25,
    27, 56, 57, 69, 70, 127, 144,
    185, 186, 209, 212, 273, 285
  strategic, 166, 203
  strategy, 205, 210, 221
  struggle, 5, 7–9, 64, 77, 82, 84,
    133, 135, 137, 138, 141, 145,
    208, 210, 214, 215, 221
  sub-fields, 6, 11, 26, 57, 206, 207,
    211
  theory, 27, 39–42, 47, 48, 50, 64,
    68, 69, 77, 78, 99, 102, 103,
    108, 109, 117, 118, 120, 124,
    126, 128, 135, 138, 139, 145,
    149, 161, 177, 195, 205, 218,
    219, 222–224, 226, 228–231,
    235–237, 249, 251, 258, 259,
    269
  of welfare work, 82, 85, 86, 88, 93
Fieldwork, 8, 22, 33, 56, 99–101,
    104, 105, 107, 109, 272
Final vocabulary, 75, 284
First Peoples, 136
French Revolution, 3

G

Garfinkel, H., 124
Gaze, 60, 105, 107, 109, 165,
    174–176, 178, 186, 240, 249,
    250, 252, 254, 265–267, 278,
    282, 287, 288
Gender, 5, 9, 12, 45, 173, 187, 188,
    191, 192, 205, 207, 208, 211,
    214, 223, 228, 253, 270
Genealogy/Genealogical, 3, 5, 6, 10,
    39, 183, 185
Generative principle, 251, 276, 278,
    286
Goffman, E., 124
Governmentality, 235, 236, 238–240,
    244–246

H

Habermas, 277
Habitus, 4–6, 10, 12, 13, 23, 40–43,
    45–50, 56, 57, 61–64, 68, 69,
    75, 101, 102, 105, 108, 110,
    119, 121, 126, 127, 133, 136,
    165, 166, 169, 171, 175, 176,
    178, 183, 186, 188, 190–192,
    194, 217, 218, 220, 222, 223,
    226, 229–231, 242, 250–254,
    259, 260, 265, 266, 272–274,
    276–278, 280, 283–287

Halliday, M.A.K., 125
Harvey, D., 222–224, 226–232
Heterodox field strategy, 138
Heuristic, 4, 55, 206–208, 212
Hexis, 281
Homology/Homologies/
    Homologous, 4–10, 31, 49, 54,
    83, 94, 133, 137, 139, 159, 160,
    165, 169, 214
Housing market, 6, 11, 22

I
Illusio, 9, 56, 74, 120, 165, 166, 169,
    182, 194, 210
Inclusion, 136, 191
Indigenous, 66, 69, 71, 73, 75, 134,
    136–139, 143–145, 160. *See also*
    First Nations
Inequality, 137, 138, 193
Insider research, 165, 167, 171, 172,
    177, 178
Intellectual love, 177, 287
Intentional definitions, 252. *See also*
    Operative definitions
Interest, 3, 4, 6, 7, 10, 35, 39, 40, 61,
    69, 74, 99, 105, 118–120, 122,
    135, 144, 152, 155, 157, 177,
    238, 242, 271, 277, 278, 288, 286
International circulation of ideas, 271
Internationalisation, 67, 77
International students, 68, 70

J
Journalism, 133–135, 137, 139, 142.
    See also Aboriginal affairs
    collaborative, 131, 132, 135, 136,
        141
    education, 133, 134, 139, 145
    legitimacy, 132
    practice, 134, 232

K
Kant, I., 281, 282

L
Learning cultures, 40, 41, 43, 46, 49
Lefebvre, F., 218, 224, 226, 229–232
Legitimate language, 121, 125
Legitimation/Legitimisation, 5, 8,
    67, 69, 139, 207, 208, 250, 254,
    257, 258, 267
Legitimation Code Theory (LCT),
    250, 254, 255, 257–259,
    265–267
Liberation, 135
Lieu, 220, 222
Literacy, 67, 72

M
Marginalisation, 144, 185
Marx, K., 222, 224, 227, 231
Masculinities, 41, 49
Mauss, M., 271
Media, 55, 64, 136, 138, 144, 145,
    149, 156, 158–160, 181, 188,
    191, 223, 239, 270
Metanoia, 165, 175, 176, 178, 249,
    286, 288
Method/Methodology, 3, 6, 23, 82,
    89, 94, 95, 99–101, 104, 109,
    122, 166, 175, 203, 236, 238,
    246, 269, 270, 272, 273, 275,
    278, 283, 287–289
Miller, A., 288
Misrecognition, 13, 133, 135, 172,
    182, 191, 246, 275
Multi-perspectival, 118, 128
Musicians, 49, 156

N

Narrative, 104, 107, 124, 125, 127, 134, 142, 143, 160, 178, 186, 188, 223, 274, 289
Neoliberalism, 11, 41
Nietzsche, F., 3

O

Objectivation(s), 99–101, 103, 105, 107–109, 134, 165, 168, 174, 177, 195
Objectivity, 2, 11, 13, 100, 101, 106, 108, 109, 134, 167, 221, 224, 270, 272, 274, 276, 278, 280, 282, 284, 287, 288
Object of research, 82, 121, 128, 166, 273, 274, 278
Ontology, 274, 278, 287
Operative definitions, 252. *See also* Intentional definitions

P

Participant objectivation, 99–101, 103, 107–109, 165, 168, 177, 195, 273, 285
Pascal, B., 219, 281
Patriarchy, 182
Patriocolonial, 181, 185–187, 191, 192, 194
Peer-led learning cultures, 39, 43, 44, 49
Phenomenology, 2, 275, 280
Philosophy, 3, 219, 226, 245, 270, 276, 282, 286, 288
Poetic habitus, 63
Policy
    housing policy, 2, 6, 7, 10, 11, 240
Position
    position taking, 7, 36, 156

Positions within fields, 3, 7, 13, 36, 45, 200, 204, 206, 208
Power
    relations, 13, 69, 72, 83, 119, 133, 134, 136–138, 144, 228, 273, 285
    statist, 9
    struggle, 7
Practical rationality, 276, 284
Practice, 2, 3, 5, 12, 13, 24, 36, 39, 41–43, 45, 47, 49, 53–60, 62, 64, 68–70, 73–77, 83, 86, 101, 103, 107–109, 122–125, 133–138, 140, 145, 151, 156, 161, 166, 167, 169, 172–174, 176, 177, 181–183, 188, 194, 206, 217, 2168, 220, 221, 224, 229, 231, 235, 238, 239, 241–246, 250, 251, 254, 255, 258–260, 262, 265, 266, 269–273, 276, 278, 280, 284–288
    logic of practice, 2, 66–68, 76, 169, 220, 243, 270
Praktik, 243–246
Praxeological knowledge, 278, 284
Praxis, 243–245
Pure gaze, 60, 282

R

Radical doubt, 3, 56, 284
Reed-Danahay, D., 106, 221
Reflexive
    development, 136
    mode of thinking, 251
    objectivity, 276, 284, 288
    reflexive sociology, 1, 2, 4
    reflexivity, 3, 269–272, 275, 276, 278, 281–283, 286–289
    relations, 2

Representation, 14, 100, 118, 128, 136, 137, 140, 165–167, 169, 171, 173, 174, 177, 178, 229, 273, 275

Resistance, 2, 25, 144, 152, 188

Rorty, 284

S

Scientific subject, 108, 283, 284

Sex, 181, 187–194

Skholè, 285

Social relations, 5, 124, 157, 185, 217, 222, 229, 258, 264, 265, 278. *See also* Specialization; Specialization code

Social space, 2, 4, 6–8, 35, 39, 45, 68, 69, 82, 94, 119, 127, 144, 153, 183, 184, 195, 212, 213, 228, 241, 244, 276, 279, 285

Social topology, 256. *See also* Specialization plane

Socio-analysis, 165, 173

Sociogenetic, 271

Spatio-temporality, 219, 223, 224, 227, 228, 230, 231

Specialization, 94, 255–257, 266. *See also* Legitimation Code Theory; Social topology
  code, 258, 260, 265, 266
  plane, 255, 256

State, 2, 3, 6, 7, 9–11, 14, 22, 26–28, 35, 47, 81, 86, 153, 160, 177, 190, 205, 206, 211, 215, 238–240, 250, 284, 287

Strategies
  hetero-orthodox, 83, 133, 159
  orthodox, 84
  strategies of players, 45, 201

Structuralism, 2, 102

Structuralist, 102, 241, 246, 271, 274, 276

Structure, 4–8, 10–13, 33, 43, 49, 90, 91, 93, 136, 150, 155, 203, 212, 221, 224, 244, 252, 263, 274, 275, 280–282

Struggles, 5, 7–9, 14, 23, 25–27, 47, 55, 64, 68, 69, 75, 77, 84, 95, 118, 119, 127, 137, 161, 207, 208, 210–214, 221, 257

Students (higher education), 67, 71, 77

Subfields, 57, 142

Subjectivity, 2, 102, 108, 109, 221, 224, 272, 274, 278, 280, 287, 288

Substantialism/Substantialist, 274, 285

Surfing, 139, 142, 181–195

Swartz, D., 4, 5, 7, 8, 10, 13, 74

Symbolic
  challenge, 133
  power, 5, 46, 47, 134, 138, 144
  struggle, 23, 47, 84, 118, 125, 134, 135, 140, 144
  violence, 8, 287

Systemic functional analysis, 125

T

Tertiary education, 61

Theory and practice/Theory of practice, 101, 133, 135, 220, 229, 231, 237, 258, 269, 271–274, 276, 278, 279, 284, 288

Time, 1, 5, 13, 14, 23, 25, 35, 44, 46, 63, 70, 74, 81, 82, 84, 93, 95, 103, 107, 127, 154, 156, 157, 159, 165, 167, 168, 172, 175, 182–184, 186, 188, 193, 194, 208, 209, 211, 212, 218, 221, 226, 227, 229, 243, 253, 258, 266, 269–272, 279, 281–284, 287

Transitivity, 125
Truth, 107–109, 136, 154, 213, 217, 218, 220, 231, 232, 282, 286, 288

U
Unification of the market, 118, 119, 128
Utopia as method, 176

V
Voice, 73, 77, 118, 136, 142–145, 156, 186

W
Weber, M., 83, 271
Welfare, 22, 81, 82, 85, 86, 88, 90, 92–95
Widening participation, 67, 70, 71, 77

Printed by Printforce, the Netherlands